This is number two-hundred and two in the
second numbered series of the
Miegunyah Volumes
made possible by the
Miegunyah Fund
established by bequests
under the wills of
Sir Russell and Lady Grimwade.

'Miegunyah' was Russell Grimwade's home
from 1911 to 1955
and Mab Grimwade's home
from 1911 to 1973.

'I have long been an admirer of William Cooper. He plumbed the pulses of political power to advocate for his people and for the Commonwealth to manage Aboriginal Affairs. Bain Attwood's meticulously researched biography is a fine tribute to an influential and canny campaigner, whose struggle for justice has gone unrecognised for too long.'

Senator Pat Dodson

'A remarkable biography of a remarkable man. Meticulously researched and deeply reflective. Bain Attwood's biography of William Cooper is a rare example of a political life told in its full historical context. We see not only Cooper's extraordinary struggle for "his people" but the entire network of activists that inspired him. It's hard to think of a biography that speaks as urgently and powerfully to Indigenous Australians' long campaign for social, economic, and political justice.'

Mark McKenna, Emeritus Professor, University of Sydney,
Honorary Professor, Australian National University

WILLIAM COOPER

An Aboriginal Life Story

BAIN ATTWOOD

THE
MIEGUNYAH
PRESS

THE MIEGUNYAH PRESS
An imprint of Melbourne University Publishing Limited
Level 1, 715 Swanston Street, Carlton, Victoria 3053, Australia
mup-contact@unimelb.edu.au
www.mup.com.au

First published 2021
Text © Bain Attwood, 2021
Design and typography © Melbourne University Publishing Limited, 2021

Cover design by Philip Campbell Design
Typeset in 12/15pt Bembo by Cannon Typesetting
Cover image courtesy Alick Jackomos collection, Australian Institute of Aboriginal and Torres Strait Islander Studies

Printed in China

 A catalogue record for this
book is available from the
National Library of Australia

9780522877939 (hardback)
9780522877946 (ebook)

For the members of the Cooper family

CONTENTS

PROLOGUE

O N SATURDAY 7 August 1937 an unusual event occurred. An Australian newspaper published a feature story about an Aboriginal man that was based on an interview one of its leading journalists had conducted with him. The Australian press often ran stories about *the blacks* or *the Aborigines*, but it was unprecedented for a newspaper to commission a staffer to seek out an Aboriginal man and write a major story in which his own words were quoted at length and his views represented faithfully. The article even included a photo of its subject, while notice of its publication was given in the pages of the newspaper the day before it appeared.[1]

The Aboriginal man was William Cooper. In his seventy-sixth year and living in a humble worker's cottage in Footscray, he was the secretary of an organisation called the Australian Aborigines' League. The occasion? Word had got around that Cooper was giving serious consideration to whether the time had come for him to present to the Australian Government a petition to the British king that he had drawn up and begun to circulate among Aboriginal people four years earlier.

The journalist was a young poet and writer, Clive Turnbull, whom many regarded as the doyen of Melbourne's newspapermen. In September 1933 his newspaper, the Melbourne *Herald*, had published a report about Cooper's petition. It was short but boldly headlined: 'MHR for Natives. King to be Petitioned: Unique Move'.

'Australia's native race—the aborigines—is taking steps for the first time in its history to secure from the King representation in the Federal Parliament', the reporter had noted before going on to explain: 'This is demanded as a right in a petition which is being circulated for signatures.'2

Now, four years later, Cooper told Turnbull that he hoped to see a change for the better before he died and that he was doing all he could to bring this about. Taking down a great roll of signatures on the petition, he observed: 'If we cannot get full justice in Australia we must ask the King … There are 2000 signatures here, from aborigines all over Australia.' Pointing to one of the pages of petition, Cooper added: 'Those who could not sign their own names have made their marks.'3

The petition called on the British king to intervene on the behalf of Aboriginal people in order to help prevent their extinction, provide better conditions, and grant them the power to propose someone to represent them in the federal parliament. Cooper explained to Turnbull: 'Up till the present time the condition of the aborigines has been deplorable. Their treatment was beyond human reason.' Cooper believed the incumbent federal government was the first in Australia to take up the cause of his people. 'But it is not enough', he observed. In his view a 'tradition of cruelty' had been 'handed down from white generation to generation to the present day'. He confessed to Turnbull, 'I sit here working hour after hour in correspondence with my people thinking. How can we save them?' He demanded to know what was being done for the principal needs of his people. 'We talk to politicians, and they say, Yes, they'll do this, and do that, but the years go on, and what is done?'4

Cooper sketched out for Turnbull the goals of the Australian Aborigines' League, which he had founded in 1933, emphasising the importance of the fact that it was an Aboriginal organisation: 'You may read the views even of sympathetic white men. But they are not our views.' For Cooper, the reason for this was clear: 'We are the sufferers; the white men are the aggressors.' He explained what he meant: 'instead of lifting up our people the early comers to our country destroyed them'. This had lasting consequences.

'Now our people have nothing: all was taken from them. They will never have anything so long as the present state of things endures.' Aboriginal people today, he went on, 'have a horror and fear of extermination. It is in the blood, the racial memory, which recalls the terrible things done to them in years gone by.' As far as he was concerned, the government had a duty towards the country's original peoples. 'You may ask where is the money to come from. But we have lost countless millions to the whites—the whole wealth of Australia. Are we not entitled to this?' This was a constant theme in Cooper's political work.[5]

Turnbull was a sympathetic listener. Had he not been, we would not have this unusually rich testimony. We do not have to search far to understand why this was the case. 'I went to talk to him', Turnbull explained to his readers, 'because I have long been interested in the problem of the aborigines.' This was so, he went on, because 'my own countrymen in Tasmania by a combination of cruelty and stupidity, succeeded in exterminating a whole race within 75 years'.[6] But if Turnbull was damning of his ancestors, he was just as critical of his contemporaries: 'although any number of people are willing to be sentimental at any moment of the day about the minorities of other countries—the Jews in Germany, the negroes in the United States, the Basques in Spain and so on and so on (provided they be sufficiently far away)—nobody of any political color, except a few religious and anthropological enthusiasts, cares tuppence about our own minority, which is perishing before our eyes.' He insisted: 'One can make a melancholy parallel between the pious sentiments of government pronouncements side by side with a record of expropriation (a polite word for theft) and oppression a hundred years ago and those of today. With the exception that aborigines are no longer publicly hunted down, their treatment has for all practical purposes changed little in a century.'[7]

This book seeks to tell the story of William Cooper's life and times, but it necessarily diverges from traditional biography to some degree. The historical sources an academic historian requires for such a study—extensive private papers that are created by the subject of the biography—simply do not exist. In Cooper's case, he was an eloquent speaker but found writing fluently something of a struggle. He was also poor and itinerant for most of his life, which made the keeping of a large collection of papers difficult, even if he had wanted to do so. The academic historian even lacks the kind of precise information that we usually require for a biographical study—for example, that regarding birth and childhood—while there are no written records for significant periods in his adult life. To complicate matters, the patchy documentary record cannot be supplemented by oral testimony. During his lifetime no oral history project of the kind that recorded the memories of former African American slaves in the United States was undertaken in Australia. The interview Cooper granted Turnbull is the only moment that he speaks at any length in the historical record.

Readers of this book should also bear in mind that biography, at least in its traditional mode, might not be an appropriate genre for telling the story of an Aboriginal person like Cooper. It has a tendency to render its subjects as unique and to disconnect their lives from those of the families, kin and communities in which they were enmeshed. In other words, a biographical approach can readily misrepresent the life of an Indigenous man or woman by casting them as loners and exceptional. Make no mistake: I believe Cooper was a remarkable man. But the political work for which he is best remembered was the product of a broad network of family, kin and community, and the outcome of a historical experience that he and his fellows had in common and shared with one another. The account of the first seventy years of his life provided in the early part of this book testifies to this fact.[8]

Traditional biography also tends to assume a particular kind of subject, one that is rather different from that found among Aboriginal people of Cooper's generation as well as later ones. As the anthropologist and historian Diane Barwick pointed out many years ago, rather than conceiving of people primarily in terms of individual egos and their personal stories (as non-Aboriginal cultures have tended to do since modernity), Aboriginal people have continued to define themselves largely in terms of their relationships with family, loyalties to particular people and communities, and enduring kinship roles.[9]

For this book I have adopted a historical approach that has much in common with a particular form of scholarly history known as Aboriginal history. This was conceived in the mid-1970s by a group of white anthropologists, archaeologists, linguists and historians who were responsible for founding a journal of that name at the Australian National University.[10] In their eyes *Aboriginal History* had several dimensions. They believed that the principal historical subject, and the subjects of this history, should be Aboriginal. This contrasted with the research that had previously been done on the history of relations between white settlers and Aboriginal people, just as it still contrasts with much of the work that white historians continue to do, which is Eurocentric in nature because it is mainly concerned with the actions of settler Australians. Those historians assumed—and still assume—that the history of relations between Aboriginal people and settlers should primarily be rendered as a story of the destruction, dispossession and degradation of this country's Indigenous people. By contrast, the founders of *Aboriginal History* took for granted the survival of a relatively autonomous Indigenous world, and they wanted to tell a story about its adaptation to colonisation, including the ways in which Aboriginal people continued to shape the world and their sense of themselves. Most importantly perhaps, these scholars saw the task of historians as one of presenting or representing Aboriginal people's perspectives in regard to that past. Likewise, they insisted that non-Aboriginal scholars should try to explain Aboriginal acts and responses in the terms that Aboriginal people themselves understood them. The founders of Aboriginal history were also intent on revealing the broad range of Aboriginal people's historical experience. This meant, for example, that they were interested in how Aboriginal people sought to reach some kind of accommodation with settlers and adopt and adapt some of their ways, not least those of Christian missionaries. They also wished to focus on Aboriginal people in the original meaning of the word *aboriginal*—that is, local or indigenous to a place. Hence, they recommended regional studies and life stories as a way of revealing the complex diversity of relations between Aboriginal and settler peoples, demonstrating Aboriginal agency and disclosing differences among Aboriginal people according to gender, race (colour or caste) and generation.

Finally, it is important to register here the fact that this book has been written within a particular intellectual tradition, namely the academic discipline of history. Above all else, this form of knowledge places great store on the traces of the past that were created at the time of the events under consideration, as it regards them as the most reliable sources of knowledge about that particular time. Practitioners of academic history tend to be sceptical about the value of sources that are created many years after the events they are discussing (whether those sources be written or oral), at least as far as the provision of historical facts is concerned. In recent decades academic historians have been more willing to accept the validity of oral history—that is, accounts of the past that are provided by people who have themselves witnessed the events of which they tell. But they remain sceptical about the facticity of oral tradition—that is, stories that are passed down over time by people who did not witness the events they narrate—though academic historians accept that these accounts can reveal a great deal about how a people have sought to make sense of and handle past events and so can provide rich insights into historical consciousness. Members of Cooper's family also tell stories about their illustrious forebear, which are based largely on oral tradition rather than oral history. As such, they sometimes differ from the stories I seek to tell here. Wherever possible, I have drawn attention to those moments.[11]

———————

This is not the first time I have written about William Cooper.[12] In my earlier work I sought to draw attention to the fact that he not only founded one of the first and most long-lasting Aboriginal political organisations in Australia, but that he and the Australian Aborigines'

League had a broad program, that they often invoked Aboriginal people's status as this country's first people in their claims for rights, that they were profoundly influenced by Christian missionaries, that they challenged the way in which Aboriginal people and race matters were conceptualised by white Australia, and that they strove to represent all Aboriginal people in Australia.

I have been drawn back to Cooper for several reasons.[13] To my mind, the passing of the years has seen the pertinence of his political work increase rather than diminish. The 2017 Uluru Statement's call for a 'voice to parliament' echoes his demand for Aboriginal representation *in* parliament, which rested on a belief that most whitefellas could not *think black* because their historical experience in this country differed radically from that of its Indigenous people. Similarly, calls for recognition of Aboriginal people as this country's first peoples, the dispossession they have suffered and the need for compensation and capital were fundamental to Cooper's campaign for justice, as the interview he granted Turnbull makes clear.

Cooper has become better known in Australia in the past fifteen years as he has been honoured in a range of public memorials. In many of these acts of remembrance—such as the installation of a sculpture in Shepparton and the naming of a legal precinct in Melbourne—he has been rightly hailed for the mighty political work he undertook on behalf of his people. However, a great deal of recent commemoration has also focused on a brief protest by the Australian Aborigines' League against Nazi Germany's persecution of Jewish people; indeed, even though most academic historians regard this act as being of little historical significance, a particular way of telling the story about it has come to dominate how Cooper is now known among most non-Indigenous people, both here and abroad.[14] This narrative has narrowed understanding of Cooper and the Australian Aborigines' League, obscured the forces that enabled his campaigning, and made it difficult to grasp what this political struggle entailed and what it stood for. As a result, Cooper's legacy risks being stripped of its far-reaching political lessons.

PART 1

1

BEGINNINGS

BIOGRAPHIES TRADITIONALLY BEGIN in time, relating the circumstances of their subject's birth and providing a date for it. Aboriginal life stories typically begin in space, telling of the place where their subject came into the world, thereby revealing that Aboriginal people in years gone by did not understand their being so much in terms of time as of space. The entry for William Cooper in the *Australian Dictionary of Biography*, prepared some forty years ago by Diane Barwick, who was the founding editor of the journal *Aboriginal History*, begins more or less in this fashion: 'William Cooper, the Aboriginal leader, was born in Yorta Yorta tribal territory about the junction of the Murray and Goulburn rivers.' Barwick was unable to be specific about Cooper's birthdate, but the omission of information was apt, suggesting that she was more concerned about *where* Cooper was born than *when* he was born.[1]

More recent research, which supplements the Yorta Yorta oral tradition that Barwick drew upon, has revealed that Cooper was born at Lake Moira, or Lake Mira as his people traditionally called it, which lay several kilometres upstream from the junction of the Murray and Goulburn rivers.[2] This is probably the source of Cooper's Aboriginal name (or one of those names), Yelgaborrnya, which means a dry leaf (yalga or yalka) that is found on the branch of a lake or river (borr[i]nyu).[3]

This contemporary photograph shows part of Lake Moira, where Yelgaborrnya (William Cooper) was born.

Lake Mira lay at the heart of his people's territory in what became north-eastern Victoria and southern New South Wales. In today's terms, this area runs from Cohuna in the west to about Albury in the east, north to a point approximately 25 kilometres past Finley and south just short of Nagambie, and it includes the towns of Echuca, Shepparton, Benalla, Corowa, Wangaratta, Glenrowan, Rutherford, Chiltern and Wahgunyah.

The riverine plains at the junction of the Goulburn and Murray rivers provided a rich combination of ecosystems that supported several large Aboriginal nations. The Murray is now thought to have nurtured one of Australia's largest Indigenous populations.[4]

Although Cooper was compelled to move away from this region at several points in his life, it remained his country and at the end of his days he returned there to die.

Cooper's birth

While the space and place of Cooper's birth should be paramount in any account of his life, many people are naturally curious about the circumstances of his birth. According to family tradition, he was born to a woman who belonged to the Wollithiga grouping of the Yorta Yorta nation and who had taken the English name of Kitty.

As far as Cooper's paternity is concerned, we know that the man who fathered him was white. The Yorta Yorta, like other Aboriginal people who acted in keeping with their own beliefs and practices, tried to establish a reciprocal kin relationship with the white invaders of their country—in this instance Henry Sayer Lewes, the founder of a pastoral run, *Moira*, and his men—in an attempt to absorb them into their community and culture and teach them the right way to behave.[5] Typically, this meant that Aboriginal groups encouraged sexual relationships between their women members and whitefellas. In the case of Cooper's seven siblings, who came to bear the English names of Aaron, Edgar, Lizzie, Johnny, Jack, Bobby and Ada, several of them adopted the surname of a white man, John Olbury Atkinson, who worked on Lewes' *Moira* run for a long time as its overseer or superintendent, as they were his offspring. The remaining children, including William himself, variously adopted the surname of Cooper or Wilberforce (the latter of which will be explained shortly). Barwick recorded Cooper's father's name as James Cooper, but recent DNA analysis has suggested that a man by the name of Edward Cooper might have been his biological father instead.[6]

From Cooper's point of view, the identity of the man who fathered him was of little if any significance. Indeed, it seems to have been irrelevant. Whereas the historical record is replete with references to Kitty, because she was at the centre of his and his siblings' familial world, there are barely any references to the white men who 'fathered' either him or his brothers and sisters. In fact Cooper, according to the historical record, barely mentioned this man. Tellingly, Edward Cooper was not registered as his father on the certificates for William's second and third marriages or his death certificate,[7] but men by the names of James Cooper and William Cooper were.[8]

In other words, there is little if any evidence to suggest that the man who 'fathered' William Cooper played any role in his life after he impregnated Kitty. If this was the case, it would be unremarkable. Most of the white men who had children by Aboriginal women in the nineteenth century and beyond were reluctant to acknowledge their offspring or take any responsibility for raising them, or they disowned them after they married white women.[9] The fact that Cooper was of so-called mixed racial descent *was* significant to the course his life took, because of the nature of white racial ideas and attitudes about 'blood'. But as far as he was concerned his kith and kin were Aboriginal, and he rejected the distinction that white people made between 'full-bloods' and half-castes'.

As far as Cooper's date of birth is concerned, some uncertainty exists as there is no birth certificate for him. (At the time he was born a large number of births in the Australian colonies went unrecorded, not least those of their Indigenous people.) Nor is there any other contemporary record of his birth. On the basis of the information recorded on his death certificate, namely that he was eighty years of age when he died, Barwick speculated that he had been born in 1861. But Cooper held that he had been born in 1860. In August 1940 he sent a letter in which he remarked: 'I will be 80 years of age on 18th December next.'[10]

But this testimony does not necessarily resolve the matter of Cooper's date of birth. A historical record created more or less at the time of an event is generally regarded by scholarly historians as the most reliable form of evidence. Furthermore, Aboriginal cultural traditions at the time Cooper was born mean that it was unlikely his people ascribed much importance to a date of birth according to the Christian calendar, as compared with the significance they gave to the place of someone's birth, their family, kinship group and totem. One can assume, though, that they remembered the season in which someone was born, and that the place in which this occurred served to remind them of this fact. Traditionally, Aboriginal people 'told the time', so to speak, according to the place in which an event happened.

Many readers will no doubt find this matter as frustrating as the author of Cooper's *Wikipedia* entry seems to have done.[11] But if we can accept that Cooper's date of birth rests on his *belief* about it, we are able to pursue a line of inquiry that will reveal more about the man, and how he understood himself, than a mere piece of paper that records his birth day. It seems likely that at a particular time in his life Cooper found himself in a position in which it was necessary or advantageous to be able to declare a precise date of birth. Aboriginal people often had to adapt to the colonial order to make their way in the world or just make do. Cooper probably chose a birth day after he became acquainted with Christian missionaries or at the point that he adopted their religion as his own.[12]

If this was the case, perhaps 18 December appealed to him for a couple of reasons: a knowledge of the season in which he was born, and a realisation that it was one of the days of Advent. Or had the missionaries alerted him to the fact that on that day in 1865 the United States Congress had declared the thirteenth amendment to the American constitution, by which slavery was abolished there? This possibility cannot be ruled out given that the missionary Daniel Matthews seems to have bestowed on Cooper and several of his siblings the surname of William Wilberforce,[13] the famous English abolition crusader,[14] and they used this name for several years before adopting the surname of Cooper or reverting to it.[15]

Early contact

By the time William Cooper was born, his people had literally been decimated as a consequence of the white man's invasion of their country. In 1788 Aboriginal people in what became the colony of Victoria might have numbered as many as 60,000, but by 1863 fewer than 2000 had survived and only a few hundred along the Murray River. Most of this depopulation had been caused by disease, especially ones introduced after British colonisation had begun. In 1788–89 and 1829–30 smallpox epidemics swept through the south-east of the Australian continent. It seems the Yorta Yorta were among those who were affected prior to their even encountering Europeans. In June 1838 the explorer Charles Sturt remarked on travelling along the Goulburn River: 'It is evident that a terrible mortality had swept [the native people] in numbers away, for … there are burial places in every sand hill, traces of which were upwards of 50 graves in every direction.' He added: 'No trace of small pox or other disorder such as obviously threatened the tribes of ... the Murray [was evident] ... Whatever [the] cause of death [it] had been busy with them.'[16]

The Yorta Yorta continued to suffer enormous population loss after European pastoralists began to occupy their land in the late 1830s. The main cause was the diseases the whitefellas brought with them. There was an increase in infant mortality and a decline in fertility as a result of the invading army of young single men infecting women with syphilis and gonorrhoea. The violent clashes that occurred as a result of conflict over land resulted in fewer deaths. This was the case on most of the frontiers in the Australian colonies, but it was especially so in this instance. As the historian Jan Penney has pointed out, some time elapsed between the initial contact that the Aboriginal nations along the Murray had with parties of European explorers and overlanders and their later encounter with pastoralists. They were able to learn from the severe losses that neighbouring nations such as the Wiradjuri had suffered in waging a war. Rather than confronting the pastoralists, the Yorta Yorta and the other nations in their part of the Murray region tried to avoid many of them, accommodate others, and force a few away. Nonetheless, there were undoubtedly instances of violence against Aboriginal people on this frontier of settlement.[17]

As a result of the pastoral invasion, Cooper's people were dispossessed of their land well before he was born. Yet throughout the 1840s the exceptionally rich ecosystem of the Murray and Goulburn rivers, upon which peoples such as the Yorta Yorta had long depended, provided them with some of the resources they needed in order to survive. This also meant that there was less competition between the whitefellas and Aboriginal people and thus less of the conflict that characterised many frontiers. Moreover, the Yorta Yorta nurtured relationships with particular pastoralists, performing some work on the pastoral runs and supplying fish and other foods in return for presents of new forms of clothing and new foods such as flour and tea. Many of the Aboriginal people along the Murray saw the large pastoral runs and the small towns as a resource they could use to their advantage. For their part, the pastoralists had a greater need for Aboriginal people's labour than elsewhere because of the region's remoteness.[18]

The relationship I have just described between the Yorta Yorta and the pastoralists continued into the 1850s. This can be attributed partly to the gold rushes in Victoria, which resulted in an increase in the demand for Aboriginal people's labour as many white pastoral workers went walkabout to the goldfields. The pastoralists were forced to offer more inducement to the Yorta Yorta in the form of wages, while the Yorta Yorta could choose whether or not they worked for them as most of their traditional food sources remained available. Much of the labour they performed was only seasonal or short-term in nature, but this suited them, as did the fact that nearly all of it could be performed outdoors and called for movement over their own land. These conditions enabled the Yorta Yorta to continue to look after their country. Moreover, in their eyes work was part and parcel of a reciprocal relationship that they sought to forge with the pastoralists, and they saw their bosses not so much as masters but as kin, often taking on their names as a way to cement these ties and the mutual obligations that accompanied them.[19]

By the mid-1850s another source of employment had emerged for the Yorta Yorta. A fishing cooperative known as the Murray River Fishing Company was founded at Lake Moira by an American man, a former miner, Joseph Rice, and managed by an Englishman, the aforementioned Edward Cooper. At this point the Murray River, lacking a deep channel, spread over several square kilometres during the winter but shrank into a series of lakes, swamps and lagoons in the summer. The resulting shallow waters created an ideal breeding ground for a great variety of fish, which attracted millions of wildfowl who returned each year to nest among the reeds and the trees. The Yorta Yorta had exploited these resources for generations and Rice was quick to see the potential of their traditional skills for a business that began to provide fish, fowl and leeches to markets in Bendigo, Melbourne and beyond. One contemporary report claimed that Rice's company was very correct in all its dealings with those who supplied it with fish, even keeping faith with the local

This wood engraving by a well-known painter and printer, Samuel Calvert, was
used to illustrate an article on the Murray River that was published in 1869
in one of the pictorial newspapers of the day. In the distance an Aboriginal
man is paddling a bark canoe, while in the foreground an Aboriginal woman
is searching for food among the reeds on the banks of the river and another
Aboriginal man is swimming towards her. The article noted that the Aboriginal
people constructed dams when the river flooded in order to prevent fish
returning to the river, thereby ensuring a food supply when they needed it.

Aboriginal people. There are good reasons to be sceptical of this
claim. Nonetheless, it is apparent that many Yorta Yorta gathered at
a small island in the lake where the company had a series of huts.[20]

Despite the fact that the Yorta Yorta were able to exploit
resources that were both traditional and new, their numbers continued to plummet. Most white observers were of the opinion that
venereal diseases, tuberculosis and heavy consumption of alcohol
were the main causes of death, while all agreed that very few
children were being born. Some of them condemned the likes of
Rice's company for paying Aboriginal people in alcohol. That many
of the Yorta Yorta men and women were reluctant to have children, and eager to consume a huge amount of alcohol, probably
testifies to the despair they felt as a result of the devastation that had
occurred since the beginning of the white man's invasion. Their
customary ways of being had been ruptured and thrown into chaos,
and they were reeling as a result. Still, they had been able to stay in
their own country, acquire new skills and maintain some degree

of independence, which would stand them in good stead in the years to come.[21]

Cooper's early world

This was the world into which Cooper was born. It seems that he spent his early years on *Moira*, the lease of which was acquired in 1862 by a leading Victorian politician, businessman and lay Catholic, John O'Shanassy. During that decade, life for the Yorta Yorta remained much as it had in the previous one. They continued to work for pastoralists and fishermen and exploit traditional food sources. But their means of survival began to diminish as the European population in the area grew—the population of the borough of Echuca increased from 221 in 1861 to 1649 in 1871—and settlers began to use the area's land and waters more intensively. For example, the Yorta Yorta's riverine resources, which had been exploited heavily by the Murray River Fishing Company, were further depleted by the growing traffic on the Murray. As early as November 1860 this had prompted several Yorta Yorta men to contemplate sending a deputation to the governor of Victoria to ask him to impose a £10

This engraving by Samuel Calvert depicts a shepherd's hut on the confines of John O'Shanassy's *Moira* run in 1869. It is unlikely that the dwellings he provided his Aboriginal workers were on a par with this one.

tax on each steamer passing up and down the river, which could then be expended on supplying food to their people in lieu of the fish that had been driven away.[22]

Yet the Yorta Yorta's loss of some of their traditional resources was offset to some degree by the fact that they were now able to draw upon the food, clothes and blankets made available periodically at depots that had been created by the Victorian Central Board for the Protection of the Aborigines (which had been formed in 1860 following a select committee inquiry about the plight of Aboriginal people in the colony). This was all the more the case because these depots were overseen by the board's honorary correspondents in the area who acted as local guardians of the Aboriginal people and whom the Yorta Yorta knew very well. James Rutherford, the lease-holder of *Ulupna*, a pastoral run at the eastern end of the Barmah Forest, and John McKenzie, the leaseholder of *Wyuna*, a pastoral run near Echuca and south of the Goulburn River, often employed them and took a paternal interest in their welfare. At one point the board also joined forces with the Victorian Commission for Trade and Customs in an attempt to limit the vast quantity of fish and fowls that were being ruthlessly killed by commercial fishermen.[23]

The Yorta Yorta people, however, continued to suffer an enormous decline in their numbers. By 1863 the board reckoned there were only 184 Aboriginal people living at Echuca and in camps along the upper reaches of the Murray. All of its honorary correspondents in the area were convinced that most of the decline could be attributed to the amount of alcohol many were consuming, which they blamed on the fact that Aboriginal people could acquire it with ease from the growing number of public houses and shanties in the area.[24]

By the 1860s much of the Yorta Yorta's traditional culture had been severely compromised and they were increasingly subject to the white man's laws. Nonetheless, they and the neighbouring Aboriginal nations continued to invoke their own law in an attempt to order relations between themselves. As an old man, Cooper recalled a meeting of these nations that numbered several hundred men, which might have taken place near Lake Moira in 1864.

Cooper also remembered an occasion in which his mother called out a warning in Yorta Yorta that meant 'white man come' and he and his brothers had 'dart[ed] into hiding until the terror passed'. This incident reveals how much the experience of violent attacks by white frontiersmen weighed upon his people, just as it makes clear that the likes of Cooper continued to be taught their own language or languages.[25]

In 1867 the seven-year-old Cooper was taken by O'Shanassy to live with his family in Melbourne (for reasons that are unknown). The O'Shanassys resided in a grand mansion in the part of the suburb of Camberwell known as the Tara Estate, which enjoyed a commanding view of the city. It is hard to imagine a greater contrast between the camps in which Cooper had been living up to this point and this eighteen-room house. Apparently he was happy there,

In this hand-coloured engraving, one of the most notable Melbourne artists of the day, George Rossi Ashton, depicted O'Shanassy's mansion in Camberwell in about 1887, some years after Cooper had spent a few years of his childhood there.

though it seems he was treated by O'Shanassy's three daughters as if he was a black doll. This was one of Cooper's abiding memories of this period in his life, but he also told one of his grandsons many years later that he had worked in the stables of the New Imperial Hotel on Elizabeth Street in the city, which O'Shanassy owned. (It is often said that Cooper was O'Shanassy's coachman during these years and that he spent much of his youth in O'Shanassy's employ in this role, but there is no reliable evidence to support either of these claims.) Cooper was sent home after three years or so, once he began to show signs that he was entering puberty.[26]

On Cooper's return to his own country, he learned horse-breaking and other such skills on *Moira*. For the next several years he seems to have worked there and at *Lower Moira* (later called *Madowla*). He was a quick learner. He was also keen to learn how to read and write. In his old age Cooper told a story that relates to this period in his life. 'I was out droving when a lad and I stayed at a hotel. While there I saw a boy "looking at something and talking". I found out he was reading those black spots on the pages of a book.' Cooper recalled: 'I was determined I would learn to read and do better than the boy did for he stumbled as he read. Someone gave me a primer and told me the names of the letters. I learned these off. I then pointed to a sign and asked what it was ... I noted it and learned how to spell that word. Then I asked what other words were and learned each one, one at a time.' This is a revealing story: Cooper tells of his eagerness to acquire the skill of literacy but also of his determination to be able to read as well as any white child, if not better.[27]

In the course of the following decade Cooper's and his people's struggle to survive became steadily more difficult. The breaking-up of several of the pastoral runs on their country after the Victorian parliament passed a succession of Selection Acts in the 1860s resulted in a further intensification in the way the settlers used the land. The demand for the Aboriginal people's labour declined and their traditional food sources were depleted or their access to them was denied. This period also saw a growth in racial prejudice as an increasing number of settlers in the area had none of the connections that had grown between the local Aboriginal people and

the first generation of whitefellas, which had often been characterised by some sense of reciprocity and even kinship of a kind.
Those such as Rutherford at *Ulupna* believed that the health of the
local people they knew had deteriorated considerably by the middle
of the 1870s.[28]

Daniel and Janet Matthews

In June 1874 Daniel and Janet Matthews established a mission on a
small part of some land Daniel and one of his brothers, William, had
selected in 1865 on the northern bank (or the New South Wales
side) of the Murray River, about 20 kilometres from Echuca. The
Matthewses and the mission they founded, which became known as
Maloga, were to have a profound influence on Cooper, and so it is
necessary to discuss both at considerable length. This is all the more
the case because the impact of Maloga on Cooper and his kin has
often been mistakenly attributed to the reserve (Cumeroogunga)
that supplanted it in the late 1880s.[29]

First, a word or two about Echuca is in order. It was a thriving
township whose name might have derived from a Yorta Yorta word
that meant 'meeting of the waters'.[30] It lay close to the junction of
three rivers—the Campaspe, the Goulburn and the Murray—and was
often frequented by Yorta Yorta people. After the Matthews brothers
opened a store there in 1864 (which stocked hardware and other
goods for the steamer trade), Daniel began to visit the Aboriginal
camp in Echuca. Shortly afterwards he made the acquaintance of
other Yorta Yorta in the Barmah Forest and at Lake Moira and
elsewhere up and down the Murray and Goulburn rivers. He seems
to have spent a considerable amount of time in their company,
joining the men in hunting and fishing, for example. He quickly
became aware of the suffering and the wrongs that had been—and
were still being—committed against them. In fact he was shocked
and sorrowed by this state of affairs. It aroused in him a desire to help
or reclaim the people, or at least their children. As a result he became
well known among the Aboriginal people in the area and many
came to regard him as one of their protectors and even a *maranooka*
(friend), calling him by that Yorta Yorta name.[31]

Daniel Matthews and Janet Matthews (nee Johnson) had both migrated to
Victoria from Britain in 1853, accompanied by siblings and at least one parent.
Daniel was a Cornishman, born in 1837; Janet a Scotch girl born in 1848. Their
families had much in common. They belonged to the British mercantile middle
class and nonconformist churches, and their parents' faith stressed the importance
of individual communion with Christ. The photograph of Daniel was taken in
1885 and the one of Janet in 1876.

As early as 1865 Matthews had begun to call on the Victorian
Government for the reservation of land for the establishment of an
institution on the Murray for the local Aboriginal people, having
become convinced that the colonists had a profound responsibility towards the country's Indigenous people. It was natural for him
to look to Victoria rather than New South Wales. The former
had chosen to take some responsibility for the Aboriginal people
it had dispossessed, establishing a board to oversee their protection
and helping to found several supervised reserves, most of them with
church or missionary organisations, whereas New South Wales had
simply neglected them, doing little more than distributing a free
blanket to each Aboriginal person once a year. In a letter Matthews
sent the editor of the local newspaper, the *Riverine Herald*, in April
1866, he argued: 'These people are the original possessors of the soil.
Granted we have as much right here as they, still theirs is the first
claim, and it is our duty as the superior race to instruct them in

those virtues which give us the ascendancy.' Two months later, he wrote in a similar vein to the editor of a Melbourne newspaper. 'As a community, have not the people of this colony, and the government, largely benefitted by the land taken from the uncivilised race?' he asserted. 'And are we not morally bound in return, at least, to ameliorate the condition of the aborigines?' He argued that large tracts of land should be set aside for them and that they be encouraged in everything that would 'raise them above their present state'.[32]

A month or so earlier, Matthews had travelled south to visit Coranderrk Aboriginal reserve, located near the township of Healesville. He was enormously impressed by the village that its religious-minded heads, John and Mary Green, and the Kulin people had founded, and the work they had done to cultivate the land. He was also excited to learn that the Victorian Central Board for the Protection of the Aborigines was planning to establish a similar institution for Aboriginal people on the Murray and that its secretary, Robert Brough Smyth, and John Green, as its inspector,

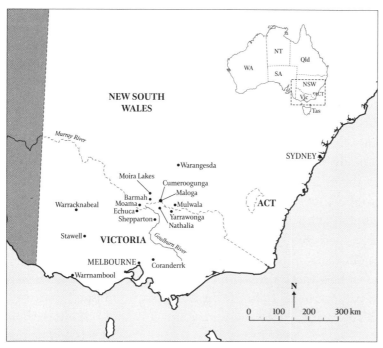

Map of key locations.

were about to visit the area to choose a site on some land that had apparently been reserved for this purpose. Nothing was to come of this plan (even though Smyth and Green's successors urged the board to adopt it several years later). In the meantime Matthews took a small number of Yorta Yorta children from the Murray to Coranderrk. Green tried to do the same, but the Yorta Yorta were extremely reluctant to allow this to occur, going so far as to hide their children when he came to take them.[33]

In January 1867 Matthews got up a petition to the chairman of the Victorian Central Board for the Protection of the Aborigines calling for a grant of land to be made to the local Aboriginal people so that they could be settled and cared for. About fifty of Echuca's most respectable and influential townsfolk signed it. Matthews had also consulted some of the Aboriginal people who worked on the various pastoral runs in the district, and they had told him that they would like to 'sit down' at a permanent camp and work the land. A couple of months later, in the course of drawing attention to his petition, Matthews tried to rouse white support by writing to the local newspaper. 'We possess their lands; we march unmolested through the length and breadth of their territory; we dwell in peace and security upon the soil which they inherited from their ancestors; we derive amusement and realise profit from what was formerly their only means of subsistence—fishing and hunting', he asserted. 'And our liberal-minded government, as compensation for these natural gifts, ... have doled out to them in the most parsimonious manner, an occasional blanket and a few paltry stores that are any-thing but timely and adequate to their needs.' Matthews received no reply from the board to his petition, and so in September 1867 he appealed to the Victorian minister for lands to reserve some land for Aboriginal people on the Murray.[34]

Matthews increasingly believed that any effort to help Aboriginal people should focus on the children. In February 1868 he discussed with some of the Yorta Yorta the value of a school for the children who were camped near Echuca. (In doing so he grasped that they were loath to leave their own country and unwilling to allow their children to be taken away.) But it was not until April 1870 that he put to the local settlers a proposal for a school and home for Aboriginal children in the neighbourhood of Echuca and the Barmah Forest. Some were sympathetic and agreed to form a standing committee to advance his plan. Matthews was a brilliant publicist and won a good deal of support from the likes of the *Riverine Herald*. The following month its editor called for support for Matthews' plan in a leader in which he asserted that it was 'a crying disgrace to us all that the unfortunate first possessors of the land should be dying out', argued that the settler community had 'carried on a war of extermination against them', and attacked those who claimed 'the race must perish'. However, the committee ran into a host of difficulties, and several years passed before Matthews was able to bring his plan for a school to fruition.[35]

During this time Matthews' plan changed. Profoundly influenced by a young woman, Janet Johnson, who would soon become his wife, he began to conceive of his venture as a *mission*—that is, a venture that would be primarily religious rather than secular in nature.[36] At the same time, though, he continued to imagine an institution that would meet the needs of young Aboriginal men and women in the district. In April 1872 he wrote to Janet: 'My mission will be by the help of God to the children but with a view to the benefit of the adults—but not in so direct a manner.'[37]

In June 1873 Matthews launched a campaign for funds to create a mission, primarily by publishing and circulating a pamphlet he had written, *An Appeal on Behalf of the Australian Aborigines*. In this he declared that the mission's object was to instruct and train the children by 'instil[ling] principles of morality and religion into their hitherto untutored minds'. But he also indicated that it would seek to impart secular knowledge 'so that they may be made useful members of society and attain the means of gaining their own livelihood', which overlooked the fact that many of the Yorta Yorta (Cooper being just one example) had already acquired many of these skills. Matthews was planning to construct a large building whose central portion would be used as a school and a place of worship and for meetings, and that would have wings that could be used as dormitories for the children.[38]

By this time Matthews had persuaded his brother William to
set aside 20 acres (8 hectares) of the land that had been selected
in William's name in 1865, to which they had since added two
adjoining blocks of 320 acres (129 hectares), the title for which had
since been transferred to their elder brother in England. This land,
which was situated on the Barmah sandhills at a beautiful bend of the
Murray River, was favoured by the Yorta Yorta since it was one of
their traditional ceremonial grounds, and the mission soon acquired
its Yorta Yorta name, Maloga. It is probable that the Yorta Yorta
had suggested this place as a site for the mission, just as Aboriginal
people elsewhere in the Australian colonies played a crucial role in
choosing land for such sites and persuading the colonial governments
to reserve them for their use. Maloga also had another advantage.
The Matthews brothers' selections lay between two water reserves
(which belonged to O'Shanassy) and so the mission was relatively
isolated and thus distant from the problems that tended to arise when
Aboriginal missions and reserves were situated too close to towns.

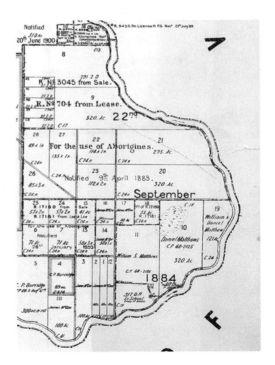

This part of a 1909
government survey map
shows the Matthews brothers'
selections and a piece of
land that was reserved for
Aboriginal use in 1883. The
latter became Cumeroogunga
Aboriginal Reserve, which
supplanted Maloga in 1888.

However, it was formerly part of *Moira* and so proved to be a thorn in the O'Shanassys' side, leading to considerable tension between the pastoral run and the mission.[39]

Maloga's early days

Cooper's mother, two of his younger brothers, Bobby and Jack, and a younger sister, Ada, were among the first to go to Maloga, sometime after the mission opened in June 1874. But William preceded them, and in early August Matthews wrote excitedly in his diary about him: 'The boy, Billy, shows great aptitude for learning. He has acquired a knowledge of the alphabet, capital[s] and small letters, in three days and then taught [his brother] Bobby—capitals only—in one day.'[40]

It is difficult to exaggerate the significance of Matthews' words. In the eyes of Christian missionaries, learning how to read and write—and converting to Christianity, building houses and farming the land—was evidence of the Aboriginal people embracing 'civilisation'. More especially, an Aboriginal boy showing an aptitude not only to read but to teach was invaluable proof that Aboriginal people *were* of one and the same 'blood' as whites and *could* be raised up, contrary to what most settlers believed. (Missions to Aboriginal people had been founded in New South Wales in the 1830s, but they were relatively short-lived and deemed to have failed on the grounds that Aboriginal people were hopelessly savage or doomed to die out.) Cooper can be regarded as Matthews' first acolyte, and a long-lasting bond between the two was forged as a result.[41]

Yet it appears that Cooper had gone to Maloga not so much for his own sake but for that of his mother and his younger siblings. He and his older brother Aaron Atkinson realised that the survival of their mother and younger kin depended on them acquiring a refuge from the sexual abuse or maltreatment they had been subjected to in camps at Barmah, *Moira* and Lake Moira. Consequently, they were inclined to join forces with Matthews in order to escort Kitty, Jack and Ada to Maloga.[42]

Cooper himself did not remain there. In the middle of September 1874, according to Matthews, he remarked: 'There couldn't be a better place than this. I want to live here always.' But he continued to work on *Lower Moira*, which lay across the river from Maloga, only returning to the mission on Sundays to attend prayer meetings, listen to Matthews read and tell stories from the Bible, and learn to sing hymns.[43]

During this period a battle over the bodies and souls of the local Aboriginal people took place between Matthews on the one hand, and pastoralists and senior Yorta Yorta men and women on the other. This kind of struggle occurred in many places as missionaries sought to establish missions to Aboriginal people. In this case Matthews, assisted by Cooper and Atkinson, repeatedly tried to persuade some of the Aboriginal women and younger kin to leave *Moira* and *Lower Moira* and move to Maloga. But he encountered fierce opposition from O'Shanassy's son Matthew and his men, who perceived a threat to their control over *Moira*'s Aboriginal labour force, or more specifically their Aboriginal sexual partners, and from senior Aboriginal men, who saw a threat to their traditional lifeways and the power and authority they exercised over their younger kin. The former group played on the fears of the latter by claiming that Matthews wanted to take away the children so that he could send them to Melbourne. They also made scurrilous but damaging attacks in anonymous letters to the editor of the local newspaper, accusing Matthews of misusing the funds that local subscribers had given to the mission and mistreating the Aboriginal people who had gone there.[44]

In this conflict Atkinson, and more especially Cooper, found themselves caught between the warring parties. In early September Matthews recorded in his diary a visit he had made to *Moira*: '[Aaron Atkinson] seems to have been biased by Mr O'S[hanassy jnr] to some extent … While we were talking Mr O'S dashed up on his horse … I approached and said "You received my note, Mr O'S." "Yes, my overseer will see to that" and he handed the note to Mr R. He then approached me closely and said, "I'll knock your damned eyes out. You sent me an insulting letter the other day and called me a coward".'[45]

Conflict between Matthews and one or more of the neighbouring pastoralists erupted again after most if not all the Aboriginal people who had gone to the mission had left. At first, it seemed that

Cooper's mother, sister and two other young women were content to remain there. Kitty apparently declared on several occasions: 'Good fellow p'ace this, plenty sing, plenty learn 'em, plenty tucker'. But it appears that she and the young women missed what Kitty called the 'pulic house', (i.e. public house) and in late September they ignored the Matthewses' remonstrances and abandoned the mission, moving first to a camp at Barmah and later to *Moira*. Matthews soon followed, but O'Shanassy jnr accused him of trespassing and ordered him off the run. Matthews had to leave Kitty, Bobby and Ada and a young boy behind. He scribbled in his diary later: 'It appears directly Mr O'S saw Bobby he caught hold of him, shook him and then took him into the house to frighten him into staying. Poor little Bobby was compelled to stay.'[46]

In early November Kitty, several of her young children and the aforementioned two young women returned to Maloga in William's company, much to Matthews' relief. However, shortly after their return, Matthews quizzed both Atkinson and Cooper about the conduct of the young women. They were both sorely troubled by what had happened. According to Matthews, Atkinson alleged that his mother had tried to induce one of the two young women to stay at the camp at Barmah, while Cooper provided 'a most dreadful account of the doings' at that camp and Rice's camp at Lake Moira. But it was a story that Cooper told Matthews about the sexual relations between one of the employees or sons of Robert Kinnear, the leaseholder of *Lower Moira*, and one of the young women that most outraged the missionary.[47] 'My blood boiled', he wrote in his diary. On hearing Cooper's recital, Matthews decided to call on the police magistrate in Echuca to prosecute the man in question and asked Cooper to make a statement that could be used to support the case. Cooper must have felt that he was being pulled into Matthews' camp. This was all the more the case after an incident that took place as he and Matthews were getting ready to leave Maloga for Echuca. The man in question came across the river and confronted Matthews, asking him for the name of the person who had given him information about him having sexual relations with the young woman. Matthews refused to answer, upon which the man realised that Cooper was his source and 'threatened that if he caught Billy on the other side of the river again he would "cut the hide off him".'[48]

This must have shaken Cooper badly. Nevertheless, he proceeded with Matthews to Echuca. There the missionary discussed with the police magistrate the possibility of a charge being brought against the man for abduction, but he and Cooper were told that no such case could be brought because Matthews could not prove he had employed the young woman under a contract. They were told that the only charge that could be brought against the man was one of illegally supplying an Aboriginal person with alcohol. But the only evidence Matthews had for this charge was Cooper's, and his testimony was inadmissible in court. The colonial order held that Aboriginal culture did not have the concept of a Supreme Being or a power that could punish or reward after death, both of which were deemed necessary by the courts for the swearing of an oath to function as a means to deter perjury.[49] (This law was to be amended in New South Wales in 1876.) The police magistrate advised Matthews to communicate the entire matter to the Victorian Central Board for the Protection of the Aborigines. This outcome must have dismayed Cooper as much as it did Matthews. The following evening they set off for Maloga, 'glad to get away from the turmoil and confusion of town life', according to Matthews. On the way home they got lost in the dark, but Cooper's superior bush skills meant he was able to guide them back onto the track and so to safety.[50]

By this time the numbers of Aboriginal people at Maloga had been reduced to six. It seems that Cooper left shortly afterwards. This is hardly surprising. The Matthewses were primarily seeking to draw children to the mission, and Cooper was already a young man. However much he felt drawn to Maloga and wanted to learn how to read and write and hear the word of God and the Biblical stories that Matthews told, the mission could not offer him any work, let alone pay him for it, and he was quite capable of getting well-paid work. But Cooper probably had to seek employment further afield now, given the breach that would have occurred between him and the leaseholders of *Moira* and *Lower Moira* on account of his connection with the Matthewses and Maloga.[51]

2
CONVERSION

COOPER SPENT THE next several years of his life working on pastoral runs in Victoria and New South Wales and further afield.[1] In the 1930s he recalled seeing the remains of the Burke and Wills expedition in the Channel Country in Central Australia more than sixty years earlier. He was probably on a droving expedition at the time. At some point he also travelled to New Zealand for work, presumably as a shearer given that there was an exodus of Australian shearers across the Tasman at various times in this period.[2]

Cooper no doubt kept in contact with his kin on Maloga during these years. He was there for a few months in 1876–77 and returned again for a while once or twice in the following few years. Late in his life he remembered leaving the mission at about this time with two of his brothers and other men to help one of Matthews' closest associates, Rev. John Gribble, establish a mission on the banks of the Murrumbidgee River near Darlington Point, some 240 kilometres to the north, which came to be called Warangesda. But it seems that Cooper saw no reason to return to Maloga on a more permanent basis until January 1882. To explain why this was so we need to consider the history of the mission during this period.[3]

For some time after its founding the Matthewses focused primarily on the recruitment of children. As a result Cooper did not see much of a future for himself there, though several men of his generation, including Bagot Morgan and Cooper's brothers Johnny Atkinson and Bobby Cooper, did. He probably realised that the mission's fortunes were precarious and so hesitated to throw in his lot with it. Maloga's poor prospects stemmed largely from a lack of money. Unlike every other mission founded in the early to mid nineteenth century, it was neither sponsored nor supported by a church or missionary society, partly because it was interdenominational. Nor did it receive any regular funds from government, not least because in those years New South Wales had no body responsible for the care of Aboriginal people and the mission was unable to make any claim upon the Victorian Central Board for the Protection of the Aborigines since it was located just across the border separating Victoria and New South Wales. Some of its people were able to make such a claim from time to time so long as they were recognised as Victorian-born, but Maloga's position on the border proved a real headache to the Matthewses.[4]

Maloga depended on subscriptions and contributions, many of which Matthews solicited from Sunday schools, and an occasional grant from the New South Wales Government. But this funding was neither large nor regular enough to meet Maloga's needs. The mission also lacked any land to run stock or raise crops for sale or sustenance. Consequently, living there was a hand-to-mouth affair. Often the Matthewses had no money to buy food for the children, let alone for the small number of Aboriginal men and women they had drawn there, or to provide them with clothes and blankets. This meant that the mission was unable to take in many of the Aboriginal people whom Matthews sought to recruit, or admit those who sought the Matthewses' help. It sometimes had to rely on the Aboriginal people hunting and gathering food in their customary way, and often it had to persuade or allow the men and women to leave the mission to get work on the pastoral runs or hunt and fish, and to ask them to postpone their return. These conditions undermined the Matthewses' attempts to Christianise and 'civilise' those who had come, and it must have deterred those such as Cooper who wanted to stay. During this period the number of deaths at Maloga outnumbered births, largely because many of the people suffered poor health, especially pulmonary diseases, and because infant mortality was especially high. This, too, must have frequently driven Aboriginal people away, given their beliefs about disease, death and place.[5]

The mission also struggled because it faced opposition in the neighbourhood. Some members of the local settler community were sympathetic, but many were hostile. They viewed the protection that the Matthewses tried to provide to the Aboriginal people as a threat to their source of labour and sexual partners. The local white men were also affronted by Matthews' complaints about their drinking and abuse of Aboriginal women and his attempts to make some of them pay for the support of the Aboriginal children they had fathered. On one occasion Matthews was assaulted by a local fisherman (and would have suffered greater harm had not a Yorta Yorta woman pulled him away to safety).[6]

Maloga also faced an uphill battle to attract or hold the likes of Cooper, as the Aboriginal men's labour was held in very high regard on pastoral runs and so they could command the same wages as white workers. Furthermore, the local people were still able to gather some food in a traditional manner and to acquire food, clothes and blankets at the depots of the Victorian Aborigines Protection Board. It was claimed that some were in the habit of going from one depot to the next to gather supplies and then selling the surplus. Moreover, at least two of the pastoralists who looked after these depots in their capacity as honorary correspondents—James Rutherford at *Ulupna* and John McKenzie at *Wyuna*—kept a paternal eye on them. These circumstances meant that the senior Yorta Yorta men and women were able to resist the Matthewses' attempt to lure children to the mission.[7]

Better days

By the early 1880s Maloga's prospects had begun to improve. In October 1878, Matthews had been able to persuade some philanthropists, clergymen and former missionaries in Sydney to form a small body called the Committee to Aid the Maloga Mission, but more importantly in February 1880 the New South Wales

Aborigines Protection Association was founded. This was a much more formidable organisation, comprising not only clergymen and philanthropists but leading churchmen and parliamentarians, and boasting the governor as its patron. The money it raised ensured that Maloga had a more regular supply of food and enabled it to build several more cottages (though the association held that missions should not be established on private land).[8]

Yet these improvements did not address a fundamental problem, namely the mission's lack of land. More land was required if Maloga was going to be able to attract more men and women, employ the men, and be a source of food and income for all the people and the mission itself. Matthews had written in his diary in August 1879: 'I am looking forward to the time when [the men] will have a grant

This photograph was one of many that a professional photographer, Nicholas J Caire, took of Aboriginal people at Maloga in 1883 as a result of a commission he received from the New South Wales Government, out of which he produced a small souvenir album, Aboriginals of Australia, comprising twelve views. Caire was most interested in depicting traditional Aboriginal culture, and so in these photographs, and the captions he wrote for them, he largely effaced the cultural changes that Aboriginal people on missions had undergone. Nevertheless, in a few of them, like this one, he revealed the impact of the missionaries' 'civilising' work in the form of the hut on the left. This probably explains why the Matthewses found these or similar photographs useful in their propaganda work, exhibiting them at the meetings they held to raise funds for the mission.

of land which they will work for themselves and reap the reward of their own industry.' He realised that this was also critical for another reason. 'Under the present circumstances', he remarked, 'it is difficult to know how to deal with the men, as any disaffection may lead to disruption and complete break up of our establishment, and the result of years' labor be entirely frustrated.'[9]

These considerations prompted Matthews to petition the New South Wales Government for a reservation of land adjacent to that owned by his eldest brother. In turn the Aborigines Protection Association took up the matter. It told the government that there was an urgent need for land to be reserved for the use of the Aboriginal people at Maloga and formed a deputation to the colonial secretary of New South Wales (later known as the premier), Henry Parkes, in which their spokesmen argued that the Aboriginal people had a right to a certain portion of land on the grounds that the colony had taken the country from them.[10]

At much the same time as this occurred, Maloga's population began to increase. A good part of this was due to the fact that a long-time Aboriginal sympathiser in Sydney, George Thornton, together with Matthews, had pressured more than twenty of coastal Sydney's local Aboriginal population to move to Maloga.[11] But most of the increase occurred because the Victorian Board for the Protection of the Aborigines had forced some of the Aboriginal people at Coranderrk off the reserve to work, and having met with hardship, they had crossed the state border to seek help at Maloga. About twenty of these people were Yorta Yorta who had sought refuge at Coranderrk in the 1860s, many of them as children, and were now returning to their own country. They were accompanied by Kulin people, some of whom they had intermarried with. All of these people had recently been engaged in a fierce battle with the board over the land and management of Coranderrk. They brought with them a bitter sense of defeat, but also a strong conviction about their rights, and considerable political experience.[12]

The early 1880s also saw the arrival at Maloga of a man who was to play a significant role in the life of the mission and its successor, Cumeroogunga, and that of its people, not least of whom was Cooper.

Thomas Shadrach James was born in 1859 in Port Louis, the capital of Mauritius, a small British colony situated about 2000 kilometres off the south-east coast of the Indian subcontinent. His parents were Tamil-speakers who had migrated from Madras on the south-eastern coast of India, probably as indentured labourers for Mauritius's sugar plantation economy. Shortly afterwards, however, James's father, who was a bright young man, began working for a local magistrate as an interpreter. Later he caught the eye of the first Anglican bishop of Mauritius, whose influence resulted in his conversion from Islam to Christianity, after which he worked for the Anglican Church—or more particularly the Church Missionary Society and its Christian Indian Association—as a catechist to his fellow countrymen and women. Thomas himself, whose birth name was Shadrach Thomas Peersahib, acquired a very good education at a private school in Port Louis, and became a Methodist before migrating to Tasmania in about 1878 after his mother had died and his father had remarried shortly afterwards.[13]

This studio portrait of Thomas Shadrach James was probably taken in the 1900s.

In January 1881 James met the Matthewses and approximately forty of the people from Maloga at Brighton Beach in Melbourne, where they were holidaying and visiting churches in the city and in the suburbs of Brighton and Hawthorn. He decided to return to Maloga with them and take up a post as the assistant teacher in the mission's school. Once there he soon performed nearly all the educational work. From the outset James was sympathetic towards the people at Maloga, probably because he identified personally with their experience of British colonisation. They in turn came to regard him as a kindred spirit and part of their kin community. The latter aspect of their relationship was cemented when he and Cooper's sister Ada married a few years later. In time James would play the roles of both advocate and mediator for the Aboriginal people at Maloga. This was probably facilitated by the fact that he learned to speak Yorta Yorta or understand it well enough to be able to translate it into English.[14]

Thomas James (far right) stands with his pupils in front of the schoolhouse at Maloga in the early to mid-1880s.

James not only taught the children during the day but the men at night, taking what he called the scholars' class in one of the men's huts. He urged the people at Maloga to embrace the opportunities that Christianity and civilisation (as he saw it) had to offer but also to assert their rights as British subjects. He was to teach several children at Maloga and Cumeroogunga who later played a major role in the fight for Aboriginal rights: Doug Nicholls, Jack and George Patten, Bill and Eric Onus, and his own son Shadrach Livingstone James, whom we discuss Chapter 5. Indeed, his work as a teacher at Maloga and Cumeroogunga is one of the main reasons why a significant number of people from this mission and reserve were prominent in Aboriginal affairs in the twentieth century.[15]

The Maloga Petition

In April 1881, soon after James joined Maloga, a petition was drawn up and signed by forty-two of the men. Among the signatories were three of Cooper's brothers: Aaron Atkinson, Bobby Wilberforce and Jacky Wilberforce. Had Cooper himself been at the mission he no doubt would have signed as well.[16]

For many centuries British subjects had used petitions to approach their political masters. By the late eighteenth century this had become increasingly common, partly as a result of the evangelical movement and its involvement in the campaign for the abolition of slavery. (I discuss the nature of petitioning in some depth in Chapter 5.) Matthews, who was familiar with the history of the fight against slavery, had probably talked to the people at Maloga about the use of petitions in this context, but the idea for the petition might have originated elsewhere, as we will see.

In the petition the Aboriginal signatories appealed to the governor of New South Wales for a grant of land. Casting themselves as the traditional owners of the land, they began by describing the dispossession and displacement of their people and its consequences: 'all the land within our tribal boundaries has been taken possession of by the government and white settlers. Our hunting grounds are used for sheep pasturage, and the game reduced, and in many places exterminated, rendering our means of subsistence extremely precarious, and often reducing us, and our wives and children, to beggary.' The petitioners declared that they wanted to cultivate and raise stock so they could settle down, build houses and support their families by their own industry, rather than continue in their former way of life. They also made reference to the fact that other Aboriginal people in the colony had proven themselves capable of supporting themselves when suitable land had been reserved for them. (Extensive networks of connection ensured that Aboriginal people had knowledge of what was happening among other Aboriginal groups.)[17]

The petitioners were probably influenced by the Kulin headman William Barak, who was visiting Maloga at this time in a desperate attempt to save the life of his ailing son, David; David became one of the signatories to the petition. The Maloga men's call for land resembled one that the Kulin people had made in 1859. Likewise, they almost certainly addressed the petition to the colony's governor because, like the Kulin and other Aboriginal people in south-eastern Australia, they believed he had a particular responsibility for them as the representative of Queen Victoria. They stated: 'We recognise in you the protector specially appointed by Her Gracious Majesty the Queen to promote religion and education among the aboriginal natives of the colony, and to protect us in our persons and in the free enjoyment of our possessions, and to take such measures as may be necessary for our advancement in civilisation.' As we will see, *protection* was a word or concept of great importance in the political work Cooper undertook in the last decade of his life.[18]

The petition might have been drafted by James, but the way it was framed probably owed something to Matthews as well. At the very least he gave the petition its final form during a trip he made to Sydney shortly after it was drawn up. The missionary had argued for some time that the Aboriginal people had been robbed of their birthright and were consequently owed compensation by the colony. 'The fact has never been fully recognised that the aborigines have valid claims upon the government and people of these colonies', he had written in 1876. 'Almost the only compensation they have yet received for the loss of their land and means of support is the blanket annually presented to each by the state … [T]he community at large is under obligation to the aborigines as the original possessors of the soil.' These ideas would also be central to Cooper's political work.[19]

After Matthews delivered the petition to one of Sydney's major newspapers in July 1881, he, in company with a member of the Aborigines Protection Association and a parliamentarian, called upon the New South Wales Government to reserve some land for the petitioners immediately. Locally, one of the honorary correspondents, McKenzie, who knew of the petition prior to its submission, also wholeheartedly supported it. So too did the editor of the *Riverine Herald*. 'There can be no doubt that if the government of New South Wales would give a grant of land to the Maloga blacks, they would only be giving what the blacks are entitled to', he declared. 'The blacks, in fact, would only be receiving back their own.'[20]

The government was slow to respond, however. This can partly be attributed to the fact that there was still no government body specifically responsible for meeting the needs of Aboriginal people. But the Aborigines Protection Association held meetings in Sydney in July and August 1881 in which its leading figures called on the government to assume some of the responsibilities for caring for Aboriginal people in the colony. This seems to have forged a body of public opinion that helped to persuade the government that it had to act. Later that year and early the following one, Matthews applied to the Victorian Government and the Land Board of New South Wales respectively for a piece of land opposite Maloga so he could erect some temporary workshops in which the men could do manufacturing work. At much the same time the New South Wales Government reluctantly agreed to create the position of Protector of Aborigines, and in June 1882 it commissioned a report on Maloga and Warangesda. In the intervening months the Aborigines Protection Association called upon the colonial secretary to reserve an area of land at Maloga for the use of the Aboriginal people.[21]

In January 1883 George Thornton, whom we met briefly earlier and who was a parliamentarian and a member of the Aborigines Protection Association, submitted a report to the government in which he called for land to be reserved for the purposes of the Aboriginal people so that they could form 'homesteads' and cultivate grain, fruit and vegetables for themselves. In fact Thornton recommended that in particular districts the Aboriginal people should not only be granted reserves of between 10 and 40 acres (4 and 16 hectares) but also provided with capital so that they could build huts and plough, plant and fence these blocks of land (though he was opposed to the work of Christian missionaries). There can be little doubt that Thornton had the petitioners at Maloga in mind as he had recently been told of their desire to get land. In February a new government headed by Alexander Stuart agreed to establish a board for the protection of the Aborigines, and in April the Department of Lands announced that it had reserved about 1800 acres (730 hectares) of land adjacent to Maloga for the use of Aboriginal people.[22]

It must have seemed to the Aboriginal men at Maloga that their petitioning had been successful. However, they were disappointed with the terms upon which the land had been granted: it had only been reserved for their use, rather than granted to them as their own property. This meant it could be revoked at any time. Moreover, whereas they had hoped that they would be able to farm the land independently, Matthews and the Aborigines Protection Association believed that the ways in which the reserve was to be used had been entrusted to *them* and so they assumed that *they* would oversee the way it was administered. On realising that this was the case, some of the Aboriginal men at Maloga made clear their dissent. Within days of receiving the news that the land had been reserved, one of them, Hugh (or Hughy) Anderson, cancelled an agreement he had made with Matthews to work on the mission—which the missionary dismissed as 'some fancied grievance about the reserve'—and Matthews complained to the Victorian Protection Board that one of the Coranderrk men 'boasted of the fact that they had … [men] … who knew how to talk to [i.e. influence] the Chief Secretary'.[23]

Cooper and conversion

It is probably no coincidence that in January 1882 Cooper decided to live more or less permanently at Maloga. From his point of view, we can assume, it had become a better prospect: the Matthewses now conceived of the mission as one that would cater to Aboriginal men and women rather than children alone; the mission's resources had increased following the founding of the Aborigines Protection Association; and there was a prospect of a grant of land that the men of the mission could farm independently.[24]

Two years later Cooper took the momentous step to convert to Christianity. After religious service one Sunday evening in January 1884 he went to Matthews and told him: 'I must give my heart to God.' After the two men knelt down to pray, Cooper declared that 'he had peace with God, through Christ'. He was one of many Aboriginal people who were involved at this time in an event that one historian, Claire McLisky, has called the Maloga Mission Revival.[25]

The conversion of a large number of the Aboriginal people between December 1883 and March 1884 was unprecedented for Maloga. So too was the fact that the majority of those who converted were men. Previously, most who embraced the missionaries' religion had been women. In August 1883 one man converted and two more men did the same two months later, but the mass conversion began a few months after this and occurred especially during a two-week period around Christmas and the New Year.[26]

McLisky has argued that several factors played a role, though she acknowledges that the causes remain something of a mystery. One of the factors, she has suggested, can be characterised as political. Some of the younger Aboriginal men played a vital role and it seems clear that they saw their embrace of Christianity as a means of strengthening their position on the mission. In the weeks leading up to Christmas two of Cooper's brothers—Aaron Atkinson and Johnny Atkinson—and Bagot Morgan, who were three of Maloga's most influential men, began the process by professing that they had embraced the word of God. What is more, they started to proselytise, even though only a short time earlier they had eschewed the faith themselves. On 24 December Johnny urged Hughy Anderson: 'You know the Lord can save you like He saved us. Tonight we will have a prayer meeting, and then you will have a chance to open your heart to the Holy Spirit. Remember we were once as wicked as you, and Jesus put us right. We will pray for you.' These Aboriginal men were not only proclaiming a very personal relationship with the Divine;

they were claiming power for themselves to act. In this respect it is surely relevant that they were all Yorta Yorta men and so were assuming authority to act on their traditional land.[27]

It is probably significant that their proselytising increased after the whole mission moved on Boxing Day to the Moira Lakes about 16 kilometres away, as it often did at this time of the year to spend a week or two camping. This was the place where Cooper had been born. It was also the place where the Yorta Yorta had traditionally held ceremonies; and, unlike most of their customary lands, which had been overrun by the pastoralists and their men and stock, it had unquestionably remained an Aboriginal place. Consequently, the young men must have felt that they had a particular right to speak there. It is also striking that some of the conversions—for example, that of Anderson—occurred during Matthews' absence. 'On visiting the camp the following day', the missionary wrote in his diary for 3 January, 'nearly the first words that greeted my eyes were "Hughy is converted. Thank the Lord!"' He added: 'It appears the previous evening, after prayers, a few gathered at Hughy's tent, and had a prayer meeting.' Matthews often seemed to be a mere bystander or

This photo was apparently taken at Maloga as the Matthewses and the people set out to camp at the Moira Lakes on Queen's Birthday in 1883. Daniel Matthews stands on the left, next to the horse and cart that would carry some of their provisions.

at best a witness to what took place. In this case, on the morning after Anderson's conversion, he noted: 'Under the shady trees, a little distance from the camp, I went with them to listen to their heart-felt prayers.'[28]

On returning to Maloga these young men continued to play a major role in what took place. This was the case with Cooper's conversion. As he told Matthews on 6 January, 'I must give my heart to God; my brothers are praying for me.' A week later Cooper's brothers Johnny Atkinson and Edgar Atkinson, Whyman McLean, Hughy Anderson and Bagot Morgan addressed the people at one of the nightly meetings, 'invit[ing] the unsaved not to delay, but at once to decide for Christ'. Two days later Edgar made clear to a meeting he addressed that in speaking God's words he was speaking as their brother, 'the same colour as you', thereby revealing that he was bypassing the missionaries in their role as spiritual mediators.[29]

The fact that the land many of the men at Maloga had sought in their petition of 1881 had been granted recently, and that the missionaries and their religious backers had played a key role in facilitating this outcome, probably contributed to these men's decision to embrace the faith of Maloga's founders. In other words, they would have grasped the fact that conversion to Christianity could bring material advantages. Three of the leading figures in the revival—Johnny Atkinson, Edgar Atkinson and Bagot Morgan—had been signatories to the petition.[30]

Matthews, like John Green at Coranderrk previously, had given these people a powerful framework to make sense of their oppression, endure it and raise their voices against it. This was a vision of society that encompassed Aboriginal people because it held that all peoples were God's children and thus potentially equal. Matthews also presented God and his religious principles as a higher form of authority than government and its secular principles. Finally, he provided what can be called a prophetic or predictive history, a vision of historical time that promised salvation in the future for the downtrodden of the earth.

More specifically, Matthews encouraged the people at Maloga to identify themselves with the Jews of the Bible. He did so through his teachings, especially from the Old Testament, and his musical work, particularly hymns and spirituals, beginning with 'There Is a Happy Land, Far, Far Away'. In his old age Cooper recalled the dramatic Biblical stories Matthews read to them. 'Your father's voice still rings in my ears', he was to tell one of the missionary's daughters. Those narratives, especially the Book of Exodus, enabled the Maloga people to imagine themselves in terms akin to the persecuted and suffering Israelites who had been dispossessed of their land. At the same time, they offered those like Cooper not just the hope but the unconditional promise of deliverance. According to God's binding covenant, the dispossessed who took their destiny into their own hands would eventually return home. The people at Maloga seem to have embraced this reassuring account of collective salvation in converting to Christianity. Late in his life Cooper made a statement (modelled on Psalm 136) in which he declared in part: 'God's mercy endureth forever. Do right. Have faith in God. Go strong and of good courage; for the Lord, thy God, and all the resources of Heaven, are with those that do His will and serve Him in sincerity and truth. Therefore incline your heart anew unto the Lord[,] His will obey, and the Lord will give thee victory over thine enemies.'[31]

It is also vital to note the spiritual dimension of the Maloga men's conversion, given their heartfelt declarations of faith, fervent praying and joyful singing at the time. 'Passages of scripture that were meaningless and obscure to them now shine out with a radiance that causes them to admire', Matthews remarked in his diary in late February 1884. 'Hymns that had been sung hundreds of times without exciting pleasure, now affected their hearts. Prayer too, was a reality, and a precious privilege.' In other words, the conversions took place, as was common in evangelical religion, in circumstances in which emotions were heightened. 'A marvellous power seemed to pervade the meeting', Matthews wrote of one gathering, concluding his account: 'It was nearly midnight before we parted, but none seemed wearied. Men and women were clapping hands for very joy. Some said "this must be like Heaven". "I never felt so happy in all my life." "Wouldn't it be nice to be always like this?" "Praise the Lord" and such like expressions.' It seems that this fervour

created a force that few could resist. Some whom Matthews least
expected to convert embraced the word of God. They included
Cooper's mother. In all probability some of these people might have
been attracted to Christianity now because they had finally been
able to see parallels between their traditional religious beliefs and
Christian mythology. Seldom was conversion to Christianity simply
a matter of Indigenous people abandoning their previous beliefs
for a new religion.[32]

The social conditions on the mission no doubt played some
role in the mass conversion as well. Throughout 1883 and into the
new year the people had been plagued by illness and had lost many
of their kin, including infants. As the historian Robert Kenny has
reminded us in his study of a nineteenth-century Aboriginal man
who converted at a nearby Victorian mission in the early 1860s,
Christianity is an especially consoling religion for those living in the
midst of sickness and death because it has suffering at its core.[33]

For his part Cooper testified to his conversion at a meeting near
the end of the revival in these terms: 'If it had not been for the
Lord, we would never have been here. We are all hard enough, but
Mr Matthews prayed for us, and we are nearly all Christians. Jesus
is more nearer to me than ever, and every chance I get I mean to
pray and speak for Him.' He urged his audience: 'Make good use of
the little faith you have got. I am very happy. Jesus died for my sins,
on the cross. Thank the Lord for saving all our family.' Like many of
the men and women who converted during the 1883–84 revival at
Maloga, Cooper remained a committed Christian for the rest of his
life, his Bible always beside his bed.[34]

3

CRISIS AT MALOGA

I N JUNE 1884, shortly after Cooper embraced the Christian faith, he married a young Yorta Yorta woman, Annie Murrie. She had come to Maloga in 1877 as a girl, along with her two sisters and her mother (who had since died of tuberculosis). She became one of the pupils in the school, sponsored by a Presbyterian Sunday school on Clarendon Street in South Melbourne (and so was called for a time Annie Clarendon Murrie).[1] Annie had been taught first by the Matthewses and then by Thomas James. Daniel Matthews seems to have been especially proud of what she had become as a result of the mission's instruction and training. He described her at the point she married Cooper as Maloga's 'first genuine Mission girl', thereby distinguishing her from other young Aboriginal women at the mission who had suffered sexual abuse at the hands of white men whom Matthews regarded as depraved. Missionaries often tried to influence who their young women charges married. If this was the case at Maloga, it reveals the high regard in which Matthews held Cooper. Annie converted to Christianity a short time after William did, and they were married at the mission by a minister from Echuca. In the next few years they were to have two children, Emma (later known as Emily), who was born in July 1885, and Bartlett, who was born in June 1888.[2]

During this period we can assume that Cooper, like nearly all the other men at Maloga, spent considerable periods of time shearing, fencing, grubbing and harvesting on nearby properties, but also fishing and catching game in and near the Murray River. Whenever they could, these men returned to the mission on Saturday evening so they could attend the following day's religious services. During one of William's absences, Annie, who suffered from respiratory problems that afflicted many of the people on the mission, suddenly fell ill, lost consciousness and was feared to be dying.[3]

The years that coincided with Cooper's return to Maloga, his conversion and marriage were a period of relative stability for the mission. Its population expanded, land was granted, and monetary aid was provided by the New South Wales Aborigines Protection Association and the Aborigines Protection Board of New South Wales. But in the next few years there was a considerable struggle between the missionaries and the Aboriginal people, particularly the men. Much of this concerned the meaning of work.

Conflict

The Aboriginal men were very capable workers. '[N]o sort of farm or bush work com[es] amiss to them', remarked a journalist who visited Maloga a few years later. 'They can put up a house, a stock-yard, a fence, a stable or a shed in a thoroughly workmanlike manner. They can also shear a sheep or follow a plough—in fact they can do almost everything required in the bush.' But, as this newspaperman noted, the men did not always work in the manner the Matthewses wanted. For the missionaries, and the culture of which they were a part, work was a means of salvation. Consequently, they expected the people at Maloga to work hard, seldom rest and always be thrifty. As time went by the missionaries and their backers in Sydney also expected the people to work in return for what was provided to them on the mission, such as rations. But work had a rather different cultural, moral and practical significance for the Yorta Yorta. Traditionally, it was regarded by Aboriginal people as a means to an end rather than an end in itself. They worked in order to survive and meet social, cultural and religious obligations, which tended to involve sharing the fruits of their labour. In recent times, moreover, they had worked for pastoralists and fishermen in order to establish relationships of kin that entailed mutual or reciprocal obligations, and to enable them to remain on their own country. They had also become accustomed to earning good wages and spending their earnings as they wished. The Matthewses never seem to have grasped the reasons for the differences between their expectations in regard to work and those of the Aboriginal people. In particular, they were oblivious to the code of reciprocity that governed the Aboriginal community at Maloga, instead complaining frequently of what they called their 'ingratitude'.[4]

The Matthewses' attempt to persuade the Aboriginal men to labour in the manner they wanted was undermined by the fact that there was seldom enough work for them to perform. Maloga lacked sufficient land and capital to exploit it, let alone enough funds to pay the men properly for their labour, especially in comparison to the wages they were able to command off the mission. The people often resisted the regime the Matthewses sought to impose. They refused to work; started late or finished early; worked slowly; did tasks in a way they considered best; complained that they were underfed (especially in regard to meat); met their need for food in a way they themselves valued, such as by hunting and gathering rather than tilling the soil; and took jobs away from the mission.[5]

Matthews and the Aboriginal people also clashed over recreation. Several of the young men began to demonstrate prowess as athletes, cricketers and footballers. Cooper was one of them. He enjoyed success as a sprinter and a hurdler, both locally and further afield, winning a series of events. Later he proved himself a good all-round cricketer. (Shortly after he died, the Riverine Herald would pose this question in one of its regular 'news tests': 'What famous athlete was buried at Cummeragunja yesterday week?', and provide the answer as: 'Billy Cooper, half-caste aborigine, famous hurdler and sprinter'.) But Matthews regarded sport as a distraction from the more serious business of work and complained that some of the men at Maloga were more interested in playing games than working. He was especially opposed to their participating in sporting fixtures

The Maloga cricket team, pictured in the mid–1880s. Thomas James, seated in the middle, might have been the team's coach while Hughy Anderson appears to have been its captain.

that took them off the mission, believing that this led them into bad company and encouraged drinking and gambling. He often tried to stop them going.[6]

Many of the Aboriginal people increasingly resisted the authority the Matthewses sought to exercise over such matters. The missionaries expected the people to submit, but they were unwilling to do so day in, day out. They periodically sought to defy the Matthewses in one way or another. For the men at any rate this included leaving the mission to work, play sport, drink and gamble. But some also sought autonomy in the religious realm. They formed an evangelistic band and took the services at the mission regularly on Friday evenings (which Matthews admitted were among the most interesting of all the religious meetings they had) and preached sometimes on Sunday mornings. Several also went out with Matthews or James to preach the gospel to local settlers, and a few expressed an interest in leaving the mission altogether to evangelise among their own people. Cooper does not seem to have been one of these men, but he might have been.[7]

Singing seems to have been one of the activities on the mission that was free of conflict between the missionaries and the people. From the outset, song was central to the Matthewses' evangelising as they taught their young acolytes, Cooper among them, hymns. (It seems that Cooper also learned to play the violin or fiddle.) Many of the hymns were composed and arranged by the American Ira D Sankey for an evangelical religious revival. By 1880 the people at Maloga could sing more than seventy of these hymns by heart. Matthews reckoned the people loved singing them, and there seems no reason to doubt him. They would perform for the growing number of visitors the mission attracted and made a name for themselves for the sweetness of their voices. Later they would give concerts in major towns in the area.[8]

In Maloga's later years the people's singing acquired another dimension for them. This followed a visit to the mission in August 1886 of the celebrated Fisk Jubilee Singers as part of an Australasian tour they were making.[9] This was a group of itinerant gospel singers that had been formed in 1871 to raise money for Fisk University in Nashville, Tennessee, which was founded after the Civil War by the American Missionary Association as the first college for emancipated slaves and other African Americans. The Jubilee Singers were both evangelical Christians and advocates for the rights of former slaves, and believed in the importance of forging a sense of solidarity among oppressed peoples.[10]

On their visit to Maloga the group sang several spirituals, 'Steal Away to Jesus' (which was their signature tune that opened every performance), 'Rise, Shine' and 'I've Been Redeemed'. According to Matthews, the Aboriginal people 'were in raptures'. The reason for this is revealed in a letter that the director of the Fisk Singers, Frederick Loudin, sent to an African American newspaper in Detroit. 'They were very shy at first and were very uncommunicative', he observed. 'But after we sang to them it seemed to be the key to their hearts, for it regularly opened their sympathies.' He continued: 'It was strange to witness the effect the old slave songs born in the Southern plantations of America made upon these people at the Antipodes.' It appears that the pain and suffering expressed by these songs allowed or enabled the Maloga people to express *their* pain and suffering. 'Many of them wept as they listened to the weird plaintive melodies ... more touched in fact by it than it has ever been our privilege in any other people', Loudin remarked. The degree to which the Aboriginal people had been moved was made plain at the end of the concert. 'After the singing was over they grasped us by the hand, many of them with the tears streaming from their eyes, thanking us again and again for what to them had been a great treat', Loudin recalled. 'When we were to leave the settlement they all came out to bid us goodbye, and as we drove away so long as we could see the settlement, handkerchiefs, hats and hands were being waved from the treetops or from whatever a native could hold on long enough to wave his hat or hand.' In fact, Matthews observed, the people sang 'Blest Be the Tie that Binds' as the Fisk Jubilee Singers departed, and the group reciprocated by singing 'Good-bye Brothers, Good-bye Sisters'.[11]

Loudin took away a pair of emu eggs beautifully carved by one of the Aboriginal people, and left behind two large photographs of the singers, a dozen books describing their travels, and copies of their songs. Matthews wrote in his diary: 'It is a time never to be forgotten.' He was right. The visit of these African American singers had a lasting influence. The Aboriginal people soon mastered some of their songs, such as 'Steal Away to Jesus' and 'Oh Brother, Are You Getting Ready'. A few of the songs were translated into Yorta Yorta and incorporated in the choir's repertoire for the concerts they gave both on and off the mission. Probably none was more important than a spiritual translated by the grandmother of Margaret Tucker (who was later a vice-president of the Australian Aborigines' League) and notated by Thomas James. In singing this song, 'Burra Phara' (or 'Bura Fera'), the people at Maloga seem to have identified with the dispossessed Jews of the Bible and envisaged that their people would one day be restored to their homeland.[12]

A challenge to authority

By this time the New South Wales Aborigines Protection Association, a small number of white workers the organisation had
appointed to the mission,[13] and the Aboriginal people themselves
were increasingly challenging the Matthewses' authority at Maloga.
This exposed the fragility of the order the missionaries had established and eventually led to the break-up of the mission and the
people's removal to the nearby Aboriginal reserve that came to be
called Cumeroogunga. This story warrants telling in detail because it
must have played a major part in Cooper's life at the time.[14]

Initially the founding of the Aborigines Protection Association in
1880 had made little if any difference to the organisation of Maloga's
affairs. But as the mission became more and more dependent on
the organisation's benevolence, it became subject to its will. (At this
stage the New South Wales Aborigines Protection Board was a small
body that had little support from government, virtually no power
and no clearly defined policy of its own, though since it eventually
provided most of the funds for missions such as Maloga it was able
to wrest control from the Aborigines Protection Association and the
missions themselves.)

Many of the Aboriginal people increasingly chafed against the
Matthewses' discipline and their expectation that they always submit
to their authority. Daniel Matthews blamed this mostly on the
refugees from Coranderrk. As early as April 1883 he had complained
to the secretary of the Victorian Board for the Protection of the
Aborigines: '[T]he presence of these people from Coranderrk is
usually prejudicial to ours at Maloga, for they (for a time at any
rate) infuse an independent and restless spirit among our people,
such as to damage the management'. A year later he would claim
that the admission of these people to Maloga invariably caused
'discord and disaffection'. But Yorta Yorta were responsible for a
good part of the unrest. Strikingly, though not surprisingly, the men
who seem to have become most antagonistic to the Matthewses'
regime were two of those who had played a leading role in the
religious revival of 1883–84: Johnny Atkinson and Bagot Morgan.
In April 1885 Atkinson and several others pitched a camp a few

kilometres up the river, having been expelled or having left of their own accord. Shortly afterwards they returned to the mission and sought Matthews' permission to remain. But several months later Morgan established a camp comprising his family and several others across the river after he had been expelled, and Atkinson soon did the same again up the river, though they all returned a few months later and were permitted by Matthews to remain, albeit on trial.[15]

In the spring of 1886 the mission again became unsettled, but for a different reason. In September the Aborigines Protection Association sent George Bellenger, a former overseer at Warangesda Mission, to Maloga. It gave him a task but no position, and so rumours began to circulate on the mission and in the neighbourhood about Maloga's superintendence and even its future. Bellenger had been sent to resolve a problem that had long bedevilled the mission and that had troubled the Aborigines Protection Association from its beginning, namely the fact that it was on private land. The association had invested a considerable amount of money in Maloga in anticipation of securing title to it, but this had proven to be very difficult, despite the fact that there was goodwill among all the parties. The association now called upon Matthews to transfer to it immediately a block of 80 acres (32 hectares) that lay between Maloga and the land that had been reserved by the New South Wales Government for Aboriginal use in 1883. But Matthews was either unwilling or unable to do so. Consequently, the association decided it had no choice but to move the mission to the land that had been reserved next door.[16]

In the middle of October Bellenger chose a site for the mission on that land and sought the association's approval, but Matthews thought this was unsuitable, just as he believed that the buildings at Maloga would suffer if they were moved. The Aboriginal people on the mission soon got wind of this proposal and were disinclined to work for the time being. What is more, they realised that authority on the mission was now divided and that Matthews' position as its superintendent had been weakened. As a result they increasingly acted towards him in ways that he considered disrespectful.[17]

In mid-November a local journalist, Keighley Goodchild, spent a week at the mission and penned a series of long articles about it.

It is worth taking into account his description of day-to-day life as it clarifies what those such as Cooper lost as a result of the imminent destruction of Maloga. Goodchild reported that the mission was assuming the proportions of a small township.[18] It comprised fourteen four-roomed weatherboard cottages, some of which were occupied by two Aboriginal families and all of which were surrounded by garden plots that were enclosed by paling fences; houses for the white overseer, the gardener and the schoolmaster; a more commodious house for the Matthewses and their children; a fair-sized building for meetings; and a small schoolroom. There was also a dairy, a woolshed, a cart shed, stables and a forge. Lastly, at some distance from this township, there was a camp that had a few huts and a couple of circular tents, one of which was occupied by young unmarried men. Goodchild remarked that several of the cottages were furnished at least as well as those of the average white selector, that some had sofas and even a chiffonier, and that pictures adorned the walls.[19]

Goodchild observed that every day, at least during the week, had a rhythm that was governed by the missionaries. Religious observance was to the fore. Each day began with a meeting that consisted of prayers and hymns and a few remarks by Matthews. Goodchild was in no doubt that many of those present at this meeting were earnest Christians. In the week he was there a camp meeting took place—that is, an evangelical religious gathering—that attracted local settlers to the mission and in which the singing of hymns and spirituals played a part. Goodchild believed these meetings were beneficial to the Aboriginal people. 'They are an emotional people, and are in need of such seasons of revival as were the slaves in America', he remarked. He was also struck by the importance of the mission's cemetery for them: 'I should say that the place is viewed with a reverence foreign to the way in which white people regard their cemeteries.' Like Loudin's observations about the people's response to the Fisk Jubilee Singers' songs, this testifies to the enormous pain and suffering the people had experienced and a deep religious sense that was attuned to the passing of life.[20]

Both these photographs were taken by Nicholas J Caire in 1883. The first reveals how a village was beginning to emerge on the banks of the Murray, while the second shows one of its cottages.

Goodchild believed that the Aboriginal people were being amply supplied with food, some of which was grown on the station, but observed that they were also able to rely on traditional foods (such as native honey) that were in abundance in a wooded area that comprised the largest part of the land. He remarked that the Aboriginal men pointed out to him a lot of things that he could not see, acknowledging that '[t]he bush was to them an open book'.[21]

Maloga, like other Aboriginal missions at this time, was a source of curiosity to many whites. Among those who visited were journalists such as Keighley Goodchild and photographers such as Nicholas J Caire. In the caption Caire gave this photograph, 'Native bark canoes, Moira', he obscured the fact that while these men were continuing to pursue traditional cultural practices such as fishing on the Murray, they were actually living on a mission, namely Maloga, where they were adopting and adapting to 'civilisation', as the missionaries conceived of this cultural change.

The 1887 petition

This was not all that several of the Aboriginal men revealed to
Goodchild during his visit. They told him that they wanted the
adjacent reserve to be divided into small farms and given to them;
that they felt they were as capable of clearing and cultivating the land
as any white man; that they wanted to be independent; and that they
found it galling to be treated as objects of charity. 'To put it shortly,'
Goodchild remarked, 'they think they are able to walk alone with a
little instruction and advice occasionally from one in authority.' By
this time five years had passed since the Maloga men had petitioned
the governor of New South Wales and since the Coranderrk refugees
had made them aware that they could be readily dispossessed of their
home by a government authority. Goodchild seems to have grasped
that there was a distinctive element in these men's plea for a piece
of land of their own, though he does not seem to have discerned
the source of it. 'They don't ask for a selling title of the land', he
noted, 'but want it granted in such a manner that they can leave it
to their wives and children.' In other words, they wanted land they
could pass on to their descendants, just as their people had done for
countless generations.[22]

Early in December Matthews travelled to Sydney to see whether
he could reach an amicable settlement with the Aborigines
Protection Association in regard to Maloga's title. He was unable
to do so, and a small minority of the association's committee voted
in favour of moving the mission to the reserved land. Later that
month the association sent a deputation to choose a suitable site and
fixed upon one despite Matthews pointing out that it was subject
to being flooded by the river. The association gave instructions
that no further work be done at the mission. In response the men
were disinclined to work, and in January several of them, including
Whyman McLean, decided to leave. According to Matthews, this
was so they could evangelise among Aboriginal people in various
camps in New South Wales and Victoria, but they probably used
these meetings to discuss the looming crisis at Maloga as well.[23]

By February the association had stopped the funds that provided the mission with much of its food. Later that month a group

of twenty-seven people chose to escape the Matthewses' rule by moving to a camp a few kilometres up the river and putting themselves, in Matthews' words, 'under Johnny Atkinson's protection'. In March Matthews and five of the mission's converts, McLean, Martin Simpson, Dan Crow, Paddy Swift and Freddy Walker, went to Sydney to attend the annual meeting of the Aborigines Protection Association. While there they formed part of a deputation that waited on Chief Secretary Parkes and met the governor, Lord Carrington, at Government House. Matthews also met the former secretary of the Aborigines Protection Association, Edward Palmer, and they drew up a document that transferred the mission's property to three trustees in the hope that this would persuade the association to abandon its plan to move the cottages and other buildings to the reserved land. But the association refused to accept this agreement. Matthews then offered to lease the association the 20 acres on which the mission sat in order to avoid the labour, expense and waste of moving all the buildings.[24]

In April and May the men worked with Bellenger to clear ground on the reserved land. In doing this some of them defied Matthews. In July the Aborigines Protection Association's secretary, GE Ardill, and its former secretary, Andrew Menzies, visited Maloga to select a site to re-establish the mission on the reserve. Matthews was loath to agree to this step, but he gave his consent after the association promised that the move would be done gradually so as to minimise the impact on the people. Nevertheless, Matthews objected to the site that was chosen on the grounds that it had flooded two or three times since the founding of Maloga. But he was overruled after the mission's white employees and several of the Aboriginal men testified to the contrary.[25]

The Aboriginal men also saw an opportunity at this juncture to press their claims. Nearly a dozen, Cooper among them, put their names to another petition that was to be addressed to the colony's governor, who was due to pay a visit to the area shortly. In this petition, which was almost certainly drawn up by a third party, probably James, the signatories described themselves as belonging not only to Maloga but also to the neighbourhood. This reflected the fact that some of them, such as Cooper's brother Johnny Atkinson, had broken away from the Matthewses and were no longer living on the mission. In a further sign of the tensions between these men and the Matthewses, they chose to acknowledge the benefits that had been conferred upon them by the Protection Association and the Protection Board but not the founders of the mission. The petitioners called for sections of land of no less than 100 aces (40 hectares) to be granted to each family, either in the form of a freehold title or at a nominal annual rent with the option to purchase later at a reasonable price. They argued that this would enable them to earn their own living but also relieve the colony of the burden of much of their maintenance, no doubt knowing that this pitch would appeal to the government. At the same time they pointed out that 'the Aborigines were the former occupiers of the land'. Finally, they suggested that the grants they were seeking would be 'a fitting memorial in connection with the [forthcoming] centenary of the colony'. Fifty years later, Cooper would invoke a similar notion in regard to the sesquicentenary of Australia, which became known as the Day of Mourning.[26]

In mid-July Matthews, James and a group of thirty or so of the Maloga people travelled to the nearby township of Moama to meet the governor. After a speech by a local justice of the peace and the presentation of an address by the white townsfolk, James gave an address on behalf of the mission's Aboriginal people. In this we get a sense of the way in which they saw an imperial figure like Carrington. '[W]e beg to express our unqualified loyalty to you in the responsible position you occupy in the land, and to Her Sovereign lady the Queen Victoria, whose name we love, and whom you have the honor to represent', the address began. It went on to assert that while they were grateful to the government, the Protection Board and the Protection Association, broader sympathy was required in order to include their brothers and sisters who had been 'deprived of the benefits of civilisation'. After the governor replied to this address, another of Cooper's brothers, Jack, presented the petition. The colonial treasurer, John Fitzgerald Burns, to whom it was handed, promised to give due attention to the request the petitioners made.

He also told them that while he did not think the government would consent to grant the land in fee simple, he believed that a portion could be granted at a very low rental and that every help would be given to enable them to settle on their own holdings.[27]

A few weeks later the Aborigines Protection Association chose to separate the spiritual and secular work of the mission, confine Matthews' duties to those of a religious teacher, and appoint Bellenger as its secular manager. This caught Matthews by surprise and he refused to accept its implications, preferring to believe that he remained the mission's superintendent. Work on the reserve continued under Bellenger's supervision, but there was unrest on the mission. At the end of September Matthews derived satisfaction from the fact that the site the association had chosen for the new mission village had flooded and so had been proven to be unsuitable. Yet his position as the superintendent of the mission was called into question by one of the mission's white workers, and a few days later he received a letter from Ardill telling him that all the Aboriginal residents were answerable to Bellenger alone. In November some of the Aboriginal people expressed their opposition to the Matthewses holding the annual religious camp at Maloga, and two men in particular defied Daniel by telling him that they were no longer responsible to him. 'I find my position very much weakened, not having the power to admonish as I formerly had', Matthews wrote in his diary. Indeed, the missionary's authority had been fatally weakened.[28]

In the same month, first Johnny Atkinson and then Cooper sent letters to their local member of the New South Wales Legislative Assembly, John Chanter, which James wrote on their behalf, asking him to use his influence to help them get pieces of land adjoining Maloga. In regard to Cooper's later political work, we should note here not only Thomas's role as a mediator or go-between but that of Chanter as an ally. At this time there were white men who were sympathetic to the needs and wants of Aboriginal people such as Cooper, and this must have persuaded these Aboriginal men, both at the time and later, that making representations to government or whitefellas more generally was worthwhile and had some chance of success.

In his letter to Chanter, Cooper remarked, 'I am anxious to get a home and make some provisions for my wife and daughter', adding that he had found it impossible to pay for a selection as the work he was doing was 'barely sufficient to maintain [his] family decently'. Both he and his brother reiterated the request that had been made in the petition to the governor a few months earlier. Cooper stated: 'I want a grant of land that I can call my own so long as I and my family live and yet without the power of being able to do away with the land.' He advanced a case for a grant of 100 acres on much the same grounds as the 1881 petition, pledging that the land would be put to 'a legitimate use'.[29]

Cooper also asserted that he was only seeking 'a small portion of a vast territory' that was the Aboriginal people's 'by divine right'. As the historian Heather Goodall has pointed out, Cooper was using the language of the religion he had recently adopted, but the authority he was invoking had a traditional Aboriginal source. Like earlier Aboriginal petitioners for land, he was insisting that the government recognise a right that rested on the Aboriginal people's prior owner-ship of the country. In Goodall's words, '[Cooper] was suggesting that the "small portion", while limited in area, nevertheless signified the whole of his people's "vast territory".'[30]

On the same day that Atkinson sent his appeal, Chanter raised the issue of such a land grant in parliament, having written to the New South Wales undersecretary the previous month. He got an encour-aging response, being told by Parkes that the Aborigines Protection Board wished to facilitate the occupation of the reserve in separate allotments and that the district surveyor had been instructed to investigate how this could be done. Chanter was also given an under-taking that the matter would be dealt with as soon as possible.[31]

Confusion

By the new year, however, confusion reigned at Maloga. Ongoing floods had made it impossible to move the mission's buildings to the site chosen by the Aborigines Protection Association, and neither Bellenger nor anyone else in authority seemed to know what was happening. According to Matthews, the people were sick and tired of the uncertainty. He also reckoned they manifested a recklessness he had never seen before. Some of the men, rather than gathering firewood to burn in their cottages, had pulled down the fences surrounding their garden plots and used them to light fires. A member of the Protection Association had come to sort out the mission's problems but had failed. Matthews claimed that the Aboriginal people did not 'know in what direction to look for the head of the mission'. Clearly, they were distressed and angry. One of the men, whom Matthews had described as among their best, had beaten his wife severely in a moment of rage. To make matters worse Matthews had dismissed one of the Coranderrk refugees on the grounds that he had neglected his religious duties. This man chose to move himself and his family onto the reserve and thus beyond Matthews' authority. Several other families who sympathised with him followed suit, telling Matthews that they were going 'to get more liberty'.[32]

In the wake of this rebellion, Bellenger decided he should implement the Protection Association's instructions to move most of the mission's buildings as soon as possible. Matthews tried to prevent this happening, first by sending a proposal to the association that he purchase the buildings for the purposes of the mission, next by calling on Bellenger to postpone any action until he had received a reply, and finally by protesting against their removal. But in early February Bellenger brought in a group of seventeen men who were now living on the reserve and ordered them to pull down the cottages. Matthews claimed they were all disaffected and so went about the work willingly. He reported later: 'My dear wife and I were grieved beyond measure at the impatience manifested in the work of demolition. Houses that had taken months in construction and years in anticipation were levelled to the ground with destructive rapidity. Fences that stood around the garden lots, and had been our pride, as being the achievement of much patient labour, were soon uprooted.' It seems that many of the people were unhappy with what was happening. While another site had been chosen for the mission on the reserved land, they were dissatisfied with it as it was on sandy ground and three quarters of a mile (1.2 kilometres) from the river. Many no doubt felt deeply ambivalent about the recent turn of events. According to Matthews, at least one couple approached him and Janet to apologise, telling them that they had been like a mother and father to them and begging their forgiveness. He also reckoned the people were 'very much divided'.[33]

At this point the Matthewses decided they would resign their positions under the Protection Association. During a visit Ardill paid to Maloga shortly afterwards, they gave him to understand that they wanted to continue the work of their mission and wished to work in harmony with the association. Matthews soon put a formal proposal to this effect to the association and took himself off to Sydney to present it personally to the members, but on arriving there learned that they had accepted his and Janet's offer to resign.[34]

In the course of March some of the cottages were moved to the reserve, despite the fact that the association had now accepted that the site it had chosen was unsuitable and had recently applied to the government for an extension to the reserve so that it could include the only piece of land in the vicinity that was suitable. While the association was waiting for a response the Aboriginal petitioners learned that their request for land, which they had made in the petition in July 1887 and which Atkinson and Cooper had repeated in November that year, had been partly granted—largely, it seems, as a result of Chanter's lobbying on their behalf. The secretary of lands had ruled that the present reservation of land was ample for the requirements of the mission but agreed that part of it could be subdivided into blocks for individual families. The petitioners probably felt that they had finally gained much of what they wanted, though the future must have also seemed very uncertain as they learned shortly afterwards that the association's application for the extension of the reserve had been rejected.[35]

In the middle of April Bellenger and the Aboriginal men pulled down most of the remaining buildings at Maloga and agreed to set aside its name and call the new mission 'Cumeroogunga', a Yorta Yorta word meaning 'our home'.[36] This must have been a poignant moment for many of the people: just as they welcomed what they trusted would be a brighter future, they mourned what was passing.

More than fifty years later Cooper told one of the Matthewses' daughters in a letter that he often cast his mind back to her parents and the place. 'When we left Maloga, it appeared to me as though we left Paradise', he told her. '[A]t times it brings tears in my eyes when thinking of the glorious hours, days and months, we spent together; the beautiful singing, the picnics, the games.' With the passing of time, Cooper might have forgotten the bitter conflict between many of the Aboriginal people and the Matthewses at Maloga, or he might have decided to put aside his memory of this in addressing their daughter. But there can be no doubt that he deeply appreciated much of what these missionaries had done for the likes of himself. He was not alone. At the time several of the men arranged a gathering at the old schoolhouse before it was demolished and removed. According to Matthews, thirteen of them 'spoke with great feeling and in the highest praise for what God was doing for them and their race'. The people sang the first hymn the missionaries had taught them: 'There Is a Happy Land, Far, Far Away'.[37]

The people must have felt that this future was now much closer, but their current circumstances were dire. They were camping at Cumeroogunga while the Protection Association made a strenuous effort to persuade the government to reverse its decision regarding the extension of the reserve. Time dragged. Winter soon came, bringing heavy rain. They lacked clothes and blankets. Many fell sick. They were dispirited. '[T]he direction they looked for help seems to fail and now they feel thrown back upon themselves', Matthews claimed. It would be several months before the association and the people learned that the government had agreed to extend the reserve and consequently the work of rebuilding the mission could begin.[38]

In the meantime Bellenger was keen to assert his authority over both the Aboriginal people and the Matthewses, who had resolved to remain at Maloga and form a mission that focused on training young Aboriginal people as evangelists. Some of the Aboriginal people were keen for the Matthewses to come to Cumeroogunga and conduct religious services, and Daniel and Janet did so for a while. But in June, Bellenger sent Daniel a note calling on him to discontinue his visits on the grounds that they were unnecessary. It seems that the Aboriginal man who carried this message to the missionaries was embarrassed and that once its content became widely known many of the people on Cumeroogunga were indignant. They must have felt they had leapt out of the frying pan and into the fire. A few months later Matthews claimed there were numerous complaints among them. There seems no reason to disbelieve him. Worse was soon to come, not least for Cooper.[39]

4

CUMEROOGUNGA

$\mathbf{D}$ ESPITE THE FACT that Cumeroogunga meant 'our home' in the Yorta Yorta language, it was far from homey when it was founded. Its early years proved to be just as troubled as its beginnings, as its superintendent and sponsor scrambled to provide the resources that were so badly needed. This took a toll on William Cooper and seems to have played a role in the fight he helped to lead against the New South Wales Aborigines Protection Board near the end of his life.

Mismanaging an epidemic

In December 1888 a large number of Aboriginal people from Cumeroogunga travelled to Brighton Beach in Melbourne. For several years they had done this to celebrate Christmas and the new year with a prolonged religious picnic in which they preached and sang hymns in local churches around the city. On this occasion Cooper's young wife and infant son Bartlett, if not Cooper and his daughter Emily, were among their number. In the past this holiday had apparently been a happy occasion for all concerned, but this time several of the group contracted typhoid fever, which was prevalent in the city in the summer. On 10 January, shortly after they returned home, Bartlett died.[1] Nine days later Annie herself died at Sandhurst (Bendigo) Hospital (where those who had previously fallen ill on

This photograph was taken at one of the Maloga Mission's holiday camps at Brighton Beach in Melbourne in the early to mid-1880s. The man on the far right might be William Cooper.

Maloga had taken been for care). After Annie died Bellenger refused William's request for a cart so that he could bring her home to be buried, and so she had to be interred in a cemetery in Sandhurst. This no doubt added to his pain and suffering.[2]

To make matters worse, the authorities were slow to act on rumours that the fever had broken out at Cumeroogunga. Only on 26 January did the New South Wales Board of Health direct its local medical officer, Dr George Eakins, to investigate. This Scottish-born and -trained doctor immediately visited the reserve. He was appalled by what he found. It was not just the fact that there were eight cases of typhoid, that a good many other people had symptoms that suggested they had also contracted the disease, and that many of the women and children were suffering from other illnesses: there was no provision for treating or isolating the infectious cases of the fever, no medical attendance or nursing, and no medicine to speak of. Moreover, the food being supplied appeared to be of the poorest quality and the supply of milk was inadequate. The conditions in and around the cottages were dangerously unsanitary, not least because there were hardly any water closets. Eakins feared that it would be difficult to rid the reserve of the epidemic and that numerous deaths were to be anticipated. He recommended to the government that a temporary hospital be erected and proper medical support provided.[3]

On learning of this shocking state of affairs, on 30 January the government's chief medical adviser instructed Eakins to attend the reserve and report further. He also referred the matter to the New South Wales Aborigines Protection Board, whose secretary telegrammed a local superintendent of police to ask him to investigate and report as soon as possible. The following day a senior constable and Eakins visited the reserve. They found it in a state of disorganisation and reported that about forty of the people had fled up the river a mile or two to escape the outbreak. Eakins urged them to remain there, advised the government that twenty or more tents were required at once, and recommended that the school be closed. He also reported that one of his patients, a child, had died since his first visit and that there were several new cases. Eakins was angered by the negligence of the Aborigines Protection Board, though the real blame lay with the Aborigines Protection Association, which was still overseeing the mission. The following day he addressed a letter to the board's secretary: 'I assume that my first report, which I sent to the Board of Health, Sydney, has been read by you', he remarked, before going on to state: 'The cause of the outbreak has been the neglected insanitary state of the camp … [T]his ought to have been looked after long ago.'[4]

Not surprisingly, the Aboriginal people were distressed about this state of affairs. In the letter I have just quoted, Eakins informed the Protection Board that he had found 'a good deal of discontent and disapproval of [the] management of the mission'. Several days earlier, Hughy Anderson had put pen to paper and written to the local newspaper on behalf of the people to express their discontent. 'We want to enlighten your minds to how we are treated', he began. '[T]he blacks are the tail of the Mission, and that is far behind, and we find that the head [of the Mission] is stronger than the tail. What the head does or says the tail has to put up with. When we lived at

Maloga we were better cared for.' Anderson was not naming names, but it is clear he was talking about Bellenger. He complained about the poor food that the sick were receiving and the lack of medical treatment, but the Aboriginal people especially resented Bellenger's refusal to help them bring the bodies of their loved ones, like Annie Cooper, back to the mission so they could properly mourn their deaths. The pain they were feeling was deep-seated. 'We have been treated very badly, and are being treated likewise at the present time', Anderson wrote. It is apparent that the people believed they had a historical right to better treatment on the grounds that they were the country's first peoples. 'We think it is a great shame for us to get the worse things, when we, the original possessors of this land, ought to get the best, if not better than we receive at present', Anderson wrote. He concluded the letter with what amounted to a threat: 'We are about to leave the station if things do not change for the better … for we cannot work any longer on a place where we are not treated right.'[5]

The Aboriginal people were by no means alone in their poor opinion of Bellenger's treatment of them. On 2 February the superintendent of police at Deniliquin, J Dowling Brown, disclosed to the Protection Board that the mission's manager had not said a word about typhoid fever during a visit Brown had paid to Cumeroogunga on 24 January, and he expressed the opinion that Bellenger did not seem to be a fit person to be in charge of a mission station. On the same day another letter by Anderson appeared in the local newspaper. Now he was prepared to name Bellenger. Anderson revealed that one of the men on the mission had recently summoned Bellenger before the local bench and accused him of maliciously poisoning two of his valuable dogs, and that Bellenger had stopped this man's rations and those of his wife after the court found in the man's favour and ordered Bellenger to recompense him and pay the court's costs. 'We think [this] is wrong', Anderson wrote.

Part of the problem as far as the Aboriginal people were concerned was the degree of power Bellenger had. In this letter Anderson remarked: 'The [Protection] association has sent the rations to him to give out as he likes; he can give it when he likes and stop it when he likes.' The people at Cumeroogunga wanted 'to ask the public if it is a right thing for the manager to impose upon us blacks in such a manner'. In the midst of the recent deaths the people at Cumeroogunga were missing the solace that the Matthewses had provided them and their kin. 'The spiritual work is going down hill fast', Anderson concluded his letter; 'singing, no prayers at the meeting house at night'.[6]

In the course of the next few days the chairman of the Aborigines Protection Board, Edmund Fosbery, who was also the inspector-general of police, and the secretary of the Aborigines Protection Association, GE Ardill, directed the various local authorities to put Eakins' recommendations into effect. But Bellenger was resistant to doing so. He sent a letter to the local newspaper in which he admitted that several of the people had died and more were ill, but he blamed the spread of the fever on the conduct of the people who had gone to Melbourne in mid-December. On the same day that this letter appeared in print, the newspaper also published a letter by a local settler who declared that there was 'a lot of truth' in what Anderson had said in his recent letters to the newspaper, and called for a thorough investigation into the management of the mission. At Cumeroogunga itself the fever continued to take its toll, especially among the children. On 5 February Eakins reported that three more had died. They included one of Cooper's nephews.[7]

Several days later Eakins reported that there were two further cases of fever and called on the Protection Board to wire instructions to Bellenger to procure a supply of milk in sufficient quantities to feed the sick. 'It is more the farce to pretend to help the sick and give them nourishment when the very article of diet most suitable is not available', he wrote angrily. 'I have written to your Board on this matter already, and no steps have as yet been taken to remedy the grievance.' Eakins also called for the appointment of a trained nurse to oversee the nursing and preparation of food for the sick. On 13 February Fosbery instructed Bellenger to procure a supply of milk but refused to engage a nurse. He did, however, direct the Deniliquin police to visit the reserve again and provide him with a report.[8]

On the same day the *Riverine Herald* published a long article about the state of affairs on Cumeroogunga, which one of its journalists had written after visiting the mission two days earlier. He too attributed the spread of the fever to want of proper supervision and was scathing about the management of the mission. While it had been established twelve months earlier, he claimed, it had the appearance of having been founded only twelve weeks previous. All the houses were in an unfinished state except those of the superintendent, schoolmaster and other such figures. The Aboriginal people's houses lacked any water closets, several elderly men and women were living in all weathers in bark gunyahs, and the young men were living in a building that was similarly open to the elements. The neat little church that had stood at Maloga had yet to be re-erected properly and lacked a roof, doors and windows. A building that had been used as the hospital at Maloga had been moved there but was now the private dwelling of one of the mission's white staff. 'How much longer', this journalist demanded to know, 'will this state of things exist at Cumeroogunga, where two men and one woman have been appointed to look after the original owners of the soil?'[9]

This report provoked a string of denials from Bellenger. But before they appeared in the local newspaper, nineteen of the Aboriginal people at Cumeroogunga had put their names to a long letter of protest to the chairman of the Protection Board. Anderson was probably responsible for this petition and Cooper no doubt was one of the signatories. It set out a series of facts about the current state of affairs on the mission and called on the board to remove the causes of the problems that they said were robbing them of their peace and impeding their progress as a community.[10]

The petitioners made a series of complaints. The manager was distributing rations only to those who worked. This was wrong, the petitioners claimed. 'We have always understood the government having dispossessed us of our land, hunting grounds, &c., gave us rations as compensation, without any condition that we should work a certain number of hours for it.' This belief was widespread among Aboriginal people on missions and reserves in south-eastern

Australia at this time. They also complained that the mission's superintendent had been granted too much power and authority. '[T]
he superintendent has all the rations in his own hands, and he can
do just as he likes', they declared; 'there is no one on the mission or
the district to question whether justice is done to the aboriginals,
or whether they receive the rights conceded to them by the government.' Finally, the petitioners felt deeply wounded by the way
Bellenger had treated them. 'We consider that he has treated us very
badly during our present time of trouble', they stated. 'During our
sickness we have received neither help nor sympathy from him …
thus destroying all our respect for him and our love for the mission
as our home.' The petitioners called upon the board to engage
Eakins' services on a permanent basis and ensure that the woman
responsible for dispensing medicine to them be trained for the task.
They also begged that several well-known and respectable gentlemen in the district be appointed to visit the mission periodically and
report to the board. 'This', they concluded their plea, 'will keep the
officers from neglecting their duties, and us from abusing the rights
conceded to us by the government.'[11]

The Aborigines Protection Board forwarded a copy of this
petition to the Aborigines Protection Association and in March a
deputation comprising members of that organisation's council visited
Cumeroogunga to conduct an inquiry into all the people's complaints. In the middle of April its secretary informed the Protection
Board that all the matters of concern the people had raised had
been settled. At the very least this was an exaggeration. Apart from
anything else, the association had refused to give any ground on the
matter of rations, insisting that its rule about them was fundamental
to its control over the mission.[12]

A few days earlier Eakins had sent a long letter to the Protection
Board. He reported that the onset of autumn and thus colder weather
had seen the epidemic finally loosen its grip, but he had no doubt
the Aboriginal people were apprehensive it would return in the
summer. He also pointed out that the conditions on the mission had
deteriorated. He then launched a fierce attack on Bellenger. 'I have
been most indifferently assisted by the management throughout

the epidemic', he complained. 'My instructions were resented as irksome, and considerable supineness was exhibited.' Eakins put his finger on the source of the problem he had encountered and that the Aboriginal people were experiencing: 'I have been, I believe, represented as unduly interfering with the prerogative of the management ... I wish to point out the danger to your Board of entrusting to any one person the power of an autocrat, and the urgent necessity of appointing a committee of local gentlemen to see that the management is effectively carried out, and the caprices of an individual may not injuriously affect a community so helpless as the aborigines.' He confirmed that the people on the mission had taken 'an intense dislike to the management, principally on account of harsh and arbitrary acts'. He was also highly critical of the Protection Association, complaining that its recent deputation to the mission had not even bothered to call on him or make him aware of its visit.[13]

The Aboriginal petitioners also enlisted the support of John Chanter, the local parliamentarian who had helped them secure the government's promise of individual blocks of land on the mission. In late April he had persuaded the New South Wales Legislative Assembly to call upon the Protection Board to table correspondence regarding the epidemic, and in early July he demanded that all of this correspondence be tabled after he realised that some of it had been withheld. However, the Protection Association chose to retain Bellenger as Cumeroogunga's manager and dispense with Eakins' services as a doctor.[14]

Recovery

After this terrible episode the Aboriginal men set to work at Cumeroogunga, laying out streets, planting trees, reconstructing the cottages, erecting new buildings, clearing land and planting crops. As a result of their labours, the mission soon began to recover. Yet only 400 acres (162 hectares) was suitable for cultivation, the remainder being heavily timbered and frequently inundated by the Murray River. A major cause of the people's discontent was removed when Bellenger resigned in the closing months of 1891 and was succeeded by Bruce Ferguson, who had been serving as the mission overseer. But some abandoned Cumeroogunga and sought refuge with the Matthewses at Maloga. By 1892 there were apparently about fifty Aboriginal people there, Anderson and his wife and family among them.[15] Others moved away from the district altogether.[16]

At Cumeroogunga the remaining Aboriginal men soon resumed their calls for the blocks of land that had been promised them in 1888. They again found a sympathetic ear in the Aborigines Protection Association. After one of its council members visited the mission in July 1891 he called on the New South Wales Government to set apart 2000 acres (809 hectares) close to the reserve and grant the men 50-acre blocks. The council endorsed this and went so far as to propose that the men be assured of permanent tenure and provided with implements, seed and rations for the first year. Yet again, the government was slow to act.[17]

In February the following year help came from another quarter, as it had so often in recent years. Chanter took the matter up in the course of a parliamentary debate about the misconduct of a manager of another New South Wales reserve, repeating the Cumeroogunga men's demands. By this time one of their number had selected land across the river in Victoria. Chanter reported that others had applied time after time to be allowed to do the same. He also repeated the 1887 petitioners' request that blocks of 100 acres be granted to them and pointed out that 25-acre blocks were too small for their purposes.[18]

By 1893 eight men had finally been granted or leased blocks of land by the association out of an area of 400 acres that it had set aside for this scheme. They eagerly set about clearing, fencing and planting them. By 1898 twenty men had such blocks. They comprised only 20 acres each but the men were able to supplement the income they derived from harvests of wheat and hay on these blocks with the wages they earned on pastoral properties, while their families were able to fish in the Murray and cultivate vegetables and fruit on the mission. The blocks provided them with a degree of independence and they were no doubt pleased to have the association's assurance of tenure.[19]

In 1894, however, the Aborigines Protection Board received
several claims that the Protection Association was mismanaging
Cumeroogunga and the two other missions under its control
(Brewarrina and Warangesda). The board deputed its chairman and
a member of the Legislative Assembly to investigate, and they upheld
the claims and persuaded the board to adopt a comprehensive set of
regulations to govern Aboriginal reserves. This eventually proved to
be the thin end of the wedge. The Protection Board soon assumed
control of the association's missions after its finances collapsed.
This was to have serious repercussions for the Aboriginal people
on Cumeroogunga.[20]

For the time being, though, Cumeroogunga flourished. By
1908 there were sixty buildings, made up of forty-six cottages that
were laid out in three streets with gravel footpaths and ornamental
trees, a church, a meeting house, a school, a dispensary, houses for
staff, storerooms, a woolshed and many outbuildings. The men had
cleared 1400 acres of the reserve and fenced more than 400 acres of
it; barges and steamers called regularly to collect hay, wheat, maize,

This photo shows some of the Aboriginal community at Cumeroogunga
standing in front of a row of cottages on the reserve. Often said to have been
taken about 1889, it almost certainly portrays the reserve at a later time, after it
had recovered from its troubled beginnings.

wool and hides; and the reserve was nearly self-supporting. With more than 300 people, it was the largest Aboriginal reserve in New South Wales.[21]

During these years Cooper seems to have done relatively well, though it is difficult to trace what he was doing as he seldom appears in the historical record. He appears to have spent most of this time at Cumeroogunga.[22] In all probability he became one of the block-holders after the scheme was introduced, but we know that he also performed seasonal work off the reserve as a fisherman, shearer, drover, horse-breaker and general rural labourer, much of which was very hard work.[23] He was a member of the Shearers' Union and the Australian Workers' Union, and it is believed that his membership of the latter saw him become a spokesman for both Aboriginal and non-Aboriginal workers in central Victoria and western New South Wales. Later in his life he would recall being active in the Australian Workers' Union on the Darling River in the call-out during the Maritime Strike of 1890, and being on the picket line during the shearers' strike of 1894.[24]

Some of the people of Cumeroogunga outside their church. Thomas James stands in the back row, fifth from the left, holding a Bible. His eldest son, Shadrach, is in the middle row, second from left, and his daughter Priscilla is seated at the piano or organ.

Just as Cooper's years at Maloga had a major influence on his later political work, so too did this period in his life. From the late nineteenth century, nearly every government in Australia followed in the footsteps of what had occurred earlier in Victoria in respect of Aboriginal affairs. They passed special legislation that governed most aspects of the lives of those who were classified as Aborigines, created protection boards to administer a growing number of regulations, and established supervised reserves and encouraged or coerced a large number of Aboriginal people to reside on them (only in later decades to force those of 'mixed descent' off them). This meant that most of what took place at Cumeroogunga in these years proved increasingly common for Aboriginal people, at least in south-eastern and south-western Australia. Cooper became acquainted with these conditions as he travelled and worked in many parts of southern Australia, and this must have deepened his appreciation of the fact that Aboriginal people increasingly had a common experience and that this could be harnessed for political ends.

For the time being, though, the most momentous events in Cooper's life were personal rather than political in nature. In March 1893 he married 21-year-old Agnes Hamilton at a Methodist parsonage in Nathalia, 30 kilometres from Cumeroogunga. Agnes had been born on the Murrumbidgee River at Balranald, a small town in Muthi Muthi country in the northern Riverina, but had grown up at Coranderrk, where her father William or Willie was one of William Barak's right-hand men in the political struggle with the Victorian Board for the Protection of the Aborigines. In the next seventeen years she and William were to have seven children, six of whom survived infancy: Jessie, Daniel, Gillison, Amy, Lynch and Maria, later known as Sally. Ultimore, the second-born, only lived a couple of months, dying of bronchitis. William's mother, Kitty, witnessed most of these births before she died at Cumeroogunga in January 1900.[25]

On the reserve Cooper participated fully in the community's affairs. For example, he had some responsibility for organising a sporting event held there in December 1894, and several years later he played in a few duets as a violinist at a prize-giving at the school and moved the vote of thanks to the chairman. At the same time his connections to Coranderrk would have been deepened after his eldest daughter, Emily, married Thomas Dunolly jnr in March 1905. This had implications for Cooper's later political work as Dunolly was the son of Thomas Dunolly snr, who had been heavily involved in the struggle over Coranderrk's future in the 1870s and 1880s. He penned most if not all of the petitions submitted to the Victorian Government and acted as one of the speakers for Barak. Later, he was among those who were expelled or removed themselves from Coranderrk. He found refuge at Maloga before moving to *Madowla Park* (several kilometres south of Cumeroogunga on the Victorian side of the Murray), where he and later his son farmed some land, thereby fulfilling a dream that Cooper shared.[26]

In this photo, which must have been taken in about 1901, Agnes Cooper is surrounded by the four surviving children that she and William had had up to this point in time: Amy, the newborn, is sitting on her knee, Daniel is to her left, and Jessie and Gillison are on her right. Emily, William's daughter from his first marriage, stands behind her.

Conflict

The progress that Cumeroogunga experienced during its first
two decades did not change the fact that the reserve had several
underlying problems. The amount of arable land continued to be
limited and most of it was flood-prone. As was often the case with
Aboriginal reserves, some of the surrounding white landholders were
hostile to the reserve and opposed to any expansion of it. Moreover,
the men's blocks of land, at 20 acres apiece and thus much smaller
than the 100 acres they had sought, were not big enough to provide
a good living for their families. (In this area at the time, about
850 acres was considered necessary to meet this need.) The men also
lacked the capital needed to develop their blocks, while the time of
the year the blocks most required their attention coincided with the
period they could earn good wages off the reserve. On more than
one occasion drought caused their crops to fail; in other years their
yield suffered because of flood; and more than once rabbits destroyed
some of the crops. Most importantly, perhaps, many of the people
increasingly resented the control wielded by Ferguson. On one
occasion several men complained, once more through Chanter, but
their protests were dismissed by the Protection Board as frivolous
and unfounded and they were warned that any further complaints
would lead to them being dismissed from the reserve.[27]

To add to these problems, beginning in 1902 the Protection
Board, having suffered a series of cuts in its funding, decided to take
greater charge of the land at Cumeroogunga. At first it ruled that the
block-holders had only a right of permissive occupancy; but if this
was not bad enough it eventually decided to abolish the farm block
system altogether, ordering the white overseer, George Harris, to
take charge of all the work done on the blocks and engage the men
as mere wage labourers under a white man. To add insult to injury,
the board claimed that the men had neglected the farm blocks
and failed to work them properly. It did so despite the fact that
the reserve's manager and the local white committee had declared
in their annual reports that progress on them was satisfactory and
attributed the problems that had arisen to the droughts and floods
that had afflicted the reserve.[28]

The board's ruling was bitterly resented by the block-holders. They held that they had a right to these small areas of land. They had been led to believe by the Protection Association that their tenure was secure, and most of the men had worked hard on the blocks. In April 1908 about a dozen of the men made representations, first of all in the columns of the *Riverine Herald*. In a letter to its editor, which was probably written by Thomas James, they complained of 'the injustice being meted out by the board in taking away the farm blocks' and declared that it was 'never intended' for the blocks 'to be confiscated' but that they had instead been promised to the men as 'a home and refuge for life'. They also pointed out that the blocks did not constitute a large part of the public estate. The following month they drew up a petition that they asked a local alderman to present to the district council with a view to it being forwarded to a local member of the Legislative Assembly, Henry Peters. Signed by nearly forty people, it pointed out that 'a grave injustice ha[d] been done' and called for a comprehensive and public inquiry to be conducted by an independent tribunal that would take evidence, consider and deal with the question of the blocks. The petitioners complained: '[We] have never been asked to show cause why the blocks should not be taken from [us].' But the Moama Council was reluctant to intervene and ruled that the matter lay outside its jurisdiction.[29]

In March 1909 several of the men again made representations to the *Riverine Herald* in a letter to the editor in which they complained that they had 'none to represent [them] on the [Protection] Board' and so they could 'only appeal to the public for justice'. They protested that they and other people at the reserve were suffering 'a great wrong' as a result of 'the unjust action of some of those in power over us'. They proceeded to provide a history of the farm blocks in order to counter the claims the board had made. 'A number of us took up blocks and cleared and improved the land for several years, and now that it is in good order we expected to reap the benefits of our work', they asserted. They conceded that some of the block-holders had been careless but insisted that the rest had worked 'hard and steadily, and [done] all that could be expected of [them]'. The letter writers held Harris responsible for what had happened, claiming that he had made up his mind to do away with the farm blocks and had persuaded the board to agree to this step by misrepresenting the facts. 'The result', they went on, 'is that after at least ten years of work we were told that the block system was abolished, and we have lost the result of our labor.' They made it clear that they wanted the blocks returned to them and concluded by expressing a hope that someone who had influence and power would see that justice was done and by making an appeal to the British notion of fair play. As we will see later, a good deal of Cooper's campaign in regard to Cumeroogunga in the mid- to late 1930s would be couched in the same terms.[30]

This protest fell on deaf ears. The chairman of the reserve's local board, John Lewis, claimed in the pages of the *Riverine Herald* that a 'full inquiry' into the block system had revealed that it had 'utterly failed'. This prompted a rebuttal and a further call for a proper inquiry by one of the men at Cumeroogunga, who might have been Cooper, using the nom de plume 'One Sufferer'. A few weeks later a local pastoralist, AE Kinsey, who had previously been the chairman of the reserve's local board and who reckoned that several years earlier he had recommended that the Protection Board grant the men the blocks, weighed into the controversy. He put his finger on the source of the problem with the blocks by remarking: 'I sent in my resignation to the central board about eight years ago, when I considered the men did not get the little assistance they required to make their undertaking a success.'[31]

In the next few months a series of confrontations took place between some of the people at Cumeroogunga and its manager that led to many of the people being expelled. Among them were original block-holders such as Bagot Morgan. Cooper might have already left the reserve by this time, never to return.[32] 'On account of the cruel administration which our people had to suffer, I was obliged to leave Cumeroogunga. I have been away … for over 30 years', he recalled in August 1940. Cooper crossed the Murray River and built a small house for his family at Barmah. There, in April 1909, he and his children suffered a profound loss of the kind that had been common among Aboriginal people since colonisation began and robbed them

Judging by the appearance of Cooper's two youngest children in these photographs (who were born in 1905 and 1907), they must have been taken in the early to mid–1910s, by which time Cooper had turned fifty, though he looks younger. In the first he is standing, tall and erect, next to Sarah Nelson (nee McRae), who cared for Lynch and Sally after his second wife had died and whom he later married. There is good reason to believe that the elderly woman in this photo is Annie Hamilton, Agnes's mother. In the second photograph William sits next to his son Gillison while Sally and Lynch are sitting, as in the first photograph. Aboriginal people treasured family photographs such as these ones and they were sometimes produced as postcards. Cooper sent the second of these photographs to Lynch many years later.

of the resources that were required for a decent living: Agnes, who had contracted tuberculosis and been in poor health for some time, died suddenly. She was only thirty-three, though the local newspaper that reported her death assumed she was much older. The years of constant child-bearing and -rearing in the reserve's straitened circumstances had evidently taken their toll on her. By this time their four older children were in their teens but the two youngest, Lynch and Sally, were barely four and two years old, respectively.[33]

After Cumeroogunga

By leaving the reserve and crossing the river into Victoria, Cooper freed himself from the clutches of the New South Wales Aborigines Protection Board. In time this made it easier for him to protest against what was taking place at Cumeroogunga, as did the fact that he never again lived on a government-supervised reserve. In April 1910 the *Riverine Herald* published a letter in the name of an Aboriginal man who used the nom de plume 'One Who Suffers'. This might have been Cooper, though if that is the case the letter was probably written by Thomas James at Cooper's direction. In it the claims that the people at Cumeroogunga had been making were cast in broader terms than they had been previously, prefiguring much of the rhetoric that James's son Shadrach and Cooper would use two decades later.

In seeking to rebut attacks that had been made in the press on the Aboriginal people of Cumeroogunga the previous year, 'One Who Suffers' asked in regard to the so-called privileges they received on the reserve: 'Are they not our rights? Do not the various states recognise them? And is it not the universal sanction, if not from a legal standpoint, from a moral one, at all events, that having dispossessed us they should bestow upon us, and justly so, the rights and privileges we enjoy?' The author of the letter continued in the same vein: 'Think of the immense wealth of this land, the vast fortunes that have been and are being made from the soil, that belonged to our fathers, or mothers if you like, and surely no sane man would begrudge us a wee portion of what by rights is our own.' Next, the letter writer attacked the way that so-called 'half-castes' (like Cooper) were being portrayed at this time, asking the pointed question of who was responsible for generating these people. 'Let him look back and he would blush to think of the batches of white men … that were let loose amongst us.' Finally, whoever was responsible for this letter decried the failure of so many in the white community to treat them as Christians should, and recalled the Matthewses and Maloga: 'We certainly lived happier under them.'[34]

In the years that followed, Cooper would have been aware of what was taking place at Cumeroogunga as many of his family and kin remained there. We must register the changes that took place there and on other supervised reserves in New South Wales at this time since they figured in much of the political campaign that Cooper and the Australian Aborigines' League mounted in the 1930s. In June 1910 the New South Wales Government gazetted regulations under legislation that had been passed the previous year, the Aborigines Protection Act. For some time the Protection Board had been seeking greater powers over Aboriginal people and Aboriginal reserves of the kind that Victoria's parliament had granted its Board for the Protection of Aborigines many years earlier. The New South Wales Act had punitive clauses that enabled the board to determine who could live in an Aboriginal reserve and receive rations; remove any Aboriginal person from a reserve who was deemed to be guilty of misconduct; force any Aboriginal person camped near a reserve to move; and prevent any non-Aboriginal person from entering a reserve. It also gave the board the power to expel any Aboriginal person whom it believed should be earning a living away from that reserve; bind by indenture any child that entered an apprenticeship; and remove any Aboriginal child from her parents who was deemed by a court of law to be neglected.[35]

In large part the board had sought these powers because they had realised that 'the Aborigines' were not the disappearing race they were widely assumed to be. Those who were called 'full-bloods' had undoubtedly diminished in number, but there had been a considerable increase of those called 'half-castes', 'quadroons' and 'octoroons'. More to the point, most of these people of so-called mixed descent were identifying themselves as Aboriginal rather than white. The existence of this racially distinct minority confounded the ideal of a White Australia that was being widely embraced by settler Australians at this time, shortly after federation of the colonies had forged the new Australian nation.[36]

Soon after the New South Wales Aborigines Protection Board acquired its new powers, there was conflict at Cumeroogunga. Its manager interpreted the Act to mean that he had the power to expel residents and prevent white children attending the school there. This prompted James and the people to protest to the board. At the same time several of the men engaged a local lawyer to represent them in regard to the loss of the farm blocks. In response the board sent a high-level deputation that included Robert Donaldson, who had been largely responsible for drafting the recently enacted legislation, and the board's vice-chairman, GE Ardill, to explain the terms of the Act and inquire into the matters the people had raised. They met the men's lawyer and heard the men themselves, but rejected the case they made for the return of the blocks and compensation for the work they had done on them. They seem, however, to have reassured the people that their children would not be removed.[37]

Yet the board soon began to use its newly acquired powers to force so-called half-castes off its reserves, just as Victoria's Board for the Protection of the Aborigines had done after similar legislation was passed in that colony in 1886. In 1911 the New South Wales Board expelled several of the people at Cumeroogunga on the grounds of misconduct, alleging that 'most of them [possessed] a preponderance of white blood, and [were] well able to provide for themselves and families'. The people at Cumeroogunga, as on other Aboriginal reserves, rejected the distinctions that government authorities made between them on the grounds of race or blood and bitterly resented being expelled from the place that had become their home. This was to fuel a good deal of Cooper and the Australian Aborigines' League's later protest.[38]

In May 1912 the people at Cumeroogunga were alarmed to read newspaper reports that the board was seeking new powers to remove children of 'mixed descent' from their parents on the grounds that this was the only means by which the children could become useful

citizens and be merged into the general population. So great was
their concern that none of the boys at Cumeroogunga were to be
seen when an inspector from the New South Wales Department
of Children's Relief came to the reserve: the people had heard he
was coming and sent the children into the bush. He reported: 'An
impression was abroad that the children were to be taken from their
parents—"babies from their mother's breasts" so it was said; some
of the old hands were in tears.' Several weeks later a member of the
Aborigines Protection Board, Thomas Garvin, came to the reserve
and recommended the removal of as many as fifty-two children
whom he classified as 'quadroon' and 'octoroon'. Among those on
his list were the children of some of the earliest block-holders: the
Atkinsons, the Coopers and the Morgans. Garvin realised that these
children were being looked after by their parents, but he nonetheless
believed that they should be taken away and absorbed into the white
population. But such was the protest at Cumeroogunga that he
realised the people would not give up their children unless they were
compelled to do so. Consequently, the board sought greater legal
powers so that it could remove Aboriginal children and send them
to a home or institution without having to prove to a court that they
were neglected. It eventually acquired these powers in 1915.[39]

To make matters worse, the Protection Board was soon restruc-
tured. From its inception in 1883 neither the government nor
parliament had closely supervised it. Instead, it was left to its own
devices to formulate the details of policy. This had not mattered
too much when many of its members were Christian humanitarians and political figures who were members of the Aborigines
Protection Association, like George Thornton, or local members
of parliament, like John Chanter, who had first-hand knowledge of
Aboriginal people and believed that government had some responsibility towards them as the original owners of the soil. But now the
board was to comprise public servants who represented departments
such as Children's Welfare and Public Health and who had scant
acquaintance with Aboriginal people. Furthermore, power devolved
to the board's small permanent staff and its inspectors, and most
of all to Donaldson, who became feared and hated by Aboriginal

people throughout New South Wales because of the role he played in removing their children—those who would become known as the stolen generations.[40]

The conflict between the board and the people at Cumeroogunga over the removal of their children added to the grievances they had felt since the loss of the farm blocks. This led them to mount further protests. But the Protection Board responded savagely by expelling more people from the reserve, which saw Cumeroogunga's population plummet. Many of those who were expelled or left of their own accord crossed the Murray and formed a camp at Barmah.[41]

By this time Cooper had moved from Barmah to Mulwala and Yarrawonga, probably in search of work as changes in the region's economy limited the opportunities for seasonal jobs. During these years he earned enough money as a fisherman and a labourer to feed the youngest of his children and acquire a small Ford truck, though he probably barely made enough to make ends meet. During these years he also suffered a series of personal losses. Having already lost his steadfast brother Johnny Atkinson in December 1910, his eldest daughter, Emily, died in August 1913, having suffered from tuberculosis for the previous two years, leaving behind a husband and two young children, Thomas and Edna, aged seven and two respectively (another child had predeceased her). The following month Cooper's oldest brother, Aaron Atkinson, also died. Then came the loss that pained Cooper the most. In September 1917 his eldest son, Daniel, whom he had named after his missionary mentor, was killed in action at Ypres in Belgium. Several years later, in December 1922, William and Agnes's first-born child, Jessie, died in Condobolin in New South Wales of peritonitis shortly after giving birth, leaving behind a husband, Charles Mann, and three children, aged just four years, three years and sixteen days.[42]

One of the few sources of solace for Cooper during these years was the sporting success of his youngest son, who was at his peak as an athlete. Lynch was a good Australian Rules footballer but running was his real forte. He won several prestigious sprint events: the Warracknabeal Gift in 1926, the Stawell Gift in 1928, and the World Sprint Championship in 1929. In fact he ran professionally for more

Daniel Cooper gave this postcard photograph of himself and two of his friends to his father, probably just before he embarked to fight in the Great War. He is the man holding the hat.

This photograph of Cooper's daughter Jessie Mann and two of her children, Cyril and Esmay, is believed to have been taken in about 1922.

This studio portrait
of Lynch Cooper was
probably taken in the
late 1920s when he was
at his peak as an athlete.

than twenty years, competing throughout Australia as well as in New
Zealand. This was a lucrative business, especially for those as poverty-
stricken as Aboriginal people. There were many carnivals in country
centres in which runners could earn £10 for winning a heat and
as much as £30 (ten times the basic weekly wage) for a final, while
the big races offered even more prize money. The Warracknabeal
Gift was worth £100 and the Stawell Gift £250. Appearance money
was also to be had and one could place bets on oneself. It has been
estimated that Lynch's career earnings might have been as much
as £3000. Cooper encouraged him to compete—Lynch once
joked that he had been 'chased into the footrunning business by his
father'—and was able to give his son some hints early in his career
before he caught the eye of a trainer.[43] William also told Lynch
stories about the great feats of earlier runners and travelled with him
to some of the major meets, such as the Stawell Gift.[44]

In these years William also found another source of solace
when he married again. His wife, Sarah Nelson (nee McRae), had
been born at Wahgunyah in about 1881 and was the daughter of

This studio photograph of
Sarah Cooper (nee McRae)
was probably taken in 1934.

Tommy McRae (who has since become a well-known artist) and
Lily Wilson. Sometime during her teens she and her three siblings
were removed from their parents and sent to reserves in Victoria (in
her case Coranderrk), after which she spent many years in service
as a farmhand. Sarah and William married in August 1928 at the
Methodist parsonage at Nathalia, after which they made a home
together at Barmah, next door to other Aboriginal families; these
included William's sister Ada and her husband Thomas James. By 1924
there were more than a hundred exiles from Cumeroogunga living
in this camp. There, William and Sarah soon assumed responsibility
for at least one of his grandchildren, Jessie's eldest, Cyril.[45]

In 1933 the Coopers decided to move to Melbourne.[46] It is often
said that they did this so William could become eligible for the
old age pension (which the federal government granted to some
Aboriginal people of 'mixed descent' so long as they did not reside
on an Aboriginal reserve) and thus acquire the independence from
government that any Aboriginal person needed if they were to fight
for their people.[47] But Cooper had left Cumeroogunga in the late

1900s and had been living at Barmah for several years by the time he moved to Melbourne, during which time we can assume that he was receiving the pension. It seems, then, that he shifted to Melbourne with just one goal in mind, namely 'to help his people', as one of his white political associates, Helen Baillie, put it. In other words, Cooper made the move because he recognised that in order to be able to pursue his political work he needed the resources that only a large city could provide.[48]

During the next seven years the Coopers were part of a small, impoverished community of a hundred or so Aboriginal people in Melbourne, most of whom lived in Fitzroy and other inner-city suburbs, having fled either Cumeroogunga or the reserves controlled by the Victorian Board for the Protection of the Aborigines. In these years Cooper came to be regarded as a father figure by these people. He and Sarah lived in a series of small houses in the working-class suburbs of Footscray and Yarraville (perhaps because

William Cooper purposefully striding down Nicholson Street, the main shopping street in Footscray, where he lived during his years in Melbourne.

one or more of William's children were living in Footscray at this time).[49] Members of the Australian Aborigines' League later recalled meeting in one of these houses. Lacking either gas or electricity, they huddled around the fire in its front room, two candles flickering on the mantelpiece.[50]

The Coopers struggled to make ends meet. As well as the old age pension, William received a war pension by dint of the fact that he had lost a son in the Great War, but even once he put these two sources of income together they did not amount to much.[51] Besides, at various times during these years he not only took Cyril under his roof but also Cyril's sister Esmay and brother Bruce and his daughter Amy's son, Alfred (Boydie) so that they were not taken by white authorities and placed in a children's home. At some point he also took in Gillison's twin sons in the hope that he could provide them with some discipline. (They had become wayward as a result of growing up in a boys' home in the wake of their mother's death.) To save money for the cause Cooper seldom rode in a tram or train but walked everywhere, despite his age.[52]

PART 2

5

PETITIONING THE KING

Soon after moving to Melbourne, Cooper took up the cause of his people. In doing so he was anticipated by his nephew, Shadrach Livingstone James, the eldest son of Cooper's sister Ada and Thomas James. Born at Cumeroogunga in 1890, James had been a student in his father's school on the reserve and later became its assistant teacher before an attack on his work by a government official and the local committee of the New South Wales Aborigines Protection Board prompted him to resign. In the late 1910s he demonstrated that he had acquired much of his father's political nous, briefing a lawyer to challenge a charge of having trespassed on the reserve, which had led to his expulsion from it. Sometime after his father retired as the school's principal teacher in 1922, the two men and their families moved to the inner Melbourne working-class suburb of Fitzroy for several years, where a small number of their kith and kin would gather sometimes to talk politics.[1]

In 1929 Shadrach James raised his voice on behalf of Aboriginal people by speaking to missionary organisations, writing to a federal minister, and making appeals to the labour movement. There were marked similarities between his political work and that of his uncle a few years later. Most of James's protest, as in Cooper's case, was informed by his own experience, or that of his family and kin, at Maloga and Cumeroogunga, and by his connections to the union

movement. (Like Cooper, he was a member of the Australian
Workers' Union and had recently been representing shearers.) But
James was also influenced by his father's ongoing connections to
India, Mauritius and the Indian diaspora and thus to the anti-colonial
struggle in India and the campaigns against indentured labour in
other British colonies, such as Fiji.[2]

James attacked government as well as white Australians more
generally for their failure to act in keeping with what he called
'their responsibility and obligation to [the Aboriginal people]'.
While he noted the violence that had been meted out to them on
the frontiers of settlement—'This massacre of my people has been
going on for years and years', he remarked on one occasion—James
focused on the state protection boards, on the grounds that the care
of his people had been entrusted to them. They were supposed to
protect Aboriginal people from harmful forces; provide for their
maintenance, education and welfare; and promote, encourage and
create the means for their moral, social and intellectual development.
But the protection boards had not lived up to their responsibilities
and had deputed them to the police instead.[3]

James primarily illustrated this contention by discussing the way
that reserves had been administered by the Aborigines Protection
Board of New South Wales, as this was the protection board he
knew the best. 'Reserves for the use of the Aborigines have been
set apart in many places throughout the Commonwealth, and they
are vested in the Aborigines' Protection Board,' he pointed out, 'but
the Aborigines are denied the right of using the land, and in some
cases these reserves are leased to white men.' James recalled what had
happened at Cumeroogunga: 'I know of several Aborigines who
were granted some 30 to 40 acres of land some years ago and were
promised larger grants if they proved their capability of clearing and
working this land. These men worked hard, their wives helping, on
scanty supplies of ration, and fenced and cleared about 900 acres
of densely timbered land, and just when they were expecting fair
returns from their land the blocks were taken away from them,
with no prospect of compensation for their labour.' James also
remembered the removal of children at Cumeroogunga. 'Our girls',

he complained, 'are forcibly taken from their homes and sent out to service.' He made clear that he was not objecting to their being trained to work but to the fact that they were sent away at a tender age, when they needed their mothers' protection.[4]

James argued that white Australians had 'a national duty' towards Aboriginal people because they had dispossessed his people of a country that belonged to them 'by divine right'. In the same vein he asserted that the weekly rations and the annual supply of blankets and clothing that they received were hardly adequate compensation for the shocking injustice they had suffered and were still suffering, especially in light of the enormous fortune Australia was deriving from resources of the land it had taken, principally through pastoralism. '[Australians] complain of our ingratitude. We ask, when will they pay the debt of gratitude they owe to us for the untold gain that has come to them through our irremediable loss?' In regard to this point, he complained that his Aboriginal people's 'natural rights' had been withheld.[5]

James attributed most of the problems facing Aboriginal people to racial prejudice and racial discrimination (though he did not use these terms). In reference to the former, he sought to correct the widely held belief that Aboriginal people were a dying race. He complained that the help provided by government rested on this misconception and claimed that it meant the people were threatened with extinction. In regard to the latter, he pointed out that it worked to deny or bar Aboriginal people from employment in many fields and accounted for the poverty his people suffered. 'With the exception of the shearing and harvesting seasons,' he remarked, 'we are practically out of employment.' For the rest of the year, 'we do some fishing and trapping' but these yielded 'a precarious living' and so most Aboriginal families were 'living in a semi-starved condition'.[6]

James also argued that the plight of Aboriginal people could be attributed to the fact that they had generally been denied opportunities for uplift. In his words, they had not been given 'a dog's chance'. While the missionaries had provided a good deal of help, especially by introducing Aboriginal people to the word of God, government

had not bestowed on them the benefits of what James characterised
as civilisation. 'So far', he observed, 'there has never been a vigorous,
resolute, decisive and intensive effort [by government] to uplift us
socially, intellectually, morally and spiritually.'[7]

James called on government to adopt such a program so that
Aboriginal people could take their place as citizens in what he called
the modern world. To this end he recommended that all Aboriginal
people be placed under the care of the federal government instead
of the states. This was a reform that missionary bodies such as the
Australian Board of Missions and Christian humanitarians such as
those belonging to the Association for the Protection of Native
Races had been making since the early 1910s. But James also called
for the appointment of what he called a *native administrator* (a point
to which I will return shortly) and itinerant missionaries who could
attend to the moral and spiritual needs of Aboriginal people who
were not connected with missions. He also called for Aboriginal
reserves to be broken up and allocated to capable Aboriginal people,
and that some monetary assistance be provided so 'they could settle
permanently and make homes of their own without fear of being
disturbed'. In making this request, he remarked, echoing the words
Cooper had used in his plea to government in 1887 (which was
written by James's father): 'We are only asking for a portion of our
own back.'[8]

James seemed to assume that the prospects for reform were
improving on the grounds that a genuine sympathy for Aboriginal
people was on the increase and government was consequently willing to act. In this respect he was probably influenced by a Biblical
way of reckoning with time. He spoke in terms of 'the hope of a
better day' and 'the dawn of a new day'. But in the last of the pleas
James made in 1929, he sought to put pressure on white Australians
to act immediately: 'The real value of a community depends on the
character of its people. The value of this country is not measured by
its material resources, but by the character of the people, and I say
to you Australians, Let not the history of the shocking treatment
of the aborigines, as it stands today, mar forever your character, but
awake, arise, shake off the reproach and shame, and be not recreant

[i.e. unfaithful] to your highest duty to protect the people you have so grievously wronged.'[9]

The following year James raised his voice again and in a way that makes clear that these matters were uppermost in the minds of the people at Cumeroogunga. Once more, he was critical of the racial prejudice and discrimination that blighted their lives, and again he attacked protection or rather the assumptions that informed the way in which it was implemented. 'Our so-called protectors are diligently attending to the care of my people with the full conviction that they are slowly but surely passing out', he complained. 'Hence all their efforts for the care of my people are mere palliatives … There is absolutely nothing … in all their activities, feeding, clothing, housing and caring, which can be counted as of vital interest to lift us up.' James also repeated his criticisms of the protection boards. 'We strongly deprecate the policy of placing us under the supervision of police', he wrote. 'Many of my people shun the aboriginal stations controlled by the Aborigines' Protection Boards because of this and [their] gaol-like conditions.' Once more he called for government policy that would give his people opportunities that would advance them and enable them to become citizens of Australia. And, yet again, he suggested that white Australians had a duty towards his people because they had 'unjustly disinherited [them] of their land' and were 'enjoying the inestimable benefits it yield[ed]'.[10]

In this protest there were some new threads. The previous year James had made little more than a passing reference to the frontier violence that Aboriginal people had suffered. Now, he talked about it at some length. 'No sooner had the white man invaded our land,' he wrote, 'than the extermination of our people began, and it has gone on, and is still going on, under various guises.' This had involved not only settlers but government forces as well, he pointed out. 'It is an undeniable fact that the early colonists not only dislodged our people from their hunting grounds, but, with the help of the police, shot down hundreds of them.' James complained that the police were still doing this with impunity. Presumably he had in mind events such as the Coniston massacre in Central Australia in

1928, which had aroused a storm of protest among white Christian humanitarians and others. He also decried the practice of recruiting Aboriginal people for native police forces, so that they '[shot] down their own people for the squatters' rum and "bacca"'.[11]

James revealed his familiarity with the conditions of Indigenous people and other racial minorities elsewhere in the Pacific: New Zealand, Fiji, New Hebrides (Vanuatu) and Samoa. He was aware that at least some of these people were faring better than his own mother's people and argued that this was not because they were more able than Aboriginal people, but because the governments of those countries had made an effort to advance 'coloured people' with 'confidence, earnestness and assiduity'. By comparison, he insisted, 'there [had] been no serious attempts for our advancement in Australia'.[12]

Among the changes that James advocated in both 1929 and 1930 was representation for Aboriginal people in the Commonwealth parliament. This warrants special attention as it assumed a central place in Cooper's campaigning later and because there has been considerable historiographical discussion about the nature of the representation Cooper had in mind. It seems clear that on each occasion James discussed this matter he was calling for an *Aboriginal* representative in parliament—that is, an Aboriginal person, rather than a sympathetic white man, to represent them. On the occasion he wrote about this matter at greatest length he spelt out the logic of this call, namely that an Aboriginal person would grasp the needs of Aboriginal people best and be most sympathetic to them. James's demand for an Aboriginal person to represent his people in the Commonwealth parliament formed part and parcel of a broader call for Aboriginal people to play a role in the administration of their own affairs. These points are evident in a letter he wrote to the editor of the *Australian Worker* in July 1929: 'I think, as the original owners of this country, we should have a share in the administration of our own race. For this reason we desire the appointment of a native administrator for the Commonwealth, because he would be in sympathy with us and grasp more readily our needs, and for the same reason we ask for a native representative in the House [of Representatives] to voice our needs and disabilities, and a native protector in each State to see that our people were well cared for.'[13]

Cooper begins his work

Cooper began his political work in Melbourne shortly after arriving there. In February 1933 he learned about the plight of Aboriginal people in north-west Western Australia from a newspaper article that reported claims made by a missionary, Rev. RS Schenk, about members of the police force indiscriminately shooting Aboriginal people. 'We have suffered quit[e] enough and the time has arrived for the natives to receive better treatment', Cooper pointed out a few months later in a letter he wrote to Rev. Ernest Gribble, who was the chaplain to the Aboriginal people on the government reserve on Palm Island in north Queensland, having spent most of his life as a missionary. (In writing to him Cooper recalled his father, JB Gribble, and the time he had spent at his mission, Warangesda, fifty years earlier. No doubt he was also aware of Ernest Gribble's passionate humanitarian concern for Aboriginal people, his calls to redress the wrongs that white society had inflicted upon them, and his reputation as a highly vocal protector of Aborigines. In the course of their correspondence Cooper would realise that Gribble shared many of his political goals and was willing to back his call for representation of Aboriginal people in parliament.)[14]

Cooper decided to protest about these killings by writing a letter to one of the leading Melbourne newspapers, *The Age*. There are similarities between this and the letters Shadrach James had sent to the press in 1929 and 1930. This can be largely attributed to the fact that James almost certainly took responsibility for putting into words what Cooper wanted to say or at least giving the letter its final form.[15] While Cooper had first taught himself to read and his literacy enabled him to do much of the work that was required to build a network of supporters for his political work, his lack of formal education also meant that he found the task of writing all the letters that were needed to accomplish his goals rather burdensome.

One of the letters
Cooper wrote to the
missionary Ernest
Gribble, and a letter
in Shadrach James's
handwriting.

On this occasion he noted that the inhumane treatment of which he was complaining was historical as much as it was contemporary. 'When the first white settlers arrived 145 years ago there were hundreds of thousands of aborigines here', he remarked. 'But brutal extermination followed, and the number of full-blooded natives was reduced to 17,000. The killing of natives is continuing to-day.' Cooper used the term *extermination* to spell out the stakes involved in this matter. '[I]f [this killing] is not soon stopped the Australian aborigine will become extinct', he argued.[16]

Cooper argued that Aboriginal people had a right to receive a great deal of consideration and attention from white Australians on the grounds that they had lost so much as a result of colonisation. Indeed, he contended that the white race and the government had a duty towards Aboriginal people, in this case to protect tribal Aboriginal people from armed attacks by providing them with sanctuaries in their own country. At the same time, given the nature of the killings he was condemning, he implicitly drew into question who was civilised and who was savage. In a similar vein, since he was aware that the reserves he was calling for could be a double-edged sword, he complained that they often did little more than provide anthropologists and sociologists with material for their investigations.[17] This was a cause of complaint among other Aboriginal advocates, such as William Ferguson, in the 1930s.[18]

Cooper was careful to point out that many missionaries had worked to both protect and uplift Aboriginal people, arguing that they would be 'remembered forever and given a honored place in the history books of the future'. But doing this gave him an opportunity to insist that it was the duty of all white Australians to follow their example and join with the likes of himself in trying to bring pressure to bear on government to protect tribal Aborigines.[19]

In the next few months Cooper sought to make contact with Aboriginal people on several missions—Yarrabah and Cherbourg (in Queensland) and Point McLeay (in South Australia)—and reached out to missionaries such as Gribble and Schenk in order to arouse support for what he called 'this cause for the betterment of ourselves'. He felt that he had a duty to fight for the better treatment of Aboriginal people throughout Australia.[20]

Before we discuss the particular campaign to which Cooper soon began to devote himself, it is worthwhile pausing for a moment to note the reception that he received from the whites whose assistance he sought, not least because this helps to deepen our picture of the man. On meeting Cooper in April 1933 Helen Baillie (whom I discuss at greater length in the next chapter) was struck by the fact that he had 'a vision for his people', 'real pride of race' and 'plans of what he [was] hoping to do for his people'. She also observed that while he was elderly he was 'vigorous' and 'a fine looking old man'. Another of Cooper's white allies would later describe him as 'very regal in bearing', and still another as 'dignified' and having 'a good presence'. Baillie also described William and his wife Sarah as 'gentlefolk in the true sense of that word', by which she probably meant that she considered them to be genteel or refined.[21]

By July 1933 Cooper had suggested to members of the nascent organisation, which he seems to have already formed,[22] that the federal government should assume responsibility for all Aboriginal people or, more specifically, that the affairs of all Aboriginal people should be overseen by a federal member of parliament as well as a federal protector of Aborigines. He also called for all the state Aboriginal protection boards to be 'do[ne] away with', arguing that they had been a burden to Aboriginal people for more than sixty years. At Federation it had been agreed that the former British colonies in Australia would retain jurisdiction over most areas of government, including land settlement, industrial development, labour relations and education, largely because the colonies were jealous of their powers and unwilling to assign anything to the federal parliament unless they believed it was a matter of common concern. In the eyes of the colonies, few of the powers that were granted to the Commonwealth seemed to have any obvious or direct relevance to Aboriginal policy. Thus, the only part of Australia for which the Commonwealth assumed a major responsibility for Aboriginal affairs was the Northern Territory, and this did not occur until 1911.[23]

This studio portrait of Cooper, which was probably taken in 1934, gives us some sense of just how dignified a man he was. This and other photographs taken of him in the 1930s also reveal his considerable gravitas.

Cooper's fledgling organisation was one of the first Aboriginal political bodies to be formed in Australia. It had been preceded by at least two such organisations in the mid-1920s: the Australian Aboriginal Progressive Association, founded in New South Wales,[24] and the Native Union, formed in Western Australia.[25] Prior to their formation there had been a not inconsiderable amount of protest by Aboriginal people in the parts of Australia that had most suffered the consequences of British colonisation, but no organisations had been formed.[26] Cooper's had much in common with the other Aboriginal organisations that were founded in the 1920s and 1930s. Many of their preoccupations were intensely local or at least regional—the mid-north coast of New South Wales in the case of the Australian Aboriginal Progressive Association, the south-west of Western Australia for the Native Union—and their representations focused on the oppression of Aboriginal communities by government protection boards and racially discriminatory laws in the southern parts of Australia, and were addressed to the relevant state authorities. This was also true of Cooper's organisation to a large degree, but his differed in that it also sought to take up matters of concern to Aboriginal people across the country, to speak for them, and to make representations to the federal government.

The emergence of Aboriginal organisations like Cooper's in the 1920s and 1930s owed something to the fact that there was an upsurge of concern about the plight of Aboriginal people among a small group of white Australians at the time, which led to the formation of new white organisations. The most influential of these was the Association for the Protection of Native Races, which was founded in 1911 but began to focus on Aboriginal people after it was revived in 1927. In the next few years the Victorian Aboriginal Group and the Aboriginal Fellowship Group were founded in Melbourne and the Australian Aborigines' Amelioration Association in Perth. Christian humanitarians were responsible for these organisations:[27] for example, the secretary of the Association for the Protection of Native Races, William Morley, was a Congregational minister. These organisations were deeply paternalistic. They believed that they should and could speak on behalf of Aboriginal people, and so they did, usually without any reference to the Aboriginal people themselves. The membership of these organisations was small, perhaps even smaller than that of the Aboriginal bodies, but they had more clout with the governments of the day, such was the depth of racial prejudice. For this reason, as well as others, Aboriginal advocates and organisations needed the help of white advocates.

In the second half of 1933, Cooper decided that the best means of advancing his cause was a petition addressed to the King, George V.

This became his most important campaign.[28] Given this, it warrants considerable attention. The petition read:

PETITION

of the Aboriginal Inhabitants of Australia to His Majesty George V by the Grace of God of Great Britain, Ireland and the British Dominions beyond the seas, King, Defender of the Faith, Emperor of India.

TO THE KING'S MOST EXCELLENT MAJESTY IN COUNCIL

THE HUMBLE PETITION of the undersigned Aboriginal Inhabitants of the Continent of Australia respectfully sheweth:

THAT WHEREAS it was not only a moral duty, but also a strict injunction, included in the commission issued to those who came to people Australia, that the original inhabitants and we their heirs and successors should be adequately cared for;

AND WHEREAS the terms of the commission have not been adhered to in that:

(a) Our lands have been expropriated by Your Majesty's Governments, and

(b) Legal status is denied to us by Your Majesty's Government in the Commonwealth;

AND WHEREAS all petitions made on our behalf to Your Majesty's Governments have failed.

YOUR PETITIONERS humbly pray that Your Majesty will intervene on our behalf, and, through the instrument of Your Majesty's Government in the Commonwealth of Australia:

will prevent the extinction of the Aboriginal race and give better conditions for all and grant us power to propose a member of parliament in the person of our own blood or white man known to have studied our needs and to be in sympathy with our race, to represent us in the Federal Parliament.

AND YOUR PETITIONERS will ever pray.[29]

We cannot be sure who was responsible for drawing up the petition. Clearly, it was the work of someone familiar with the form that a petition was expected to take. Arthur Burdeu, who was later to become Cooper's most valuable white collaborator, reckoned that the Catholic Archbishop of Melbourne, Daniel Mannix, had drafted it. We know that Cooper met with Mannix, probably the best-known churchman in Australia, at this time (as a result of an introduction provided by Baillie) and that he was sympathetic to the Aboriginal people's plight.[30] But more likely than not it was Thomas James who drafted the petition, given his experience in drawing up such documents, not least for his brother-in-law.[31]

As far as Cooper was concerned, the key claim in the petition was its call for representation in the federal parliament. This was also the aspect that the press concentrated on. This is probably no coincidence as Cooper himself focused on it in writing to news-papers to alert them to the petition.[32] It was also the aspect that he emphasised in the interview he granted to Clive Turnbull several years later (see Prologue).[33]

As readers will have noted, the petition sought the power to propose a member of parliament who was *either Aboriginal or white* in order to represent the Aboriginal people in the Commonwealth parliament. How do we account for the fact that Cooper qualified the demand for parliamentary representation that Shadrach James had previously made? This can be attributed to the fact that the white people who were seeking to guide him at the time, most notably Baillie, were anxious about his appealing to authorities in Britain and so advised him to temper his political demands so that the demand for parliamentary representation made in the petition diverged from what Cooper and his Aboriginal offsiders really wanted. In talking about the petition on its release, Cooper declared that its object was 'to place the aborigines on the same footing as the Maoris'—that is, to gain the right to choose a parliamentarian of their own race to represent them in parliament. (Cooper knew that there were four Māori MPs in the New Zealand parliament, that they were elected by voters who were Māori, and that this had been the case since 1867.) If this is not the case, at the very least what Cooper had in mind was a member of parliament who was, in his words, 'to be chosen by [his] people to represent them in the federal parliament'. That is, it was a means to ensure that the federal parliament was aware of *their* views. In this regard it is surely significant that Cooper decided that the petition should be signed only by Aboriginal people.[34]

Aboriginal representation had long been regarded as crucial by those such as Cooper. They knew that government policy was determined without any consideration of their views, and so they envisaged a member of parliament speaking on their people's behalf. They also believed that their perspectives differed markedly from those of white Australians, and so they assumed for the most part that only an Aboriginal person could truly represent them. This consideration was related to what Cooper more than once called 'thinking black'.[35] A few rare exceptions aside, Cooper told the minister for the interior, Thomas Paterson, and his successor, John McEwen, white men could not 'think black'.[36]

But why did Cooper and his associates choose a *petition* as the means of presenting their plea for representation in the Common-wealth parliament? Petitioning government was a common political technique in Britain and its colonies during the nineteenth century, not least among evangelical Christians involved in the campaign for the emancipation of slaves. Cooper must have known this, given how often he used the word *emancipation* in his calls for change. They were also no strangers to petitioning. Those at Maloga and Cumeroogunga had been party to several acts of petitioning in the 1880s and 1890s, and no doubt believed that they had gained a good deal from adopting this political method.

While petitioning by Aboriginal people seems to have become less common in the early to middle decades of the twentieth cen-tury, Jane Duren, an Aboriginal woman from Batemans Bay in New South Wales, had petitioned King George V in 1926 about matters that included the loss of her people's reserve lands,[37] and Fred Maynard's Australian Aboriginal Progressive Association dis-cussed this petition at a meeting in Sydney the following year. In all likelihood Cooper knew of the work of Maynard's organisation and the advocacy of other Aboriginal men and women on the north coast of New South Wales (though there is no trace of this in the

historical record).[38] In the same month that he launched his petition, another Aboriginal man, Joe Anderson, at Salt Pan Creek near
Sydney, called for a meeting of all the Aboriginal people of New
South Wales to discuss sending a petition to the King. The petition
he had in mind also called for representation in the federal parliament. It seems likely that Anderson and Cooper had been talking
to one another, probably for quite some time. Anderson was the
stepson of a Dharawal woman, Ellen Giles, who was one of many
people Daniel Matthews had induced to move to Maloga in 1881
(see Chapter 2), and Hughy Anderson, one of the Yorta Yorta men
who had assumed a role as leader at Maloga and Cumeroogunga.
In the 1890s Hughy Anderson had tried to form a mission on land
in the Kangaroo Valley near Barrengarry in the southern highlands
of New South Wales, but the land was poor and he and his young
family were forced to return to Cumeroogunga. However, after this
they seem to have moved between the two places before shifting to
Sydney in the 1910s.[39] There, they encountered a white organisation called the Aborigines Inland Mission, which had been founded
to evangelise among Aboriginal people at La Perouse. Shortly afterwards they purchased land on Dharawal country at Salt Pan Creek
and made a home that became the basis of a small community of
Aboriginal people that in the 1930s included Joe Anderson but also
Cumeroogunga men like Jack Patten, who were to play a major role
in the struggle for the rights of Aboriginal people in both Victoria
and New South Wales.[40]

It is probable that Cooper and his Aboriginal associates also knew
that Indigenous peoples in other parts of the Empire had petitioned
the monarch. For example, in the late nineteenth and early twentieth
centuries Māori had petitioned Queen Victoria and her successor
on several occasions and even travelled to England to present their
appeals to her authority. More recently, Māori leader Tahupōtiki
Wiremu Rātana had done the same, seeking to present a petition
to King George V in regard to the Treaty of Waitangi and the
confiscation of land in New Zealand (while one of his offsiders had
travelled to Geneva in an attempt to present this petition to the
League of Nations).[41]

This said, the most recent petition Cooper was aware of was one drawn up by a fellow septuagenarian, JC Genders,[42] a white Christian socialist who was the honorary secretary of a South Australian organisation, the Aborigines' Protection League, which has been described as one of the most radical of the groups advocating for change in Aboriginal policies and practices at the time. Genders' petition called for the creation of a model Aboriginal state and parliamentary representation for it, and he also cited the New Zealand example. Shadrach James had endorsed this petition in 1929.[43]

Yet the roots of Cooper's petition go deeper than what I have been discussing so far. Consequently, it is worth our while considering the history of petitioning and the assumptions that tend to inform it. As a form of claim-making, petitions are inherently legal or moral in nature. They never merely comprise a request to some kind of authority to redress a grievance: they involve an appeal to some sort of right or standard of justice that is considered to be legitimate. Thus, while a petition is usually couched in a deferential manner as befits an appeal from an inferior to a superior—Cooper and his associates characterised their plea as 'humble', sought to 'respectfully sheweth' the matters it presented, and 'humbly pray[ed]' the King would intervene—it often suggests that the ruler has an obligation to respond; Cooper and his associates styled this as both 'a moral duty' and 'a strict injunction'. Furthermore, petitioners tend to imply that they and the ruler they address belong to a common moral order. Consequently, we need to pay attention to the way petitioners represent the moral world in which their appeal is made.[44]

Cooper's petition, and his political campaign more generally, rested on several moral premises, nearly all of which were informed by, or drew upon, Christianity as a normative force. He assumed that white Australians recognised that they had a duty to Aboriginal people because they shared a common nature. As Cooper told Gribble during the first stages of his petition campaign, 'the Aboriginals are men, women and children and same as [whites] are in God's sight. God has made us after his own image.' Further, he assumed that white Australians were inherently benevolent but had forgotten their Christian duty to Aboriginal people, which meant that those like himself had to teach or shame them so they would act in accordance with those responsibilities. As Cooper remarked rather ambiguously to Gribble in the letter I have just quoted, 'I am sure they know their responsibility for the Aboriginal people … If every man had the same respect as you have for the Aboriginal race there would be no suffering for [my] race of people.' Cooper also believed that white Australia had a duty towards Aboriginal people because the British Crown had given a particular undertaking at the outset of colonisation but had not fulfilled it. As the petition stated, the Crown had issued a commission to all Britons that 'the original inhabitants and their heirs and successors should be adequately cared for' and that 'the terms of [that] commission had not been adhered to'. In the early years of his campaign Cooper repeatedly spoke of this duty, pointing to a proclamation that the first governor of South Australia, John Hindmarsh, had made on his arrival in that colony in 1836. This premise was shared by white Christian campaigners. Two months after Cooper launched the petition, several South Australian churches and philanthropic organisations presented a petition to the Commonwealth parliament in which they demanded, first and foremost, '[t]hat the pledges given by Governor Phillip to the natives in his first proclamation at the beginning of white settlement in Australia, be redeemed'. (Genders' petition had done the same.) In respect of each of these assumptions, Cooper was relying on a sense of a common moral order in order to justify his petition's claims, or he was seeking to enlarge the moral order so as to persuade his audience of the legitimacy of its claims, and in some instances he was doing both.[45]

Petitioners often tend to rest their claims on an assumption that there is a higher form of authority to whom they can appeal to put things right. In this case Cooper had imperial authority—or more particularly monarchical authority—in mind, hoping that the British Crown would overrule the local authorities in the form of the federal or state governments. He and his associates, like other Aboriginal petitioners in south-eastern Australia, believed that, despite the fact that British responsibility for Australian affairs had largely ceased as a result of the founding of the Australian nation in

1901, the British monarch continued to have a special right to intervene in Aboriginal matters in Australia, and that they had a right of appeal to the British Crown on the grounds that the King or Queen had reserved certain powers in respect of the Aboriginal people.[46]

There was also a belief among Aboriginal people at Coranderrk and other reserves in Victoria and New South Wales that they had a special relationship with the Crown and that Queen Victoria herself had given them certain undertakings, which included a promise in regard to the lands that had been reserved for them.[47] Cooper undoubtedly thought this to be the case. Late in his life he asked one of the Matthewses' daughters if she could find what he called 'the Queen's proclamation for the protection of the aborigines' (as he believed that Daniel Matthews had had a copy of this at Maloga), adding: 'It would be of great use to me if I could get it.' Thus, it is hardly surprising that Cooper and his associates proposed a petition to one of Queen Victoria's successors.[48]

In all probability Cooper had an even higher form of moral authority in mind than the British monarch: a transcendent one, namely that of God. It has been suggested by one scholar, Ravi de Costa, that the strong commitments of Indigenous peoples to a cosmological order that governed the world influenced their encounters with European moralists such as Christian missionaries, that these enabled syncretic forms of belief to emerge, and that this in turn prompted them to fashion petitions in the way they did.[49]

The work of the petition

Many newspapers carried reports of Cooper's petition after it was launched. Most were sympathetic, the labour press especially so. For example, the *Australian Worker* asserted that the petition's principal demand—that is, a representative of Aboriginal people in the Commonwealth parliament—had 'much to recommend it' given that 'the aborigines [were] the best judges of how they are being treated in the land that ha[d] been taken from them'.[50]

For the next several months Cooper spent an enormous amount of time doing the work that was required to obtain signatures on the petition. In the first instance he believed he had to get the permission of the protectors of Aborigines in Victoria, New South Wales, Queensland, South Australia, Western Australia and the Northern Territory to circulate it, if only because he recognised that Aboriginal people living under the Protection Acts might be apprehensive about signing the petition unless they knew that this had been sanctioned by these authorities. The task of securing their permission proved a frustrating one, at least in the beginning. Two or more of the protectors were slow to reply. One felt it necessary to seek the advice of the Commonwealth Government; another told Cooper that practically all the Aboriginal people in his jurisdiction would be unable to understand the petition because they were unable to read; and yet another refused to give his consent for quite some time. This prompted Cooper to appeal to the prime minister, Joseph Lyons, for help. One of the protectors was so apprehensive about who might be behind the petition that he made inquiries of his Victorian counterpart, who called upon that state's police force to investigate. Cooper must have been surprised to open his front door one day to find a plain-clothes policeman who proceeded to ask him a series of questions even though all he had done was exercise a fundamental democratic right. He would experience more of this kind of surveillance in 1936 and 1937.[51]

It was several months before the New South Wales Aborigines Protection Board finally granted Cooper permission to circulate his petition, and even then it insisted that nothing be done 'to cause disaffection among the Aborigines on the board's stations and reserves'. This would have reminded Cooper of the autocratic rule at Cumeroogunga. But it was the chief protector of Aborigines in Queensland, JW Bleakley, who proved to be most reluctant to agree to his request, prompting him to solicit the help of Gribble and a leading South Australian Labor MP, Norman Makin, who had pressed for Genders' petition to be considered by the federal government. In March 1934 Bleakley's recalcitrance provoked an outburst from Cooper in a letter that Shadrach James penned on his behalf: 'Why can't Mr Bleakley give me something definite as regards my petitioning my own people for signatures in Queensland, as each of the other states have done. It is just upon six months since

I first applied.' Clearly exasperated, Cooper went on: 'Surely it does not take all that time to get an answer.' He told Makin he would seek to publicise Bleakley's unnecessary delay if he did not get a proper answer soon.[52]

Much of the work required to get signatures on the petition involved Cooper writing to missionaries such as Gribble to ask for their help in circulating it, and to Aboriginal spokesmen such as Norman Harris, one of the principal figures in the Native Union, and Bill Ferguson, a leading New South Wales Aboriginal spokesman, to request their help in getting other Aboriginal people to sign. He trusted that the missionaries would help and believed that it was the duty of every Aboriginal man and woman to sign. He hoped to secure the signatures of all the Aboriginal people in the country, or at least those living on missions and reserves. But in undertaking this work Cooper was hampered by a lack of funds. In order to save money on the cost of postage, he asked at least one missionary to arrange for the printing or copying of the petition forms, rather than providing them himself. He also found the sheer task of writing so many letters arduous. '[M]y education is not what I would like it to be', he confessed to Gribble; 'it seems a struggle for me to keep up to the standard I ha[d] got the work up to.' James lent a hand by writing the required letter on more than one occasion. In the early months of this work Cooper was discouraged by the poor response he got from the local churches, confiding in Gribble: 'I did not get any sympathy from any of the Church people here in Melbourne.' But he was nothing if not tenacious, calling what he was doing 'this great work' and 'this good cause'.[53]

By January 1934 Cooper was heartened by the response he was finally getting. 'Copys [sic] of the petition have been circulated well by [my friends] all around in different parts [of] Australia and all are signing fast, so we are doing well so far', he told Gribble. Several months later he tried to form a delegation of Aboriginal people representing each state to wait on the Commonwealth Government before forwarding the petition to the King, a move he seems to have had in mind from the outset. This plan, however, was also hamstrung by a lack of funds. Cooper begged for a free railway pass for each delegate, but one government department after another refused to grant his request. Nonetheless, resilient as ever, he pressed on, sending several letters to Prime Minister Lyons.[54]

In September 1934 Cooper sent a circular letter to all his supporters to tell them how the petition was progressing. 'The petition is in perfect order and we are getting along with it as well as we can expect', he stated. 'I am pleased to say I have now in hand signatures amounting to 2,500 and we are expecting another 2,500 which should bring the total to about 5,000.' In December that year Cooper claimed he had 3000 signatures to hand and that petition sheets were still coming in from all the states. At this point he believed the petition would be completed by the end of January and he was still hoping that a deputation of Aboriginal spokespeople would be able to wait on the Commonwealth Government to discuss its terms before forwarding it to the King.[55]

In the end Paterson agreed to meet a deputation in Melbourne in January 1935. This meant it could only comprise Aboriginal spokespeople who lived in Melbourne or relatively nearby. According to some press reports the deputation numbered five Aboriginal people—Cooper, Shadrach James, Caleb and Anna Morgan, and Doug Nicholls—but it is apparent that it comprised many more.[56] They were accompanied by at least four white sympathisers—Makin, who introduced the delegation, Baillie, Morley and Claude B Smith, the president of the Footscray Historical Society—but the deputation nonetheless struck several newspapers as novel simply because it included Aboriginal men and women. It was claimed that this was the first time Aboriginal people had ever waited on a federal government minister, which was probably correct.[57]

The matters raised by the deputation were wide-ranging, but representation of Aboriginal people in parliament was at the forefront of the minds of the principal Aboriginal speakers. On this occasion they broadened their demand to include representation in both the federal and state parliaments. In a statement that Cooper prepared for the meeting he explicitly called for 'aboriginal representatives to protect [their] interests'; James argued that Aboriginal people should have 'a say in the making of laws'; and Baillie stated that it

This photograph, in which many of the League's members and one or two of its supporters pose, was probably taken on the occasion of the delegation to Paterson in January 1935. Front row, left to right: Cooper, Martha Nevin, Hyllus Briggs, Sarah Cooper, Anna Morgan, an obscured figure (who might be Helen Baillie), Doug Nicholls; back row, left to right: Caleb Morgan, Ebenezer Lovett, Claude B Smith, Annie Lovett, Shadrach James. Many of the people Cooper drew to his organisation came from Cumeroogunga as well as being family: for example, Nicholls, who had made a name for himself as an Australian Rules footballer, was one of Cooper's grand-nephews while Briggs was one of his grand-nieces.

was preferable that 'one of their own people' rather than a white person 'represent their interests in parliament'. Cooper once again pointed out that Māori had representatives in the New Zealand parliament and on this basis he suggested that Aboriginal parliamentary representation was long overdue. It also seems that the deputation called for formation of a special advisory council in each state that would include an Aboriginal representative. Yet the petition itself was not presented to Paterson. In fact, it was not even mentioned. This can probably be attributed to Cooper accepting the advice of Baillie and Morley that it would be a mistake to do so. (The latter did not believe there was any chance the request to the Commonwealth

Government for parliamentary representation would be granted given that responsibility for Aboriginal affairs in the country was divided between the federal and state governments.)[58]

We need to note here the response of both the minister, Paterson, and his most senior adviser, JA Carrodus, to this call for parliamentary representation, as it influenced the way in which Cooper and his organisation presented their demand for parliamentary representation two or more years later (which is discussed in Chapter 8). At the meeting Paterson, after remarking that the federal government only had responsibility for Aboriginal people in the territories, pointed out that Aboriginal people were not alone in having no parliamentary representation: the Australian Capital Territory had no member and the Northern Territory had a member who had a voice but no vote. Several months later Carrodus claimed in a memorandum he prepared for Paterson that there were no

This cartoon, which appeared in the Melbourne *Herald* on 25 January 1935, suggested that the political class would refuse to face up to the problems that the delegation led by Cooper had presented to the government.

Aboriginal people in the Northern Territory competent to take a seat in the Commonwealth parliament.[59]

Cooper and his associates hoped to get definite replies to the matters they had raised in this meeting. In May, having heard nothing, Cooper was authorised by the Australian Aborigines' League to approach Paterson. Ten days later he received a letter in which the minister began by addressing the matter of parliamentary representation. Paterson informed him that the state governments were the only authorities that could decide whether representation of Aboriginal people could be granted in their parliaments, repeated his observation that representation of Aboriginal people in the Commonwealth parliament had to be confined to the Northern Territory, and expressed the opinion that there were no Aboriginal people in the Territory competent to take up a seat in the Commonwealth parliament. He suggested that an alternative was to elect or nominate a white person to represent the Territory's Aboriginal people in that parliament, but also remarked that he could see no advantage accruing from such a measure.[60]

On receiving this letter Cooper must have felt very discouraged, but he believed that the government was going to give further consideration to the matter and so he wrote to Gribble asking whether the missionary could recommend 'a[n] Aboriginal or a sympathetic white man to take the seat to represent our people in the NT'. Several months later, perhaps at Cooper's request, the federal Labor MP for Melbourne Ports, Jack Holloway, used question time in the House of Representatives to ask Paterson whether he had raised with Cabinet the deputation's request for 'a special representative' in the Commonwealth parliament; Holloway was emphatically told that the government could not accede to the request. At this point Cooper seems to have set the petition aside, but he had by no means forgotten about it.[61]

6

THE LEAGUE

Cooper's name is inextricably bound up with the Australian Aborigines' League. This organisation was fundamental to his work. It is often confused with another organisation with the same initials, the Aborigines Advancement League (of Victoria), that was formed in Melbourne much later (1957).[1] But while they had some figures in common—most notably Cooper's grand-nephew Doug Nicholls, who co-founded the Advancement League and became one of the leading Aboriginal political figures in the postwar period[2]—and some of the same concerns, such as securing reserve lands for Aboriginal people, they were distinct organisations.[3]

Several historians have argued that the Australian Aborigines' League was founded in 1935 or 1936 once a white man, Arthur Burdeu, became involved in Cooper's work.[4] But this overlooks the fact that Cooper had formed, however loosely, an organisation earlier, perhaps even prior to the drawing-up of his famous petition, though it appears that at least eighteen months passed before any material was issued in its name. In November 1934 Cooper sent a circular letter in the name of the 'Australian Aboriginal League' and the following month he submitted a letter to *The Age* as the honorary secretary of the 'Australian Aborigines' League'. By March 1935 it might seem 'Australian Aborigines' League' or 'Australian Aboriginal League' had become common usage among its members given that

Cooper signed a letter as the secretary of the 'A.A. League' and that the following month a very brief newspaper report made reference to a member of the Australian Aborigines' League.[5] Yet in April 1935 Cooper authorised the sending of letters in the names of both the 'Real Australian Aboriginal Association' and the 'Real Australian Native Association'. Nevertheless, one way or the other, it is clear that he and his Aboriginal associates had formed an organisation and called it from time to time the Australian Aborigines' League before Burdeu assumed a role in its affairs and it was formally constituted as an organisation.[6]

This said, there can be no doubt that Cooper relied a good deal on the help of Helen Baillie in the early phases of his work in Melbourne, just as there can be no question that in order to sustain it he depended on Burdeu's help after Burdeu became involved in the League in 1935. The lack of opportunities Cooper had suffered in his life and the resulting paucity of resources he had at his disposal made this necessary. In order to be able to understand why Cooper welcomed both Baillie's and Burdeu's help, and why they proved such useful allies to him, we need to know something about them.

Helen Baillie

Baillie, born in England (c. 1893) but raised in Australia, was in many respects typical of white women who took up the cause of Aboriginal people in the 1920s and 1930s. She was a fervent Christian, single, middle-aged and financially independent. She travelled frequently between Australia and England for both pleasure and politics. After training to become a midwife in London and being inspired by the famous philanthropist Octavia Hill to work among London's poor, she returned to Australia in 1932 looking for what she called 'new work'. She found it, at least partly, in what she cast as 'the call of the Aboriginal', to which she believed she had been guided by God. In this period in her life Baillie took up many causes. She was someone who needed a cause to which she could devote herself. 'It is *great* to have a good cause to work for', Baillie once remarked to her local Anglican clergyman. One might say that she needed to be needed and that she preferred to work for a cause in which the needs of

This photograph of Helen Baillie was taken in Melbourne in 1936 when she was the secretary of the local Ethiopian Relief Committee, which had been founded to help the Indigenous peoples of that country after Mussolini's invasion of Abyssinia. Later she would volunteer as a nurse for the Republican forces in the Spanish Civil War and work for the Spanish Relief Committee on her return.

others, rather than her own, were to the fore. In this respect Baillie might have reminded Cooper of his missionary mentors, Daniel and Janet Matthews.[7]

After returning to Melbourne Baillie established an organisation she called the Aboriginal Fellowship Group, and worked alongside another Christian humanitarian organisation, the Victorian Aboriginal Group, which, despite its name, comprised only white folk, just like Baillie's was. (Both these groups worked with several women's organisations, including the Women's Citizens' Movement, the Young Women's Christian Association and the Women's International League for Peace and Freedom.) Soon afterwards Baillie forged a connection with Rev. William Morley, the long-time secretary of the Sydney-based Association for the Protection of Native Races, which she joined and whose policies she endorsed, including its strong support for missionary work among Aboriginal people. She also began what became a long-lasting correspondence with the clergyman and anthropologist AP Elkin, who had recently become the president of the Association for the Protection of Native Races. She embraced his call for a constructive government policy in Aboriginal affairs and endorsed the task he prescribed for missionary workers—that of understanding Aboriginal people's culture sympathetically.[8]

In espousing principles that mirrored those of other white Christian humanitarians at this time, Baillie cast Aboriginal people as the original inhabitants of the land, argued that white Australians had a duty towards them, and emphasised the appalling history of white Australians' treatment of Aboriginal people. She stressed the importance of upholding Australia's reputation in the eyes of the world, argued that the federal government was morally responsible for the Indigenous people of Australia and those of New Guinea under a mandate from the League of Nations, and called upon the government to consider policies that had been adopted by enlightened colonial administrators in Africa. Baillie believed the Commonwealth Government should assume control of Aboriginal affairs or at least coordinate the policy of the states, and recommended an increase in the number of reserves for Aboriginal people, the removal of police as protectors and their replacement by women, the training of protectors in anthropology, and greater support for missions. In nearly all these respects Cooper and Baillie would have seen eye to eye.[9]

This was all the more the case because Baillie differed from most Christian humanitarian campaigners. Her political connections lay as much with the labour movement and left-wing organisations as they did with Christian humanitarian ones. (She once described herself as a Christian communist.) Most importantly, she also supported the political work of Aboriginal people, even though this meant that she was considered to be eccentric by fellow Christian humanitarians and treated accordingly. After meeting the New South Wales Aboriginal leader Bill Ferguson in Melbourne in 1934, she offered to help him organise Aboriginal people and later became a strong supporter of the organisation he founded (with Jack Patten), the Aborigines Progressive Association. Baillie also corresponded with Norman Harris, one of the Aboriginal spokesmen for the Western Australian Native Union. By contrast, William Morley, who was one of the most influential Christian humanitarian campaigners of this period, distanced himself from Ferguson and regarded the Aborigines

Progressive Association as an organisation that could harm the cause. Finally, Baillie's work for the Aboriginal cause was not only political but philanthropic in nature. She laboured among the Aboriginal community in Fitzroy as an unpaid social worker, trying to meet its needs by organising clothes and food for them, seeking help for the people from state relief funds, and making applications for pensions on their behalf. (Later in her life Baillie provided accommodation for young Aboriginal people in her house on Punt Road Hill in South Yarra.)[10]

Baillie had sought Cooper out shortly after reading the letter he had sent to *The Age* in March 1933 and offered to help him in his political work. It must have quickly become clear to Cooper that she could be an invaluable source of information. Baillie could tell him the names of relevant agencies and officials in Aboriginal affairs in the federal government, and knew a great deal about matters that affected Aboriginal people elsewhere in Australia as a result of her travels. Cooper would also have realised that she had useful contacts and was willing to share them. She personally knew people who could help him in his cause, such as Ernest Gribble, William Morley and Morley's son, Norman, who was the secretary of a white Christian humanitarian organisation in Western Australia, the Australian Aborigines' Amelioration Association, and she was eager to put Cooper in touch with them. Cooper would also have grasped that Baillie was able to arrange interviews with political figures, most notably the federal Labor leader James Scullin and the minister for the interior JA Perkins. She was almost certainly responsible for the legwork that made the deputation to Minister for the Interior Thomas Paterson in January 1935 possible (see Chapter 5). Cooper must have also come to appreciate Baillie's considerable organisational skills, not least in helping to arrange concerts that raised funds for his cause and for local Aboriginal people in particular need.[11]

In performing all this work Baillie was often paternalistic, like practically all the whites who sought to help Aboriginal people at this time. But, unlike most Christian humanitarians who tended to assume that they had the right to represent Aboriginal people, she was aware that the relationship between white campaigners like herself and Aboriginal campaigners like Cooper could be fraught. Moreover, she understood the forces that constrained Aboriginal people's political work; 'because of their lack of education and political influence, [they] have not the power or ability to speak for themselves', she once remarked. In her campaigning Baillie often sought to include Aboriginal people's utterances in her pleas on their behalf. On occasion she noted their support for the political demands she was making, and she regularly praised their leaders. In short, Baillie believed that whites like herself could 'help best by assisting the Aboriginal people to press for their rights'.[12]

Baillie also contributed to the League's work by recruiting at least one of its members. 'I was just an Aboriginal maid and getting to love parties', Margaret Tucker, who became one of its vice-presidents, once recalled. 'And then a white society lady Miss Helen Baillie found me and asked me to sing in a concert … in aid of our Aborigines in Fitzroy and that was the beginning of understanding and working for my people.'[13]

Helen Baillie helped the Australian Aborigines' League to organise conferences and concerts. This photograph of Cooper, Margaret Tucker, Cooper's son Lynch and Cooper's wife Sarah was taken when they sang at one of these—a conference held at the Society of Friends' Meeting House on Russell Street, Melbourne—in order to coordinate the work of groups concerned about the plight of Aboriginal people. It appeared in one of the Melbourne broadsheets, *The Argus*, which called Tucker by the Yorta Yorta name Cooper had given her: Lilardia. On occasions like this in which oral or visual performance was to the fore, Aboriginal culture was more evident than it was in the written texts produced by or in the League's name, in which white people had a major hand.

Anna and Caleb Morgan

Baillie also played a part in encouraging other Aboriginal women to speak and enabling their voices to be heard. This is especially true in regard to Anna Morgan (nee Bowden), who, along with her husband Caleb (one of Bagot Morgan's nephews), was a member of the League. A discussion of the Morgans serves to highlight key points in our story. The matters that Cooper took up when he formed the League had a national dimension, but it was local matters that tended to occupy the thoughts of many of his Aboriginal associates. Further, the cause for which Cooper fought and the arguments he made in doing so were common to the community of Aboriginal people to which he belonged.[14]

This photograph, which largely comprises members of the Australian Aborigines' League, was clearly taken at the same time as the photograph of the League members shown earlier (page 113). Many years later, one of those who kept a copy of it, Margaret Tucker, captioned it 'The start of the Aboriginal League in Melbourne'. She identified the people as follows, from left to right: Shadrach James, Ebenezer Lovett, Annie Lovett, one of Claude B Smith's sons, William Cooper, Claude B Smith, Sarah Cooper, Hyllus Briggs, Caleb Morgan, Anna Morgan, Martha Nevin and Doug Nicholls.

Most of the local matters the Morgans took up concerned Cumeroogunga. This is hardly surprising. The people for whom this reserve was home were the bearers of a historical tradition that asserted that they had fought for and recovered land, and farmed it well as blocks, only to lose this land and have their independence undermined and their families and community broken up by a repressive Protection Board. As early as 1912 Caleb had spoken out in a letter he wrote to one of the Australian Workers' Union newspapers, *The Worker*, from Bringle, near Dubbo, where he, Anna and their family had taken refuge after they were expelled from Cumeroogunga. In this letter he had begun by saying how glad he was that at least one white Australian (a Labor MP, William Higgs) recognised that white Australians owed Aboriginal people 'a duty as a compensation for the land they deprived [them] of'. But he soon recalled the bitter experience of being told by the overseers at Maloga and Cumeroogunga 'that we ought to be thankful for our privileges', asking: 'What privilege is it to us, who are enlightened, to be herded together like sheep on a few hundred acres, and fed on what the managers think fit to feed us?' He went on to point out: 'Should we offend them in any way, they give us a few days' notice or jail us for trespassing on our own land.' Morgan was undoubtedly referring to his own experience at Cumeroogunga, but he made it clear that his complaint was not confined to this mission or even to missions or reserves more generally. 'We feel it acutely when, walking across a squatter's ground, he comes along and hunts us off, and if we don't go, summons us for trespassing', he wrote, adding 'It is bitter indeed to think of, that this beautiful country of Australia was ours by birthright, and we can't call an acre our own.' Like Cooper had done in 1887, Morgan appealed for a tiny fraction of that land to be returned to them: 'We would be infinitely grateful [if] the federal government [was to] give those of us who are capable and willing to work a block of our own land and a start.' Fifteen years later, after returning to the Murray, Morgan renewed a call to the New South Wales Aborigines Protection Board for the restoration of the farm blocks at Cumeroogunga.[15]

In October 1934, by which time the Morgans had been living at Coldstream, near Coranderrk, for several years,[16] Anna published an article in the Political Labor Council of Victoria's newspaper, *Labor Call*. In it she described the bitter experience of living under what she called 'the Black Flag' of the so-called Aborigines Protection Board of New South Wales, contrasting this with being a subject living under the British flag. (In 1923 Aboriginal people on Coranderrk had made a similar comparison.) 'We have not the same liberty as the white man, nor do we expect the same justice', she stated emphatically.[17]

Morgan proceeded to tell the story of the farm blocks at Cumeroogunga: 'My husband was given a 30-acre block of land; he cleared and fenced it … There were only two teams of horses to do all the work for ten such farms, and no assistance from outside was allowed. When at last we did get in a crop the Board took away the land from us. We wanted to remain on the land and make our living however we could. But … the Board would not have it … saying that the men were too lazy to work the land.' As we know, worse followed. In her words: 'Those who protested against this injustice were classed as agitators, an expulsion order was made out against them, and it was served by the local police. My husband was among the victims.' A few months later, Caleb returned to the reserve in order to get their belongings, which they had left at his father's place, and stayed the night. '[T]he next day', Morgan recalled, 'my husband got a summons for trespassing. He was taken and gaoled for fourteen days.' In fact Caleb was gaoled for a fortnight with hard labour.[18] As far as Anna was concerned, her husband had not broken any British laws but rather the laws of the New South Wales Protection Board. In her view, this smacked of the prejudice Aboriginal people suffered more generally: 'When a white man is charged with a crime, he is taken to court and judged. If innocent, he is allowed to go home to his family, and there the matter ends.' This was all the more unjust, Morgan explained to her readers, because the people had been told 'This is your home and your children's as long as there is an aboriginal left.' Indeed, she declared, in the case of her husband, 'the land had been reserved for my husband and his people' and now he could 'never go back to his own people' because the two of them had been 'expelled for all time'. More generally, she pointed out that the Aboriginal people had been dispossessed: 'You have taken our beautiful country from us—"a free gift".' And, like Cooper, as we will see, she appealed to white Australians by calling on those who prided themselves on British fair play to think of the plight of the Aboriginal people.[19]

In an interview Morgan granted a journalist and in the speech she gave in January 1935 at a meeting held at the Unity Hall in Melbourne under the auspices of the International Women's Day Committee, she spoke in more general terms before returning to the local matters that no doubt prompted her remarks. 'The blacks of Australia are trying to emancipate themselves', she stated, but '[t]he authorities are hindering them at every turn.' What they wanted was education but instead they were confined to what she called compounds. Furthermore, they had no means of redress there and dared not complain. 'Is this British fair play?' Morgan asked. 'Is it right for a government to give a man the power of repressing a community such as ours? We are British subjects the same as the white people in this hall, and are entitled to justice.'[20]

This photo of Anna Morgan appeared in the Melbourne newspaper *The Herald* after she spoke to the meeting organised by the local International Women's Day Committee. Sadly, she died suddenly just a few months later.

On these occasions Morgan spoke not only of the prejudice and injustice against which Aboriginal people were struggling but of the poverty they were suffering. She attributed the latter to the way that the likes of herself and her husband were treated by the government. On turning sixty years of age she had applied to the Commonwealth Government for an old age pension, but had been informed that she was regarded as an Aborigine and so was not entitled to one. On appealing to the Victorian authorities for assistance she was told she was ineligible because she was *not* considered to be Aboriginal.[21]

Morgan launched an attack on the forced removal of Aboriginal girls from their families and kin as soon as they turned fourteen years of age, which once again owed much to the experience on Cumeroogunga of many of those who comprised the League. She accused the government of trying to 'wipe out the black race' and 'build a white Australia'. In doing so, she made it clear that Aboriginal people were 'proud of their race' and 'anxious to extend aboriginal culture'. This was the point of most of the writings Morgan produced, which took the form of Aboriginal legends, several of which she delivered on the Australian Broadcasting Commission's Melbourne radio station at this time. Using one of her Aboriginal names, Ghingobin, she declared that these were stories 'handed down, from generation to generation [which] we never let our children forget'.[22]

Arthur Burdeu

By the middle of 1935 Cooper was feeling the burden of leading the League's campaign and discouraged by the tardy response of the federal government to his calls for change. Actually, his work had more or less ground to a halt. Part of the problem lay in the fact that he and his Aboriginal associates, who were similarly poverty-stricken, lacked the financial means to sustain it. In June Cooper appealed to Paterson for help. 'Since taking up the work on behalf of the Aborigine cause, to endeavour better conditions, I have been under the whole of the expense of postage, letter writing, travelling, and other expenses besides my time', he wrote. He asked for some remuneration or advice as to how he might fund his work. But he was told that the government could not help and that he should seek reimbursement of his expenses from the League.[23] He tried to carry on, but found it increasingly difficult to do so.[24]

In the closing months of 1935 Cooper got the help he needed as a result of meeting Arthur Burdeu.[25] Burdeu's assistance was to prove even more valuable than Baillie's. Unfortunately, we know less about him. But it is enough to get some sense of what compelled him to assist Cooper. Born in 1882, the eldest of eight children, Burdeu was a trade unionist. Above all else, though, he was a fervent Christian. '[T]hat', he said once, 'comes before all other considerations.' He had once been an Anglican vestryman but had become a member of the Church of Christ. This was a church that was accustomed to giving each congregation considerable autonomy. It also worked on the grounds of the 'priesthood of all believers' and thus had no hierarchy. Its non-denominational nature probably reminded Cooper of the Matthewses. The Church of Christ also sponsored an Aboriginal pastor at Cumeroogunga, Edwin (Eddy) Atkinson, who was one of Cooper's grand-nephews, and Doug Nicholls would also later join and become one of its pastors.[26] Like Baillie, Burdeu was pro-missionary, though unlike her he was apprehensive about left-wing influences subverting Aboriginal organisations. As with Baillie, Cooper and his Aboriginal associates probably welcomed Burdeu to the cause because his connection to the work was not only political but philanthropic in nature and so they regarded it as more genuine. 'I came into the ameliorationist [sic] world from the Aboriginal sphere. There I made my first contacts, there I did my first work', Burdeu once told Elkin, the anthropologist, church-man and advocate. 'I thus came into the work with a knowledge of the heartthrobs of the people and a [practical] knowledge of their disabilities', he explained. 'There is a whole world between my outlook and that of the academic ameliorationist.' Cooper and the rest of the Aboriginal community in Melbourne came to regard Burdeu as a 'firm friend and councillor [sic, i.e. counsellor]'—at least this is what Baillie believed—and affectionately called him 'Pop'. A Melbourne newspaper remarked that they even called him 'the white blackfellow'. Burdeu took great pride in the fact that they regarded him in that way.[27] This, along with other evidence, suggests

This rare photograph
of Arthur Burdeu was
probably taken in 1934.

that he, like Baillie, was driven to help Aboriginal people—if *help* is really the right word—by emotional needs of his own.[28]

The fact that both Cooper and Burdeu were strong labour men and devout Christians provided the two with common ground for the work they were to do together. Other factors probably played a part as well. While they were of a different generation, they both belonged to large families and had lost a family member in the Great War. They also lived relatively close to one another—Cooper in Footscray and Yarraville, Burdeu in Essendon (and later in Moonee Ponds)—but it seems that they used to meet at Spencer Street Railway Station (where Burdeu worked as the president of the Victorian Division of the Federation of Salaried Officers of Railways Commissioners), conferring during Burdeu's lunch hour.[29]

It seems that the League was formally constituted as an organisation not long after Cooper enlisted Burdeu to help him with his cause. As a result of Burdeu's work, by February 1936 the League had acquired a constitution, a program, a slogan and office-bearers, though the formation—or what really amounted to the re-formation—of the League had been announced a few months earlier. Cooper became its secretary and Doug Nicholls its treasurer; Lynch Cooper was appointed its assistant secretary, Margaret Tucker, Mary Clarke and Nicholls became its vice-presidents,

Doug Nicholls, August 1931. About a year after this photograph was taken, Nicholls converted to Christianity and joined the Church of Christ, which had a chapel in Fitzroy. A few years later, Cooper persuaded him to join the League and fight for his people's rights.

and the executive committee comprised these people and Annie Lovett, Hyllus Briggs, Marie Lovett, Julia Niven, Alice Clarke and Caleb Morgan.[30]

The nature of the League's work also began to change at this point. 'Under my influence a campaign of seeking amelioration by goodwill has been carried out', Burdeu was to explain later to a government minister. 'I have argued that governments reflected the mind of the constituency and that we should work to secure our aims by convincing the administration of the justice of our claims in the first place.' The League's program also changed to some degree after Burdeu became involved, at least as far as the way it was articulated in the organisation's constitution and formal statements of policy. The League's 'ultimate object' was said to be 'the removal of all disabilities, political, social or economic, now or in future borne by aboriginals and to secure their uplift to the full culture of the British race', and its 'immediate programme' was described as 'the progressive elevation of the aboriginal race by education and training in the arts and crafts of European culture'.[31]

Burdeu's involvement also saw the League become much more strategic in the way it went about its work. This resulted in a considerable expansion in its activities. It made many more approaches to government but also overtures to other like-minded white organisations, which Burdeu called Aboriginal amelioration societies. The League also became a more effective champion of Cooper's cause as its appeals to government acquired more focus: problems were specified, supporting arguments provided, particular solutions recommended.[32]

Burdeu's role in the League's affairs was formalised by his appointment as its president. Its constitution stipulated that administrative positions should be filled by full members and that full membership was only open to Aboriginal people, but it allowed associate members (who were characterised as people sympathetic to the League's aims) to play these roles. Its Aboriginal members apparently asked Burdeu to take the position of president and re-elected him to it year after year. One can assume that they did so because they realised he had skills they lacked, primarily those of a fluent writer.[33]

On the League's re-formation in 1935–36, it acquired a slogan, 'A fair deal for the dark race', which Burdeu seems to have suggested, and a letterhead, which he probably designed.

AUSTRALIAN ABORIGINES' LEAGUE

"A fair deal for the dark race."

WILLIAM COOPER,
Hon. Secretary

DOUG NICHOLLS,
Hon. Treasurer

43 Mackay Street,
SEDDON, W.11.,
Victoria,

June 25th 1937

The Hon. the Minister
for the Interior,
CANBERRA,

Dear Mr. Paterson,

I do thank you for your willingness to discuss the matter of the aborigines with me by letter. It is but another token of your genuine desire to do the right by my people. You say my previous letter was in a pessimistic strain. Mr. Paterson, I am an old man and I did hope to live to see my people in a fair way to uplift, hence my hopes are not being realised, hence my despair. If my claims for my people are just, why should I not look for immediate relief. If they are unreasonable cannot I claim to be shown in what way they are. I am being assured all round that what we ask is only our right and therefore I feel that I am right when I persistently press for this right.

I am delighted at the assurance that your colleagues in the Federal Cabinet are likeminded with you and the Prime Minister in sincere desire to do the very best by our people.

I understand that the Federal Parliament has jurisdiction only over such aborigines as may live in the Territories. There are over 18,000 full bloods in these parts and I venture the opinion that if the Federal Government deals adequately with the problem as it affects the aborigines under its control a definite lead will be given to the State Governments and a favorable psychology will be developed in the general public.

Mr. Paterson, your kindness is so genuine that I feel I can respectfully say to you, without impropriety, that you should, just for the moment, forget that you are a white man so that you may look at the matter as we do. To see things as we do, to feel as we do, is the best way to realise the extent of our disabilities. We do not want our people to remain primitive, uncultured and a prey to all comers. Why should we remain in the near Stone Age ? The British were once where we are now. The conquering power of Rome, whatever else it did, lifted the British to culture and civilisation. We want that same uplift. Are we unreasonable ?

We have proven our capacity, all over Australia, to become capable in every form of husbandry. In places we have made ourselves indispensable. We have acquired the faculty for the arts

Once it is recognised how important Burdeu was to the League carrying out its work after its re-formation, a couple of questions necessarily arise. First, did the League remain the voice of Cooper and its other Aboriginal members? There can be little doubt that they were keen to ensure that the organisation represented *their* views. This is indicated by the possessive apostrophe in its name: the Australian Aborigines' League. Its rule that only Aboriginal people could be full members is also telling in this regard. So too are the statements that were made shortly after the League was re-formed: Cooper remarked that this was 'the Dark Man's own ameliorative effort for his own race' and the League's first annual report bluntly asserted: 'This is Our Movement'. For his part Burdeu believed that Aboriginal people should be in the forefront of the political struggle for change and that the role they played advanced the cause considerably. He also saw the League as a distinctive organisation because it sought to represent matters from the Aboriginal point of view. As he declared once, in the context of explaining differences between the various organisations campaigning on behalf of the Aboriginal people, 'The League is the Aboriginal Voice'. In the same vein Burdeu realised that Aboriginal people tended to have views and aspirations that were, as he remarked once, 'completely different from the white man's', and he conceived his job as one of faithfully presenting those views. He actually went so far as to claim that he saw the problems of Aboriginal people 'through Aboriginal eyes'[34] and that their cause was his cause, asserting on one occasion: 'to that cause I have devoted all I am and have and all I hope to be'.[35]

Second, did the material the League presented in Cooper's name, mostly in the form of letters to government, represent his views?[36] To answer this question, we need to consider how Cooper and Burdeu went about their work together for the League. There is actually no historical record of how they did this, but it seems likely that they prepared letters to government ministers and the like in this way: Cooper began by drafting a letter, explaining to Burdeu in the 'crisp sentences' in which he usually spoke what he wanted to say; Burdeu read Cooper's drafts or listened and took notes; the two men then discussed how the points Cooper wanted to make might best be expressed; and, finally, Burdeu prepared the drafts of letters by hand, typed them out, and returned them to Cooper to sign.[37]

It is also important to reiterate in this regard that Burdeu was committed to helping Cooper say what he wanted to say. After Burdeu died, Baillie remarked: 'I remember attending many committee meetings [of the League] in which he patiently assisted the native people to express their needs.' (She also recalled that he 'never spared himself in his work for the aborigines and the amount of correspondence he got through was amazing'.) It is also critical to note that Cooper would have been unwilling to authorise the letters that were sent in his name if they did not represent his opinions. 'He was a real leader, with definite views and capable of strong expression of those views', Burdeu recalled after his death. 'He had opinions and the courage of expression.'[38]

It thus seems reasonable to conclude, then, that the letters in Cooper's name by and large *did* represent his views faithfully. This is less true, though, of the League's formal statements, which Burdeu was undoubtedly responsible for composing. 'He was particularly nettled by talks of "long range policies"', Burdeu recalled after Cooper died. 'He used to say that what was wanted was "a policy for the present".' It also needs to be borne in mind that Burdeu, like Baillie, sought to ensure that the League was always 'constructive' in its political work and so tried to moderate what Cooper wanted to say. But they did not always succeed, not least in regard to his famous petition.[39]

7

RACE AND RIGHTS

AFTER ARTHUR BURDEU became involved in the work of William Cooper's organisation, the way in which it often couched its demands increasingly echoed the language of rights that was used by other parties that were campaigning for, or on behalf of, Aboriginal people. In the 1930s most of those calling for changes in government policy and practice were inclined to emphasise that Aboriginal people shared a common humanity with white Australians and to advance claims to rights on that basis. This means, as the historian Russell McGregor has emphasised, that the nature of the rights that organisations such as the Australian Aborigines' League and the Aborigines Progressive Association claimed were, in large part, rather different from those that Aboriginal people have been claiming in recent decades.[1]

The rights that Cooper and his fellow Aboriginal campaigners mostly called for were the same rights that other Australians enjoyed—what they called 'equal rights' or 'citizenship rights'—rather than Indigenous rights, which are the rights that only Indigenous people can claim on the basis of being the descendants of the country's First People. Furthermore, whereas many people have now become accustomed to demanding that rights be granted to them immediately, they tended, at least in the formal statements made of the League's objectives, to advance claims for rights that were conditional in the sense that they rested on the *capacity* of their people to exercise them. Consequently, the League's spokesmen and women were inclined to accept that those rights would be granted to all Aboriginal people only in the fullness of time. To be specific, the demands they expressed for the rights of citizenship were premised on Aboriginal people having the capacity to assimilate European or British culture and thereby acquire the essential prerequisites of what was deemed to be 'civilisation'.[2]

Given this nexus, rights were not so much regarded as an entitlement as something to be earned. In the course of presenting a long statement to the minister for the interior, Thomas Paterson, in October 1936 the League asserted: 'he [the Aborigine] is not seeking anything else than the right to obtain what he proves himself to be entitled to by his capacity to use it'. This stance was in keeping with what the League's spokespeople envisaged as 'the *progressive* elevation of the aboriginal race by education and training in the arts and crafts of European culture'. In this regard they sometimes distinguished between three groups of Aboriginal people—'primitive aborigines', 'semi-civilised and de-tribalised natives' and 'civilised natives'—and called for particular rights in accordance with the level of 'civilisation' each group had attained, with 'full rights' only being claimed for 'civilised aborigines'. Thus, we find Cooper calling on Prime Minister Robert Menzies in September 1939 to introduce legislation that would grant 'full rights to aborigines', but only to those who had 'civilised status', and asserting that 'many [Aboriginal people] are not able to understand these matters and as little able to benefit from [these rights]'.[3]

Despite the qualified nature of the claims the League made, they were radical in the context of the time. Most white Australians regarded Aboriginal people as an inferior race that had no capacity to adapt to a superior civilisation, while some even held that they were subhuman. This means that the claims Aboriginal campaigners made for rights on the basis that their people were similarly human and had the same capacity as white Australians constituted a challenge to the racial order of the day.

How are we best to explain the nature of these calls for rights
for Aboriginal people? Their discourse can probably be attributed
to several factors. First, they wanted to reduce the salience of race
in their people's affairs, at least as far as the ways in which race was
defined by whitefellas. For instance, Cooper frequently complained
of being treated as inferior on the grounds of his race. He explained
once to one of the League's white sympathisers in Britain: 'as
regards the public as a whole … there is ignorance, indifference and
even the same old superiority complex of the white man toward
the coloured—for, as you know, the White Australia policy excludes
us, the aborigines of this continent'. In other words, their highly
visceral experience of discrimination on the grounds of race meant
that Cooper often called for rights on a basis that transcended any
notion of racial difference.[4]

Second, though Cooper and his Aboriginal associates in the
League sought to represent all Aboriginal people in Australia, much
of the League's focus was upon Aboriginal people like themselves,
namely those who had acquired the status of civilised subjects but
who had been denied the rights and privileges that Australian
citizens enjoyed. Given this, it is probably unremarkable that they
called for those kinds of rights and privileges and assumed that this
would enable them to overcome the disabilities they suffered.

Third, tying their claims for rights to cultural capacity—or, to be
more specific, the attainment of British or European civilisation—
provided Cooper and his Aboriginal associates with a means of
challenging white Australia's denial of 'uplift' to them on the basis
of colour or race. This is so because that denial rested on an assumption that the current condition of Aboriginal people was permanent
rather than one that could readily change (as the League suggested)
if only white Australia were to provide them with the necessary
assistance. Consequently, Cooper and the League were inclined to
demand: 'Let the determination be, not color, but capacity.'[5]

Finally, since the dominant racial discourse cast Aboriginal people
as fundamentally different and denied them rights and privileges
on those grounds, the best or perhaps even the only viable political

strategy available to campaigners for rights for Aboriginal people was to represent Aboriginal people as having the same nature as white Australians and call for the same rights and privileges as those held by their fellow Australians.

Difference

While Cooper and the League laid claim to the same rights as other Australians enjoyed and did so on the grounds that Aboriginal people shared a common nature with them, this is by no means the sum of the way in which they claimed rights. In calling for the same rights that other Australians had, they often made an argument for the granting of those rights that focused on what we can call *difference*. For example, their calls for equal rights were often accompanied by pleas for a new government policy to remove all the disabilities suffered by Aboriginal people so that they could be 'uplifted' to the 'full' or 'modern' or 'British' culture. According to the League's constitution, the removal of those differences was its primary objective. The League had two kinds of disabilities in mind. There were civil ones, which were largely the product of the legal measures contained in the various special Aboriginal Protection Acts. These prompted it to call for the same political and legal rights enjoyed by Australian citizens. And there were the economic and social disabilities that Aboriginal people suffered, which were a result of racial attitudes, policies and practices that severely diminished their opportunities in respect of education, employment, housing, health and the like, thereby incapacitating them and causing extreme poverty and hardship. These disabilities prompted League spokespeople to demand that sustenance (or unemployment) benefits, maternity bonuses, invalid pensions and old age pensions be made available to Aboriginal people—that is, to call for the same economic and social provisions as Australian citizens enjoyed—but also to make a special case for Aboriginal people in the name of uplift and gaining 'full equality in every way with the white race'. This explains why Cooper and the League welcomed the federal government's 'New Deal for Aborigines' in these terms (in a letter to Menzies): 'Mr Lyons' government produced our MAGNA CARTA in the new policy. We do trust that your government will take the logical final steps for the outcome of the federal policy must be the civilisation of the race who thus must ultimately come to a full Australian status.'[6]

Difference was also at the heart of the League's rights talk in other, more obvious ways. It sometimes made reference to the fact that other Indigenous peoples, namely Māori, as well as naturalised aliens, had been granted the rights of Australian citizens and yet Aboriginal people had not. In calling attention to this, the League implied that it was manifestly wrong that they—Australia's aboriginal or first people—were being denied the rights that all other Australians enjoyed. (In the postwar period, in the context of massive non-British migration to Australia, Cooper's protégé Doug Nicholls often deployed the newly coined term *New Australians* to press the claims of Aboriginal people as the *Old Australians*.)[7]

More commonly, the League explicitly invoked the fact that the Aboriginal people were the country's first people in the course of claiming the rights of Australian citizens. Cooper argued that Aboriginal people had 'a right to the best' because they were the descendants of those who had peopled Australia for hundreds of years and were thus their heirs; he asked 'in any case who should have this right before the dark race itself?'; and he declared: 'We claim that the native has a right to live in the "Land of His Fathers".' At other moments, he explicitly argued that Aboriginal people had a right to uplift on the grounds that they had been dispossessed as the country's original peoples. In August 1937 he remarked to the journalist Clive Turnbull: '[W]e have lost countless millions to the whites—the whole wealth of Australia. Are we not entitled to this?'; and in December 1938 he complained to the minister for the interior, John McEwen, 'yet the white man holds the land of our fathers without compensation', and went on to refer to 'the debt of the white man to the dark one'.[8]

The League most often raised Aboriginal people's status as Australia's Indigenous people in the course of making claims in regard to land. Cooper spoke of 'the right to a share of our father-land', 'the right to a little of [our] fathers' lands' and 'the soil of the country inhabited for centuries by his forefathers'. On occasion he and the League argued that the granting of the rights of British subjects to Aboriginal people was a quid pro quo for their people's loss of sovereignty, just as they claimed that transfer of sovereignty should not have expunged their title to land (a view that the High Court of Australia was to accept in its famous *Mabo* ruling in 1992). In October 1936 Cooper told Paterson, 'They [the Aborigines] are the lineal descendants of their fathers. The change in ownership by conquest should not invalidate their title to reasonable part of those lands and these rights should be admitted without cavil.' The following month he remarked to the editor of the Australian Aborigines' Amelioration Association's magazine: 'The coming of the white race and the passing of the sovereignty should not have affected the title to his share of the soil, and his coming, by conquest, under British rule, should have brought him British citizenship with all the rights and privileges thereof' (which echoed what Christian humanitarians such as the British secretary of state for the colonies, Lord Glenelg, had asserted almost a hundred years earlier). And in February 1938 he bluntly told McEwen: 'Aborigines are entitled to a quid pro quo for the loss of their lands and liberty. This is implied in the term BRITISH JUSTICE. If the aborigines are merely a conquered and enslaved people it is not consonant with British justice.'[9]

On more than one occasion Cooper and the League went further and made a claim to the right to an Aboriginal state. In the interview Cooper granted to Turnbull in August 1937, he asked why the federal government would not give Aboriginal people a chance 'to make our own state in our own country'; and in January 1939 he asked McEwen: 'Can we not have a "Balfour declaration" for natives of a national home in Australia?'[10] As readers will recall, Shadrach James had endorsed JC Genders' call for such a state ten years earlier.[11]

The area these advocates had in mind for such a state was the north of Australia. In recent years more than one historian has paid attention to the position that the League adopted in regard to northern Australia.[12] In the 1930s the country's white political leaders were deeply troubled by the fact that this vast area seemed empty of people and that this constituted an invitation to a non-white foreign

power to invade. Consequently, they advocated its development by
the white race. Aboriginal people barely featured in these plans. But,
as McGregor has pointed out, the League seized upon the calls to
develop the north as a means to impress upon the federal government the need to adopt a systematic plan to uplift Aboriginal people,
arguing that they were as able as white men to play a major role in
this project, and claiming that they could thereby become worthy
citizens and prove themselves to be an asset to Australia. In February
1937 Cooper told Paterson: 'In the aboriginal you have all the man
power required for the development of Australia's unsettled parts if
they are given due training, direction and leadership … You are yet
to find that the aboriginal race of Australia … [are] units making for
the stability of Australia and defence of our heritage.' A month later
he asserted in a letter to the secretary of the Anti-Slavery Society, Sir
John Harris: 'We are the potential solution of the neglected empty
spaces … a virile race capable of developing the vast resources of
Australia.' In June that year Cooper informed Paterson: 'We claim
that, given a trial, we will prove that we are capable of producing a
yeomanry that can open up and develop the outback better than
anyone else.' And he presented the same arguments to McEwen
once he succeeded Paterson as the minister for the interior. In doing
this, Cooper suggested that Aboriginal people like himself could
help redeem both the land and their people by populating and cultivating the earth, a notion that had deep roots in the Christianity
to which he had converted and that rested on a particularly English
interpretation of the Biblical injunction 'Be fruitful, and multiply,
and replenish the earth' (Genesis 1:28).[13]

Yet in the case that Cooper and the League made for Aboriginal
people playing a role in the development of northern Australia they
also invoked the matter of race in a way that rested on claims of
difference in one sense or another. From the outset the League's
case implied a criticism of the White Australia policy that denied
Aboriginal people the status and the rights and privileges that were
accorded to Australian citizens, even those called non-British aliens.
In October 1936 Cooper told Paterson: 'We submit that a practical ideal should be the development of the North and Centre by

Colored Australians instead of the proposed immigration of Nordic peoples and Southern Europeans.' In February 1937 he contended that Aboriginal people were better suited to develop the north than any European migrants because they were 'truly British'. And a year or so later he made the same point emphatically to McEwen: 'NO OUTWORKING OF THE WHITE AUSTRALIA POLICY SHALL WORK DETRIMENTALLY TO THE NATIVES. FOR THE PURPOSES OF THIS POLICY, THE ABORIGINAL IS WHITE ... WE BELIEVE AND CONTEND THAT ABORIGINES, NOT SOUTHERN EUROPEANS, ARE THOSE WHO SHOULD DEVELOP THE OUTBACK.'[14]

A month later Cooper and the League started to make a case for Aboriginal involvement in developing the north that rested not only on the claim that Aboriginal people were British and thus as Australian as any white or British Australians, but also on claims that Aboriginal people had much to offer because they were indigenous. There were several aspects to this argument. In the first instance Cooper contended that, just as Europeans were unsuited to the peopling of the north (since it was in the tropics), Aboriginal people were particularly well suited to the task, indeed more so than anyone else, because they were 'acclimatised'. In making this argument a further contention was never far away: the land or country in question belonged to the Aboriginal people. On one occasion Cooper referred to 'your land and ours' but at another point he remarked that the land in question was 'peculiarly his own'—that is, the Aboriginal people's. On another occasion he remarked that 'We Aborigines feel we have a right to a place in Australia and we feel we are robbed of that place'. On yet another he observed that this area was 'home' to the Aboriginal people. But it seems that Cooper and the League realised that they had to temper these arguments as they could damage their case by arousing a matter that hovered (and still hovers) at the edge of white Australia's consciousness, namely its knowledge that it had dispossessed the Aboriginal people of their land without any compensation and that Aboriginal people deeply resented this and so had little reason to be loyal subjects. Consequently, Cooper and the League repeatedly offered assurances that Aboriginal people *were* loyal citizens, though this often had a barb to it for they said they were loyal to the throne and person of the British king rather than to the Australian state. Finally, in the context of setting out the League's general policy, Cooper suggested to Prime Minister Joseph Lyons at one point that 'the proper method of dealing with the primitive people would be to send educated and cultured Aborigines' to northern Australia, as '[t]hese men, of the same blood, would understand their people and would be able to suggest to the government means whereby the hardships and sufferings of these people could be alleviated or removed'. In other words, the development of the north needed Aboriginal people like himself because their difference meant they were peculiarly well suited to work with the local Aboriginal people.[15]

Race and caste

The point upon which Cooper and the League most profoundly challenged the racial assumptions of the day was their rejection of the widely held distinction between so-called full-bloods and half-castes. This matter tended to arise in the context of the League discussing the federal government's plans for the uplift of Aboriginal people. The government, and white Australians more generally, held that the pathways that were available for Aboriginal people depended on whether they were 'full bloods' or 'half-castes'. But the League would have none of this distinction. Indeed, Cooper would claim that this was the League's 'chief bone of contention over the years'.[16]

Time and time again Cooper and the League took up this matter. In March 1936 they reacted to an announcement in the press of a proposal to relax legal restrictions imposed on Aboriginal people of 'mixed descent', such as the right to buy alcohol, by expressing concern that measures of this kind should make no distinction between 'full bloods' and 'half-castes'. They refuted the belief that 'half-castes' were more capable of advancement, and requested that future measures to ameliorate the Aboriginal people's conditions and uplift them be made available to all Aboriginal people capable of benefiting from them. Two months later a public meeting organised by the League passed a resolution endorsing its claim that

'all aborigines, of full or mixed blood, should be afforded opportunities … in common with other citizens of the Commonwealth',
and another one protesting 'against the discrimination still being
exercised against the aboriginals of Australia' and urging that 'full
citizenship rights be accorded to those of full aboriginal or mixed
blood who may be qualified to exercise them'. Several months later
Cooper told Paterson: 'To the extent that there has been discrimination in the past or the advantage of one section without regard to
the other, we are in protest. We claim for each section the full rights
of British nationality.' The following month the League temporarily
extended its motto so that it read: 'Full equality for the dark race
with the white race, and no differentiation between the full blood
and those of mixed blood.' A month later it reiterated this principle
in a statement it prepared for the first-ever meeting of all the chief
protectors of Aborigines in the country. And in June the following year Cooper beseeched Paterson: 'looking at our problems
from the point of view of the native, please forget the white man's
discrimination between the half caste and the full blood. Except
where the notion is put into the head of the half caste no one thinks
of the white strain at all.'[17]

Cooper and his Aboriginal associates in the League not only
rejected the dominant racial thinking of the day but asserted their
sense of themselves as Aboriginal people. In November 1936
Cooper told WJ Chinnery, the editor of the Australian Aborigines'
Amelioration Association's magazine: 'The coloured person has no
feeling of repugnance toward the full blood, and in fact he feels more
in common with the full blood than with the white.' And, he added:
'We dark folk have no regret that we are coloured … We are proud
of our race.' On another occasion Cooper told McEwen that he
should not 'suppose that the colored folk have, generally, aspirations
to be white or possess any regret as being colored'.[18]

Given this, the League had no truck with any policy that anticipated that Aboriginal people would be absorbed or assimilated into
the general population.[19] In June 1937 Cooper told Paterson that
Aboriginal people had no desire to be incorporated into the white
race but had instead a vision of '[t]he two races, side by side yet

distinct'. Nearly two years later, after the commissioner for native affairs (formerly the chief protector of Aborigines in Western Australia), AO Neville, pressed forward with a policy of absorption, Cooper told McEwen that the League viewed this most unfavourably. He declared that Neville was regarded by the League 'as the greatest enemy of our race'.[20]

Cooper's organisation devoted a great deal of time in 1938 and 1939 to mounting attacks on the Western Australian Government's administration of Aboriginal affairs. In large part this can be attributed to the fact that it was apprehensive that the federal government was intending to adopt that state government's policies and practices. 'For God's sake,' Cooper pleaded with Lyons in May 1938, 'don't have us pushed back to West Australian status, but rather show that state that their [regressive] legislation is foreign to Australian sentiment.' Two months later he went so far as to accuse the Western Australian Government of 'out Hitlering Hitler in the way of hounding a harmless and well meaning race'. Presumably Cooper and the League had the 1935 Nuremberg race laws in mind, which excluded Jewish people from German citizenship and prohibited them from marrying or even having sexual relations with people of so-called Aryan blood.[21]

Minority rights

In November 1938, in the course of mounting a further attack on the Western Australian Government, Cooper and the League adopted another way of framing their claims for Aboriginal people.[22] 'With so much talk of the rights of minorities,' Cooper wrote to the editor of the *West Australian*, 'it seems hard to believe that another minority can be ground to dust.' This protest followed a heightened awareness of Nazism among the League's members, which was the result of a growing connection they had with left-wing forces. This saw some of them take part in the May Day march in Melbourne in 1938 in which fascism and Nazism were denounced.[23]

In regard to minorities and their rights Cooper and Burdeu might also have recalled a passage in the article Turnbull had written a year or so earlier. As readers will recall, the journalist had stated that while many people in Australia were troubled by the plight of minorities in other countries, such as the Jewish people, African Americans and the Basques, no one of any political persuasion, except for a few Christians and anthropologists, cared less about Australia's own minority. In November 1938 Cooper echoed this sentiment in telling Rev. William Morley: 'We want respect for the rights of minorities to be conceded in Australia just as much as Australia contends that this right be conceded to European minorities.'[24]

In this context a meeting of the League that was held at the end of November 1938 passed a resolution protesting against the persecution of Jews by the Nazi government and calling for this to be brought to an end.[25] Several days later, on 6 December, the League sent a deputation, which presumably included Cooper,[26] to the German consulate on Collins Street in Melbourne so they could present a petition that contained this resolution. According to a newspaper report of the day the consul refused to admit them, but they left a letter asking him to forward the League's petition to the German Government; Yorta Yorta oral tradition suggests that Cooper returned the following day and presented the petition.[27]

This fleeting event is now the one for which Cooper is best known among non-Aboriginal people.[28] Yet this is only the case because of the myth-making that has occurred recently in the context of particular acts of commemoration.[29] As a result, the protest is now conceived as a unique act as well as one in which Cooper bears witness to the suffering of Jewish people that had resulted from a series of pogroms Nazi Germany launched against them in cities throughout Germany, Austria and Sudetenland on the night of 9–10 November 1938—an event that is now known as Kristallnacht and which has come to be cast as the prelude to the Jewish Holocaust. But this story misrepresents the League's protest in several respects.

By the time the League had drawn up its petition, let alone waited on the German consulate, several left-wing groups in Melbourne had in fact already raised their voices against Nazi Germany's persecution of Jews. What is more, about two weeks prior to the League formulating its petition, two deputations representing left-wing anti-fascist organisations (the Australian League for Peace and Democracy and the Spanish Relief Committee) had visited the consulate to protest against the treatment of Jews and left messages asking the consul to forward their resolutions to the German Government. At much the same time, the Labour Council of New South Wales passed a resolution attacking the persecution of Jews in Germany, Austria and Czechoslovakia. It also seems likely that the Australian Aborigines' League was influenced by a declaration that leading churchmen, communists, trade unionists, pacifists, anti-fascists and civil libertarians had sent to Lyons on 23 November calling on the federal government to remonstrate against the per-secution of the Jewish people in Germany, given that Burdeu had signed this resolution on behalf of the League.[30]

There are undoubtedly other reasons why the League mounted this protest. The Yorta Yorta people had previously identified themselves with the dispossessed Jews of the Bible, and now Cooper and his associates were dismayed by the contemporary persecution of the Jewish people and other minorities. In keeping with this sentiment, part of the petition the League presented to the consulate stated: 'We are a very small minority, and we are a poor people, but in extending sympathy to the Jewish people we assure them of our support in every way.'[31]

Most importantly perhaps, Cooper and the League, as we noted earlier, had recently been seeking to draw a parallel between Hitler and Nazi Germany's persecution of the Jewish people and the Western Australian Government's treatment of Aboriginal people and thus their mutual suffering.[32] In other words, the League's protest to the German consulate was probably devised in large part in order to advance their own people's cause. Consequently, its petition stated: 'Like the Jews, our people have suffered much cruelty, exploitation and misunderstanding as a minority at the hands of another race.'[33]

This reason for the protest is also evident in what the League did shortly afterwards. Barely ten days after it delivered its petition to the German consulate, Cooper sent a letter to the federal government in which he remarked: 'We feel that while we are all indignant over Hitler's treatment of the Jews, we are getting the same treatment here and we would like this fact duly considered.' (He no doubt had in mind what was happening at this very time on Cumeroogunga, which will be discussed in Chapter 9.) In a similar vein Cooper commented to Menzies several months later: 'I do trust that care for a suffering minority will ensure that kindliness of treatment that will not allow Australia's minority problem to be as undesirable as the European minorities of which we read so much in the press.' Not long after, he spelt out the kind of connection he and the League were seeking to make in protesting the plight of those such as the Jewish people, declaring in another letter to Menzies: 'Australia is linked with the Empire in a fight for the rights of minorities … Yet we are a minority with just as real oppression.'[34]

History

In concluding this consideration of Cooper and the League's approach to the matters of race and rights, two further points warrant discussion. Cooper seems to have been critical of some aspects of traditional Aboriginal culture. At the very least he had reservations about the public performance of particular rituals and ceremonies that white Australians deemed to be primitive. Furthermore, like most contemporary anthropologists, Cooper also seems to be of the opinion that Aboriginal people tended to lose 'the aboriginal culture' as they became 'civilised' and so thought it was destined to 'perish'.[35]

How are we to make sense of these views? In large part they can be attributed to Cooper's embrace of both Christianity and British culture. But they might also be attributed to particular strategic considerations. When Cooper and other League spokespeople made critical remarks about aspects of traditional Aboriginal culture or referred to the loss of Aboriginal culture, it was usually in the course of their trying to persuade government ministers of the capacity of Aboriginal people for uplift. For example, Burdeu told McEwen on one occasion: 'The Aboriginal loses his culture with the greatest facility. He quickly acquires the culture of the superior race he contacts.' This was a sensible position to adopt as the dominant racial discourse assumed that the continuation of Aboriginal culture ruled out such a future for Aboriginal people.[36]

It also seems that Cooper did not believe that traditional Aboriginal culture constituted the core of what it meant to be Aboriginal. Instead, he defined being Aboriginal in terms of his people's historical experience since 1788. As we noted at the beginning of this book, Cooper told Turnbull that a fear of extermination was 'in the blood', a 'racial memory', which recalls the terrible things done to [us] in years gone by'. Among Aboriginal people, Cooper confided on another occasion, this was a collective memory that was passed from one generation to the next: 'believe me, aboriginal folk do feel the indignities put on them and many a camp fire has heard the old folk tell the younger ones of the baptism of blood that has been our portion'. Above all else, this history of oppression lay at the heart of what it meant to be Aboriginal.[37]

Thus, Cooper did not reject the notion of 'racial difference'. On the contrary, he redefined it—in historical terms—and invoked this in the course of demanding rights for his people. Both his racial consciousness and his sense of history are evident in his petition to the King. Aboriginal people were represented as a 'race' of people who were the 'heirs and successors' of 'the original inhabitants' of Australia, and their prior presence was juxtaposed with that of the colonists who had 'expropriated' their 'lands' and failed to comply with the 'strict' undertaking enjoined upon them by the British Government to treat the Aborigines justly. Cooper was to give expression to these sentiments when he took up his petition to the King again.

8

THE PETITION AND THE
DAY OF MOURNING

THE PLACE COOPER'S petition to the King occupied in his political agenda receded for a while after Burdeu became involved in the League's affairs. But by the middle of 1936 it had resumed its position as the matter uppermost in his mind and dearest to his heart. At this time he had called on Burdeu to have a chat about the petition and impress its importance on him. He informed Burdeu that he had secured about 2000 signatures, that he and his son (almost certainly Lynch) were currently pasting one sheet under another in order to make a roll of signatures, and that he expected it would soon be ready to submit.[1]

Burdeu, however, had reservations about this course of action. He had recently approached the military secretary to the governor-general, Lord Gowrie, to inquire about the procedure for submitting such a petition, but got a reply that he found discouraging. He could envisage a situation in which the petition might be sent to the Prime Minister's Department or the Crown Solicitor's Office but never be seen by the governor-general, let alone forwarded to the King. At the meeting of the two men in the middle of June Burdeu asked Cooper whether he would be willing to go to Canberra to present the petition personally to the governor-general. He also suggested that it would be a good idea if Rev. William Morley or another member of the Association for the Protection of the Native

Races could accompany Cooper, believing that the association's name would lend weight to the document and ensure it got a good hearing. Cooper must have welcomed this proposal. But Morley was sceptical that the federal government would act on the petition given that the states had most of the responsibility for Aboriginal affairs. As a result it appears that Burdeu recommended to Cooper that he hold the petition back for the time being, pointing out that the federal government had made a promise to consider the future of the Aboriginal people at a meeting of the prime minister and the state premiers in August. And, when this promise was not fulfilled and consideration of the matter was deferred to the first meeting of all the administrators of Aboriginal affairs in Australia that was scheduled for February the following year, Burdeu probably urged Cooper to wait until that meeting took place.[2]

Not bread but a stone

Cooper had high hopes in regard to the later meeting, though the matter of parliamentary representation was not among the list of proposals the League put forward for consideration, presumably because Burdeu had recommended that it be omitted. But this meeting, after being postponed by a couple of months, proved a bitter disappointment to Cooper, prompting one of the angriest letters he ever sent to the federal government. 'I am addressing you personally for the matters I have to communicate are so important from the Aboriginals' point of view', he began a letter to Thomas Paterson in mid-June 1937. 'You may have heard,' he continued, 'that I have a petition to the King signed by some 2000 members of my race, setting out our disabilities and praying the intervention of His Majesty to intervene for the prevention of the further extinction of our race and that we be granted representation in the federal parliament.'[3]

Cooper proceeded to explain that the petition had been ready for some two years but that he had postponed submitting it in the hope that the government would act. But the meeting of the administrators had yielded nothing. 'We feel that all the delay, all the expense, all the talk is just to result in "As you were"', Cooper complained

before going on to explain the cause of his frustration: 'We looked
to the political field, representative of public opinion, and we were
shuffled on to the Administration, which has never been sympathetic, but always repressive … We did look to this move as marking
an epoch in our history. We asked [for] bread. We scarcely seem
likely to get a stone.' The government's response to the League's
numerous appeals had obviously reminded Cooper and Burdeu of
the passage in the Book of Matthew: 'Or what man is there among
you who, if his son asks for bread, will give him a stone?'[4]

Cooper proceeded to set out for Paterson the essence of what he
had been holding back by postponing the submission of the petition.
'We have got nothing definite except the refusal of our claim for
representation in the federal parliament—no result but a refusal—
and no prospects but continued exploitation. 80,000 aborigines in
Australia deliberately kept from uplift and refused one representative in parliament. Yet in New Zealand the same number of natives
have four members and one minister for Native Affairs. Our need is
greater because our people are scattered.'

At this point in his letter Cooper remarked that the League was
asking only for a member with the same status as the representative
for the Northern Territory in the federal parliament—that is, an MP
who had a voice but no vote. There is little to suggest that this is what
he previously had in mind in calling for parliamentary representation
for Aboriginal people. It seems that the nature of the League's
demand had shifted because Burdeu had noted the government's
response to the League's plea in 1935 (see Chapter 5)—namely that
the Commonwealth only had responsibility for Aboriginal affairs
in the Northern Territory and that the representative for this region
had no vote in the federal parliament—and so urged Cooper to
temper his demand for parliamentary representation.[5]

It is also evident that Cooper partly conceived of the petition
as a political weapon and to regard it as a means of forcing the
government's hand. 'We did the reasonable thing in withholding
our petition to His Majesty for two long years', he told Paterson,
'[but] unless we are assured that something definite will be done
without further delay we will go ahead and solicit the intervention

of His Majesty, which we believe we have the right to do and which prerogative the King has the right to exercise.' Cooper proceeded to summarise the League's program before concluding his letter in this vein: 'We are further withholding the petition for a little longer while we ask what is the utmost you are prepared to do in the way of remedying our injustices.' In other words, Cooper was willing to withhold the petition altogether if he could be satisfied that the government was going to implement the League's program.[6]

A couple of days later Cooper received a long and sympathetic reply from Paterson. The minister had noted his letter's 'very pessimistic strain' and once again claimed that the activities of any representative of the Aboriginal people in the federal parliament would be greatly limited by virtue of the fact that the Commonwealth only had jurisdiction for Aboriginal people in the territories. A week or so later Cooper took the opportunity to explain to Paterson why he was so frustrated and angered by the government's tardy response to his calls to implement a program for Aboriginal uplift: 'You say my previous letter was in a pessimistic strain. Mr Paterson, I am an old man and I did hope to live to see my people in a fair way to uplift. My hopes are not being realised, hence my despair. If my claims for my people are just, why should I not look for immediate relief … I am being assured all round that what we ask is only our right and therefore I feel that I am right when I persistently press for this right.' Cooper refused to concede that a parliamentary representative for Aboriginal people would provide very little. 'I understand that the federal parliament has jurisdiction only over such aborigines as may live in the territories', he remarked, but went on to say: 'I venture the opinion that if the federal government deals adequately with the problem as it affects the aborigines under its control a definite lead will be given to the state governments and a favorable psychology will be developed in the general public.'

Cooper called upon Paterson to forget that he was a white man so that he could look at the matter as Aboriginal people did. This done, he set out again the League's program before returning to the matter of why Aboriginal people wanted a parliamentary representative in the federal house. 'We feel that a member representing our race can maintain contact with our people, study their needs and present their claims. He can watch legislation with a view to seeing that his constituency is not omitted or penalised. He can initiate legislation. Though he would have no voice in respect of other states ... his opinion might be of value as an interpretation of aboriginal thought.' Finally, Cooper added a remark that both makes clear that what he had in mind was considerable, and reflected his conception of parliamentary representation at the time the petition was originally formulated: 'THE ABORIGINAL WOULD ONLY HAVE WHAT THE MAORI NOW HAS.'[7]

On receiving this letter Paterson suggested to the secretary of the Department of the Interior, JA Carrodus, that Cooper might be told that his request for parliamentary representation for Aboriginal people would be put before Cabinet at the earliest convenient opportunity. But Carrodus thought this course of action unwise. He suggested that a bland letter be sent in response, saying that the minister would write to Cooper regarding the matters he had raised after returning from a trip to the Northern Territory. (As the historian Andrew Markus has remarked, Carrodus was a public servant whom government ministers could rely upon to ensure that the status quo was upheld with an appearance of reasonableness.) There are no historical sources that reveal why Paterson had been prepared to take the matter of the petition to Cabinet, just as there are none to suggest that Cooper ever learned that this was the case.[8]

Several weeks later Cooper showed the journalist Clive Turnbull the roll of signatures he had gathered for the petition. 'Some tell us that the King has no power now in these things,' he remarked, 'but we shall try anyway.' He proudly told Turnbull that he had gathered 2000 signatures 'from Aboriginal people throughout Australia'. He also informed him that he and his associates were 'coming to the end of [their] tether' and were going to send the petition to the King. Another few weeks passed, though, before Burdeu wrote to Prime Minister Joseph Lyons to tell him that Cooper had a petition he wanted to submit to the King and ask how it should be sent. Three weeks later Cooper sent the petition to Lyons by registered mail and asked him to forward it to the King. It must have been an anxious moment for both Cooper and Burdeu; at any rate they forgot to date the covering letter. The day after Lyons' office received the petition his secretary acknowledged receipt of it, but this letter must have miscarried as a month later Burdeu wrote to Lyons to ask if he had received the petition. As they waited for an acknowledgement Burdeu had confided to Ernest Gribble that Cooper had become depressed by the slow progress that was being made in his work, but added: 'Still, God is not dead, as the old negro woman said when the dark champion [Frederick] Douglas[s] was about to give up the fight in despair.'[9]

In the meantime the Prime Minister's Department had called on the Department of the Interior for advice. There, Carrodus took responsibility for preparing a response. He was inclined to give short shrift to proposals for any significant change in government policy and practice, not least those presented by Aboriginal people, of whose prospects for advancement he had a very poor opinion. On this occasion Carrodus began his task by subjecting the petition to an analysis that seems to have been designed merely in order to dismiss it. He observed that 1814 Aboriginal people had signed the petition but that many of the signatories had simply affixed their mark. He also claimed that it was reasonable to assume that the signatories were people of 'part aboriginal blood', thereby implying that the petition could not be regarded as an expression of Aboriginal opinion.[10]

Carrodus also drew attention to the fact that approximately half of the signatories were from Queensland, 550 from Western Australia, about 350 from South Australia, less than 100 from New South Wales and Victoria, and only nine from the Northern Territory. He pointed out that all but a dozen of the Queensland signatories were from the government's Aboriginal reserve on Palm Island, and that all the Northern Territory signatories resided on the Goulburn Island mission.[11] Further analysis would probably have revealed that most of the signatories in the other jurisdictions also dwelled on missions and reserves. The relatively small number of signatories in both New South Wales and Victoria is puzzling. Cooper believed that many more Aboriginal people would have signed had they not been fearful of the consequences, and this might explain what occurred in those states. In October he told a journalist that in the case of some missions 'no one had dared to sign' even though the Aboriginal protection boards had allowed the petition to be circulated to them.[12]

Carrodus proceeded to comment on the contents of the petition, though only after pointing out that the Department of the Interior could merely act in regard to the Aboriginal people of the Northern Territory. In reference to the petition's plea for the King to intervene to prevent the extinction of the Aboriginal race and provide Aboriginal people with better conditions, he claimed that the Commonwealth and state governments were doing everything they possibly could and that this had been evident in the recent conference of administrators of Aboriginal affairs. On this basis, he pronounced: 'It is not seen what good purpose would be served by submitting those request[s] to His Majesty the King.'

Carrodus was even more supercilious in commenting on the petition's principal demand. 'The granting of the request that aboriginals should be represented in the federal parliament', he declared, 'would not have the beneficial results which the petitioners apparently think would accrue from such representation.' Besides, he claimed, such an MP could only 'deal with the natives in [the Northern] Territory' and the minister for the interior was 'virtually a representative of the aboriginals of the Northern Territory'. Carrodus probably also still held the view he had expressed in April 1935, namely that there was no Aboriginal man in the Northern Territory competent to represent his people in parliament and that the analogy Cooper and the League had drawn between the rights of Aboriginal people and the rights of New Zealand's native people was nonsensical because '[t]he Maori [was] a much more highly developed native than the aboriginal'. Accordingly, he concluded that nothing would be gained by forwarding the petition to the King, though he suggested that in the event that the Prime Minister's Department agreed to do this it should give the state governments (other than Tasmania) an opportunity to express their views on the pleas of the petitioners.[13]

Lyons was reluctant to accept all of Carrodus's advice. In a letter the secretary of his department, Frank Strahan, sent Cooper on his behalf, he repeated Carrodus's remark about the limited nature of the Commonwealth's responsibility for Aboriginal affairs and his claims that the various governments were doing all they could to prevent the extinction of the Aboriginal race and provide better conditions for Aboriginal people. Nevertheless, it seems that the prime minister was willing to give serious consideration to the petition's key demand. He headed a conservative United Australia Party government but had previously been a leading figure in the Parliamentary Labor Party and had embraced radical causes as a young man. A well-informed political observer who noted Lyons' response to the petition attributed it to the sympathy he felt towards Aboriginal people and suggested that this was partly due to the fact that he remembered the wholesale slaughter of Aboriginal people in his own state, Tasmania. Whatever his reasons, Lyons directed Strahan to tell Cooper that he had 'the fullest sympathy' with the League's wishes that the interests of the Aboriginal people be 'adequately safeguarded', and advise him that the government was going to give full consideration as soon as possible to the matters he had raised in the petition.[14]

Cooper must have been both heartened and troubled by this response. On the one hand, the government seemed to be taking the petition's principal demand seriously; on the other hand, it implied that it alone had the authority to act. In replying to Strahan's letter in late October, Cooper thanked Lyons for his promises but immediately shifted tack to raise a number of points, in the course of which he at the very least implied that he expected the petition to be forwarded to the King. Cooper asserted that the King had responsibility for Australia and so the states' control over Aboriginal affairs in most of the country should not prevent proper consideration being given to the petition. 'With all respect, since our petition is to the King of Australia, it should not be possible for divided control [in Aboriginal affairs] hurting us in this instance', he argued.[15]

Cooper proceeded to dismiss the government's claims about the recent meeting of the Commonwealth and state protectors of

Aborigines. 'From our point of view the conference was only a waste of time', Cooper informed Lyons. 'We did expect a Magna Carta from the Premiers' Conference but from the conference of Chief Protectors we only got the confirmation of our humiliation.' Cooper also claimed that the League had been alarmed by that conference's suggestion that advice be sought from South Africa and the United States. 'To add to our sorrows the humiliation [that] our dark brethren [suffer] in the curfew and the pass system would be [de]gradation indeed', Cooper informed Lyons. He declared that the League was 'in protest against the whole result' of the conference.[16]

Cooper promptly moved to the League's claim for parliamentary representation. 'We are persisting in our claim for one who can speak for us in parliament,' he told Lyons, 'influencing legislation on our behalf and safeguarding us from administrational officers who, with notable exceptions, interpret their responsibilities to the aborigines in much the same way as a gaol governor does his criminal population.' This remark reveals that the petition was deeply rooted in the oppression that Cooper and his Aboriginal associates in the League had endured on Cumeroogunga, just as it makes clear that they were seeking a means by which Aboriginal people could play a role in governing their own affairs more generally. Indeed, this letter of Cooper's demonstrates once more that the League's demand for parliamentary representation was not limited to the federal parliament but actually included at the very least a claim to representation in all the Australian parliaments.[17]

Cooper called on the government to overcome any problems the Australian constitution posed to it granting the League's request by passing the necessary legislation. In doing so he raised the possibility that their member of parliament could be a member of the Senate given this was, as he put it, 'the States' Rights house'. Here, perhaps, is the trace of a belief on Cooper's part that Aboriginal people had a claim to rights that rested on their being something other than mere subjects of the Australian nation.[18]

At the moment Cooper sent Lyons this letter, the League sought to put pressure on the government by informing the press that it had submitted to the governor-general a petition to the King and that

Lyons had promised to give it early consideration. In Melbourne a journalist from *The Age* interviewed Cooper about the petition while a large number of newspapers around the country carried reports about it, as did the influential British newspaper *The Times*. Many of them were sympathetic to its call for protection and parliamentary representation, especially the labour and left-wing newspapers, and more than one newspaper devoted editorials or commentaries to it. During the next few months the petition was given more serious consideration by the press than historians have hitherto realised.[19]

"THE LOST HORIZON"

More than one newspaper published a cartoon after Cooper submitted his petition. This one appeared in *The Argus* on 27 October 1937.

Yet some newspapers were scornful. One doubted whether many of the signatories had understood a word of the petition. But what really vexed Cooper was the fact that one of the white organisations involved in Aboriginal affairs, the conservative Aborigines' Friends' Association, launched an attack on the petition in an interview that its secretary, Rev. JH Sexton, gave to an Adelaide newspaper. In this he claimed that sending the petition to the King would stain Australia's good reputation for treating the native race fairly. Like the patronising and high-handed Carrodus, Sexton doubted whether political representation for Aboriginal people would further advance their wellbeing and alleged that the signatories to the petition were mainly people of 'mixed blood'; he also made it clear that he thought the signatories were uppity and should be 'content like the old aborigines to accept their fate in the old uncomplaining spirit'. Sexton went on to make other remarks that must have angered Cooper even more. He claimed in effect that 'half-castes' would and should be absorbed into the white race and so disappear as Aboriginal people; drew attention to one of the resolutions of the recent conference of administrators of Aboriginal affairs that declared that 'the destiny of the natives of aboriginal origin, but not of the full blood, [lay] in their ultimate absorption by the people of the Commonwealth'; and recommended that 'all efforts be directed to that end'.[20]

In early November, perhaps as a consequence of the attention the petition had received in the press, Lyons called upon the Department of the Interior to take the necessary steps for it to be considered by Cabinet. Several days later, acting on a suggestion made by Strahan, Carrodus called on the Attorney-General's Department for advice in regard to the constitutional question raised by the petition's request for parliamentary representation for Aboriginal people. A week later, Carrodus, on the advice of the secretary of the Attorney-General's Department, called on the Commonwealth Investigation Branch to prepare a report on the League that would provide information about the make-up of its executive, the number of financial members it had, and so forth. His purpose seems to have been one of casting doubt on the credibility of those responsible for the petition. The secretary to the Attorney-General's Department seems to have been of the same mind. 'I should say that there are very few people connected with it [i.e. the League]', he remarked in the course of suggesting that this information be incorporated in the Cabinet submission.[21]

Two months passed before the solicitor-general, George S Knowles, provided legal advice to the Department of the Interior. In his opinion the Commonwealth, according to sections 51 (xxvi), 7, 24 and 127 of the constitution, had no authority to pass legislation granting representation in parliament to Aboriginal people *as* Aboriginal people in the various Australian states. However, in respect of the question as to whether the Commonwealth could enact a law granting them representation in the Northern Territory, Knowles, referring to rulings in two legal cases, expressed the view that section 122 of the constitution granted the Commonwealth the authority to provide for Aboriginal people electing an Aboriginal member to represent them there.[22]

Ten days later, on 25 January 1938, the acting secretary of the Department of the Interior drafted a submission to Cabinet in McEwen's name. While he noted the solicitor-general's legal opinion that allowed that parliamentary representation for Aboriginal people could be granted in the Northern Territory, he reiterated Carrodus's opinion that McEwen was really the representative of Aboriginal people of the Territory and thus there was no point in submitting the petition to the King. As a result, he recommended that no action be taken.[23]

The Day of Mourning

Cooper had no knowledge that Lyons seemed to be giving his petition serious consideration. His letter to the prime minister of late October had been met with a deafening silence. Consequently, by the middle of November he was feeling even more dispirited. Consequently, he called a meeting of the League to discuss further action, and its members agreed to hold a 'day of mourning' simultaneously with the sesquicentennial celebrations of Australia's founding in Sydney on 26 January the following year. 'While white men are throwing their hats into the air with joy', Burdeu informed the press, 'aborigines will be in mourning for all that they have lost.'[24]

This meeting of the League was attended by William Ferguson, the secretary of the Aborigines Progressive Association, and he acted as the principal spokesperson for the Day of Mourning after plans for it were announced shortly afterwards. But in all probability the idea to hold this protest was Cooper's, given his historical sensibility. Yorta Yorta people like him had a predictive or prophetic view of history, derived from the Biblical stories they had been told by Matthews. This envisaged the relationship between past, present and future as a long trajectory marked by epochs and days—of Judgement and Restitution, Mourning and Hope—at the end of which there would

surely be deliverance for the Aboriginal people from the suffering
that was theirs, as it was for the Jews of the Bible.[25] This religious
perspective constituted an alternative history—a different view
of how events would unfold in time—that resisted the colonisers'
account of Australia's history as the triumph of white progress.[26]

More immediately it seems that Cooper's idea for a day of
mourning on 26 January 1938 was prompted by his recent experience of another celebration of white Australian history. On the
afternoon of 24 January 1937 he and other members of the League
had attended a 'Grand Pioneer Rally and Historical Service' that had
been organised to celebrate John Batman's founding of Melbourne
and Australia more generally. This event (attended by some 2000
people) was orchestrated by Isaac Selby, the secretary of the Old
Pioneers' Memorial Fund, an organisation devoted to the commemoration and celebration of the so-called founders of Melbourne.
But one of Cooper's white supporters, the benevolent president
of the Footscray Historical Society, Claude B Smith, was probably
responsible for inviting the League's members to participate in it.
They were to lead the singing that began the afternoon's program,
which was to include 'Rule Britannia' and 'God Save the King', and
play the part of 'the aborigines' in a pageant at the close of the
celebration that re-enacted Batman's so-called discovery of the Yarra
River, upon which Melbourne was founded.[27]

Cooper and his people probably agreed to take part in this
pageant reluctantly. It turned out to be worse than they might have
expected. Several speeches formed the centre of the programme.
Selby's address would not have troubled them much, for while he
spoke of Batman as an 'Empire Builder' it is likely that he referred
to Batman's treaty with the Kulin,[28] which was regarded highly by
Cooper and the members of the League since in their eyes Batman
had recognised that Aboriginal people were the owners of the land
and undertaken to pay an annual rent for the land he claimed to have
purchased by dint of the agreement.[29] But a speech entitled 'Our
Island Continent' by the chief president of the Australian Natives
Association, the organisation that had championed the cause of
white Australians since the 1870s, dismayed and angered Cooper.[30]

This carefully posed photograph was taken by one of Melbourne's leading commercial photographers of the day, Edwin G Adamson, who had a studio on Collins Street, one of the city's classiest streets. We know nothing about when, where or why it was shot, though it was almost certainly taken in Melbourne in the late 1930s and it is possible that Helen Baillie might have commissioned it, as she arranged for Adamson to take other photographs for her at this time. Clearly, the photograph mostly comprises members of the League. Margaret Tucker stands on the far left; the woman next to her might be Hyllus Briggs; and on the right are Norman Clarke, William Cooper, his wife Sarah, and two other Aboriginal people, one of whom might be Mary Clarke. The man shaking Cooper's hand might be Claude B Smith while the bespectacled man looking on is Arthur Burdeu. It has been suggested that the woman in the centre is Helen Baillie but she bears little resemblance to a studio photograph of her taken in 1936 (see Chapter 6).

A few days later he sent a letter to Selby, protesting in no uncertain terms. He began by complaining that he and his associates had been 'regaled with an address on the White Australia policy, no mention of the aborigines occurring' and called upon to celebrate the anniversary of 'the coming of the whites [that had] spelt disaster to [their] forebears'. He then proceeded to tell a very different history from the one he and the other members of the League had been subjected to on this occasion. 'We were here before the whites', he pointed out, yet their coming had caused 'extermination' and 'complete subjection', which had taken the form of 'shooting, poisoning [and] the like'. And while 'the crime' of those days was 'now happily gone', Aboriginal people had since suffered 'disabilities not put on the white race' and were still 'being barred from the full rights of the white race' by the 'White Australia policy'.[31]

Yet Cooper did not write to Selby merely to give him a history lesson. He wanted him to change his ways. 'I am writing to suggest that in future gatherings the notice of the white people be called to the presence of a residue [of Aborigines], left after the white man satiated himself [o]n the blood of the aboriginal, and that there should be a call for more than sympathy on their behalf', he declared before adding: 'We claim that the day of restitution has come and that we should be accorded full equality of opportunity and responsibility with the whites.' Selby, he was sure, would recognise the justice of the League's claim and would know how to call attention to the wrongs of the past and the present.[32]

If the seed of the idea for a day of mourning lay in Cooper's response to the celebration of White Australia on 24 January 1937, and of this there can be little doubt given that Cooper told Selby that 'what is a memorial of the coming of the whites is a memorial of death to us', something of its germination can be attributed to Selby's response to Cooper's appeal and what followed. Selby passed Cooper's letter onto the Melbourne *Herald*, which, oblivious of any need to gain his permission, published it under the headline 'APPEAL FOR ABORIGINALS'. This caused quite a stir. Several newspapers referred to it and a number of people were prompted to contact the League's leader. A pleasantly surprised Cooper, now addressing Selby as a friend, told his fellow septuagenarian that he had 'been able to do more for us tha[n] we … have been able to do ourselve[s]'. It seems Burdeu also found common cause with Selby in the coming months, which might have been facilitated by the fact that Selby had once been a pastor in the Church of Christ.[33]

Selby, who made his living from public lectures, lantern shows and pageants on local historical subjects, now invited the League's members to participate in the celebration of Melbourne's 102nd birthday in May. In response Cooper suggested that the League could stage a concert on 31 May—the day Batman had famously come up the Yarra River and declared that this would be 'the place for a village' (Melbourne)—that would feature a choir made up of members of the Melbourne Aboriginal community as well as their kin who formed the Cumeroogunga Choir. The latter was about to undertake a concert tour of Victorian country towns, just as Matthews and the Maloga Choir used to do, and give a series of radio broadcasts. It was directed by a railwayman and Church of Christ evangelist, WB Payne, who was closely associated with Burdeu.[34]

This concert, sponsored by the League, was seen by Cooper as an opportunity to present Aboriginal people as civilised and the equals of their fellow Australians. Presumably he had this in mind when he decided that the programme should include many English songs. However, there is little doubt that he also regarded the occasion as a chance to reveal the pride that Aboriginal people took in their race and persuade the audience that they were, in his words, 'a people for whom the best should be done in the way of restoring something in place of what was wrested from us'. To this end the concert was to have 'a definitely aboriginal background'. There were to be songs composed by Aboriginal people and songs sung in the Yorta Yorta language; gumleaf accompaniment for these and the English songs; and spirituals that Cooper had first heard the Fisk Jubilee Singers perform fifty years earlier.[35]

The concert was held in the Australian Church in Russell Street, thereby anticipating the Day of Mourning that was held in the Australian Hall in Elizabeth Street, Sydney, the following January. It opened with a 'corroboree song' by the full company, 'Billy Go Bangalee', and a song accompanied by a harp and gumleaf orchestra; and continued with English songs, African American spirituals such as 'Massa's in the Cold, Cold Ground', and 'Cummergunja Chimes', a feature of the Cumeroogunga Choir's repertoire. At this point the programme was punctuated with an address by Selby, 'The Pioneers and the Aborigines', after which one of the members of the choir sang a song, 'Stay in Your Own Back Yard', in which an African

American woman gives her son advice about how to deal with the
pain of racial segregation in the American South. More African
American spirituals, a song in the Yorta Yorta language, 'U Burra
Gah', and English duets followed before the concert concluded with
the whole company singing 'Burra Phara', the hymn based on the
African American spiritual sung by the Fisk Jubilee Singers that was
discussed in Chapter 3.[36]

Cooper laying a wreath
on John Batman's grave
in January 1940. Isaac
Selby stands second on
the right.

Cooper and the League must have regarded the concert as a
success.[37] Certainly, they agreed to participate in further events that
Selby organised in the next few years. In November 1938 members
of the League contributed to another 'Grand Pioneers' Day Rally
and Concert'. Once again they performed 'U Burra Gah' and 'Burra
Phara' as well as a song styled as an 'Aboriginal Interlude' (performed
by Margaret Tucker), a 'gum leaf solo' (played by Doug Nicholls),
'Billy Go Bangalee', and a Yorta Yorta version of 'Song of Australia'.
On 'Aboriginal Sunday' in 1940 (which was a day of reflection that

Cooper had previously urged to be held every year, in the manner of the Day of Mourning, on the Sunday closest to 26 January) they were involved in a pilgrimage to Batman's grave, where Cooper laid a wreath and Nicholls gave an address. And the following June they sang 'U Burra Gah', 'Burra Phara' and other songs at another historical service held at Batman's grave, while Cooper placed a wreath on the monument and Nicholls spoke.[38]

It is probably no coincidence that Cooper's proposal for a day of mourning and his petition to the King have a similar historical content in that both emphasised prior Aboriginal ownership of the continent and the Aboriginal people's subsequent dispossession by the British, just as they interpreted the plight of Aboriginal people as originating in that historical process. Their similarity, or at least the way in which they were connected in Cooper's mind, is suggested by his simultaneous issuing of two appeals in December 1937, one headed 'Petition to His Majesty', the other 'Australia Day 1938. Aborigines' Day of Mourning'.[39]

AUSTRALIAN
Aborigines Conference
SESQUI-CENTENARY
Day of Mourning and Protest
to be held in
THE AUSTRALIAN HALL, SYDNEY
(No. 148 Elizabeth Street — a hundred yards south of Liverpool Street)
on
WEDNESDAY, 26th JANUARY, 1938
(AUSTRALIA DAY)
The Conference will assemble at 10 o'clock in the morning.

ABORIGINES AND PERSONS OF ABORIGINAL BLOOD ONLY ARE INVITED TO ATTEND

The following Resolution will be moved:

"WE, representing THE ABORIGINES OF AUSTRALIA, assembled in Conference at the Australian Hall, Sydney, on the 26th day of January, 1938, this being the 150th Anniversary of the whiteman's seizure of our country, HEREBY MAKE PROTEST against the callous treatment of our people by the whiteman during the past 150 years, AND WE APPEAL to the Australian Nation of today to make new laws for the education and care of Aborigines, and we ask for a new policy which will raise our people to FULL CITIZEN STATUS and EQUALITY WITHIN THE COMMUNITY."

The above resolution will be debated and voted upon, as the sole business of the Conference, which will terminate at 5 o'clock in the afternoon.

TO ALL AUSTRALIAN ABORIGINES! PLEASE COME TO THIS CONFERENCE IF YOU POSSIBLY CAN! ALSO SEND WORD BY LETTER TO NOTIFY US IF YOU CAN ATTEND

Signed, for and on behalf of
THE ABORIGINES PROGRESSIVE ASSOCIATION,
J. T. PATTEN, President.
W. FERGUSON, Organising Secretary.
Address: c/o. Box 1924KK, General Post Office, Sydney.

A poster advertising the Day of Mourning and Protest on 26 January 1938.

After Cooper and Ferguson had agreed to hold a day of mourning, the Aborigines Progressive Association determined its terms and dictated these to the League, so much so that Cooper came to see the day as the association's conference. Nevertheless, he fiercely defended it in the face of an attack by David Unaipon, the South Australian preacher, author and inventor, who was closely associated with Sexton and the Aborigines' Friends' Association and who might have been the best-known Aboriginal person in Australia at this time. Unaipon believed in gradual change and regarded the Day of Mourning as a mistake. He claimed it was overly political and emotional, and expressed concern that it would give Australia a bad reputation overseas. His remarks, which were publicised by Sexton and widely reported in the press, perturbed Cooper and other members of the League as they felt they were prejudicial to the cause of Aboriginal people. Cooper immediately sent a letter to McEwen in which he pointed out that the League had always 'kept [its] hands and pen clean'. A day or so later, he made his resentment clear when he complained to a journalist about the attack on the Day of Mourning as a day of wailing. 'Aborigines were not fools, and knew that in the Briton there was a deep sense of fair play', he said. 'They had been "getting there" steadily over the years, and resented the attempt to break down the value of their work [i.e. their lobbying] in such an underhand way.'[40]

Cooper and his two acolytes, Nicholls and Tucker, attended the Day of Mourning in Sydney. Helen Baillie took them there in her little car, driving at breakneck speed for much of the treacherously narrow and sometimes twisting Hume Highway while she chatted incessantly. The Aboriginal members of the League arrived shaken but just in time to attend a meeting organised by the Rationalist Association, which passed a resolution condemning the government for coercing Aboriginal people from the Menindee reserve in far west New South Wales to participate in the celebrations that were to take place the following day. On the morning of 26 January, from a street near the Town Hall, Cooper, Nicholls and Tucker watched a procession of floats that was part of a series of events in the city and on the harbour celebrating 150 years of white settlement,

Pictured here outside the Australian Hall on 26 January 1938 before they
commenced their meeting protesting against the white man's celebration of the
sesquicentenary of Australia's founding, Bill Ferguson and Jack Patten appear on
the far left and right respectively. Others identified in this photograph are Jack
Kinchela, Helen Grosvenor and Selina Patten.

and then made their way to the Australian Hall for the Day of
Mourning protest meeting that took place later. They were to play
relatively minor roles in its proceedings, which were dominated by
Bill Ferguson and Jack Patten. Cooper hoped he would have the
opportunity to advance his claim for parliamentary representation
as part of a deputation that was to wait on Lyons several days later.
But Ferguson made it clear that he was opposed to the primary
claim in Cooper's petition. 'I say definitely that we do not want
an Aboriginal Member of the Parliament', he declared. 'We want
ordinary citizen rights, not any special rights such as that.'[41] (The
Sydney Morning Herald highlighted these remarks in its brief report of
the conference.) Given this, it is hardly surprising that parliamentary
representation was omitted from the measures a twenty-strong
delegation put to Lyons.[42]

The 1938 Day of Mourning meeting. Doug Nicholls and William Cooper
(seated) listen to Jack Patten read the resolution. The other men pictured are
Tom Foster and Jack Kinchela, partly obscured.

Soon after the Day of Mourning protest concluded, Cooper,
Nicholls and Tucker returned to Melbourne,[43] this time taking the
train rather than risking life and limb with Baillie. On 31 January
the League held its own meeting that it styled as a Day of Mourning
conference, passing a series of resolutions in keeping with the
organisation's program.[44]

The petition and Cabinet

The following day McEwen approved the draft that the acting
secretary of his department had prepared for its submission
to Cabinet about Cooper's petition. Shortly afterwards Lyons and
the Cabinet endorsed its recommendation that the government
hold on to the petition rather than forward it to the King. It seems
the government was unsure whether it had the authority to do
this even though there was no convention that required it to send
such a petition to the British monarch. Whatever the reason for its

decision, the government decided not to inform Cooper of it.[45] Instead, three weeks later, Lyons' secretary sent Cooper an ambiguous letter informing him that the welfare of Aboriginal people was receiving full and sympathetic consideration by the Commonwealth Government in conjunction with the state governments. It declared that the government thought that 'no good purpose would be served by transmitting the petition in the meantime', and asserted that any action in this regard was 'therefore being held in abeyance'.[46]

The letter exasperated Cooper and prompted him and Burdeu to prepare a lengthy statement, 'From an Educated Black',[47] which Cooper sent to Lyons at the end of March.[48] This statement can be regarded as Cooper's political testament. Even though it repeats much of what we have already learned about his political program, it deserves our attention, not least because it reveals the degree to which the principles that informed Cooper's political work in the 1930s were fundamentally the same as those that shaped the Yorta Yorta people's appeals to government, and especially their petitioning, fifty years earlier.

Cooper's purpose in producing this statement was, as he remarked in a covering letter to Lyons, 'to give the aboriginal mind on the problem of the native race'. This was necessary, he observed, because so often the public statements by white Australians, however well-meaning they might be, were made from their point of view and thus did not 'reflect the opinions of natives'.[49]

In seeking to provide an Aboriginal perspective, Cooper's premise—as it had been in all his political campaigning—was that white Australians, or the Christians among them, might be sympathetic to Aboriginal people but were ignorant of what had befallen them. 'Believing that there is a spark of human kindness in nearly every heart and knowing that the vast majority of men are opposed to oppression,' Cooper remarked on this occasion, 'I think that the majority of Australians, and British people in general, need only KNOW what my people have suffered and are suffering to bring the relief long sought and now much overdue.' This meant that the task of those such as himself was to educate white Australians about the truth concerning the conditions of his people. 'My earnest ambition', he wrote, 'always has been to publish abroad the truth about my people, the Australian Aborigines, in order that the white people might know something of the facts concerning the treatment of my race.'[50]

But, Cooper went on, therein lay a problem. 'I have addressed numerous letters to the editors of the various newspapers and find that my pleas for better conditions are, in nine cases out of ten, "pigeon-holed"', he explained. Nonetheless, he claimed, he lived in hope that some day the press would 'begin to publish the truth concerning Aboriginal affairs so that the public, being informed, [would] see that the great evils' from which his people were suffering would be 'remedied'.[51]

He proceeded to set out what he believed lay at the heart of the Aboriginal condition, namely that they were a people who had come under the 'protection' of government and yet had been poorly served by their protectors. What was required, Cooper argued, was something he called 'TRUE PROTECTION'. 'I understand that the correct meaning of the word "Protector" is: "One who protects from injury—one who protects from oppression; a guardian; a regent; one who rules for a sovereign"', he stated. Clearly, he had an expansive understanding of what protection meant, a point to which we will return. For the moment he simply observed that the protectors of Aboriginal people had not lived up to their responsibilities as guardians. He gave an example of a policeman who was responsible for the relatively recent massacre at Coniston of more than thirty Aboriginal people, and claimed that these killings had been justified by a justice of the peace.[52] Yet, he insisted, there were much higher forms of authority than that of the laws of the white man. As he often did, Cooper invoked British justice as well as God.[53]

At this point he started to provide a brief account of the history of Australia from an Aboriginal point of view. 'History records that in the year 1771 [sic] white men first landed on the shores of what is now called Botany Bay. They claimed that they had "found" a "new" country—Australia.' But, Cooper pointed out, '[t]his country was not new, it was already in possession of, and inhabited by, millions of blacks'. Moreover, he declared, as he had fifty years earlier in calling for a grant of land, the Aboriginal people 'owned the country as their God given heritage'. Thus, he revealed once again that his protest often had a dual basis: not only the rights of his people as aboriginal but the rights that were bestowed by God. 'From the standpoint of an educated black who can read the Bible upon which British constitution and custom is founded,' he remarked, 'I marvel at the fact that while the text book of present civilisation, the Bible, states that God gave the earth to man, the "Christian" interferes with God's arrangement and stops not even at murder to take that which does not belong to them.'[54]

Cooper proceeded to give a short history of contact. White men had dispossessed Aboriginal people of their hunting and camping grounds, destroyed their food resources, and murdered them with guns and poison. 'The treatment meted out to us has been so bad', he stated, 'that the present generation of blacks lives in a state of fear and horror.' Early contact, he continued, was followed by a period in which Aboriginal people were looked down upon 'with disdain as unworthy of consideration—as "Abos", a race of another colour', and as 'a useless race'. They were subjected to laws marked by 'prohibitions and restrictions' and denied protection and the opportunity to prove that they could adapt and become good citizens. 'If we are a burden on the country it is not our fault,' he declared, 'but due to the fact that various governments have not adopted the practical considerations which have been offered from time to time by men who know.'[55]

Cooper argued that 'what [was] really needed' to bring about change was for government to 'view the life of the Aborigines as the Aborigines [saw] it themselves'—in effect to 'think black'. This meant, Cooper contended, that it should draw upon Aboriginal people like himself: an 'educated black'. He insisted that the likes of anthropologists had failed to bring about relief and that their work was useless as far as the Aboriginal people's present needs were concerned because they were only really interested in scientific research. It would be better to engage 'educated and cultured Aborigines' as they were of 'the same blood' as other Aboriginal people and more able to understand them and suggest to government the means by which their hardships could be relieved or removed. Up until the current day, Cooper went on, this group of Aboriginal people had not been given the opportunity to help their 'less fortunate brethren in their hard struggle, because [they had] been left homeless and penniless'. Moreover, they had been denied a political voice. 'Many of us have not been given the right to vote', he observed. 'We are not even counted', he added, presumably in reference to a section in the Australian constitution (a matter that would later be taken up in the postwar campaign for a referendum to alter clauses in the constitution relating to Aboriginal people).[56] He declared: 'We are not recognised as British subjects and have therefore no rights.'[57]

Cooper turned next to the matter at the heart of his petition to the King. As he had done before, he compared the lack of parliamentary representation for Aboriginal people to the fact that Māori had had such representation since 1867. The latter meant, he argued, that Māori could 'place their grievances before the authorities'. Moreover, Cooper seemed to suggest, it had played a role in the fact that the descendants of some of those who had been dispossessed in the early days of New Zealand had since been financially compensated for their loss. 'How much compensation have we had? How much of our land has been paid for? Not one iota!' he declared. Once more, he stated, 'we are the original owners of the country. In spite of force, prestige, or anything else you like, morally the land is ours', and claimed again: 'We have been ejected and despoiled of our God given right and our inheritance has been forcibly taken from us.'[58]

At this point Cooper repeated his contention that the government had an obligation towards Aboriginal people because of the undertakings the British Crown had given at the outset of colonisation. Even though he made no reference to the Treaty of Waitangi in discussing the fact that some Māori had been compensated for their loss of land, one might wonder whether his invoking of the British Crown's undertakings in the case of Australia was not informed by a knowledge of the commitments that the British Crown was believed to have given Māori in that treaty. This, at any rate, is what he stated:

The time is long overdue when the Aborigines should be considered as much and as fully under the protection of the law as any other citizen of the Empire, and equally entitled to the privileges of British citizenship.

This more particularly in view of the fact that history records that in the commission originally given to those who came from overseas the strict injunction was given that the Aborigines and their descendants had to be adequately cared for.

This benevolent intention of his most gracious Majesty towards his primitive people was not carried out. We, therefore, now plead for moderation and forbearance to be exercised by all people in their dealings with the native people, and hope that the Government will seize every opportunity to carry out His Majesty's original intention to facilitate our approach toward civilisation.[59]

He went on to point out that the contrast between those instructions and the manner in which Aboriginal people had been treated during the past 150 years had severely shaken their confidence in 'the professed Christian nation—standing for good government, justice, and freedom'. From there it was but a short step for Cooper to argue that Aboriginal people, '*as a people*, … should be dealt with by the Commonwealth government and NOT by the states'. What did he mean here in using the phrase 'as a people'? We cannot be sure, but it seems to have been a function of an argument he next made, namely that the Commonwealth controlled all that originally belonged to Aboriginal people and as such had an obligation to provide them with 'reasonable compensation'. Was he implying some kind of equivalence between the Australian nation as a nation of people and Aboriginal people as a nation of people, or was he merely suggesting that the Commonwealth of Australia rather than the states was the true inheritor, so to speak, of the commitment the British Crown had originally made in regard to Aboriginal people? Whatever the case, he called on the federal government to take responsibility for his people's affairs before moving on to claim that there was a noticeable change in the amount of interest in Aboriginal people, especially in the sphere of the federal government. 'For the first time in history,' he contended, 'the will to do a fair thing is evident and we trust that this good-will will work out for our emancipation.'[60]

In concluding 'From an Educated Black', Cooper revealed once again the degree to which his statement was both animated by his Christian faith and addressed to his fellow Christians. He turned to his readers and addressed them personally, asking whether they would act and whether Aboriginal people would get the help they deserved: 'Will you, by your apathy, tacitly admit that you don't care, and thus assume the guilt of your fathers? ... OR are you prepared to admit that, since the Creator said in his Word that all men are of "one blood", we are humans with feelings like yourselves in the eyes of Almighty God ... If you admit that, will you like true men do your bit to see a great injustice at least mollified by agitating to get a fair deal before it is too late?'[61]

Obfuscation

Nearly two months later Cooper wrote to Lyons again to raise a series of matters, the first of which concerned his petition. After noting that it had received a good deal of publicity in the press, he expressed concern that the League had got no further word from the prime minister. 'Would you please tell us how it now stands', he pleaded. In reply, the Prime Minister's Department once again told Cooper that he would be contacted on all the matters he had raised as soon as possible, and referred his letter to the Department of the Interior, who set it aside. A month later, after being prompted by the Prime Minister's Department, Carrodus drafted a letter in reply to remind that department that the Cabinet had decided that the petition was not to be forwarded to the King.[62]

In early July Cooper relayed to Lyons several resolutions that had recently been passed by the League, one of which concerned the government's delay in replying to the petition to the King, and requested an early announcement. Ten or so days later the Prime Minister's Department responded to his letter of late May but made no reference to the petition, fobbing Cooper off again by saying that McEwen was currently on a visit to the Northern Territory during which he proposed to discuss the future policy relating to Aboriginal people there with the administrator and chief protector of Aborigines. In response Cooper appealed to McEwen in the last week of July, telling him that he had been 'deeply concerned about the policy for aborigines and particularly in respect of the reply to our petition to the King for representation in Parliament'. It is apparent that Cooper and the League took the story they had been told at face value. 'From the replies to my correspondence I gather that nothing will be done in the matters of our concern till you return from the North and have drawn up the observations you will have to make in the matter', he wrote. As he had done previously, Cooper appealed to the minister for the interior to frame his recommendations for change 'from the point of view of the interests of the natives' and went on to state once again that Aboriginal people needed someone in parliament 'able to speak for the native and to represent native interests'.[63]

In the months that followed Cooper must have reluctantly concluded that the principal demand of the petition was a lost cause, at least for the time being. According to Doug Nicholls' biographer, Cooper's health began to falter at this point, no doubt because he felt frustrated, angry and dejected. But shortly after Lyons' death in April the following year, Cooper rallied, as he had so often done in the past, sending a letter to Robert Menzies that concluded by asking the new prime minister to become conversant with the petition and recommend some of the requests made in it, which really meant the request for parliamentary representation. A few weeks later Menzies told Cooper that he had sent for the petition so he could familiarise himself with it and that he would bring it under the notice of the new minister for the interior, Harry Foll. But he was much less sympathetic to the cause of Aboriginal people than Lyons seems to have been. Foll, in turn, pointed out to Menzies that the Cabinet had already agreed that no good purpose would be gained by submitting the petition to the King. Yet once again this information was withheld from Cooper; he was told instead that the officers of the Department of the Interior were fully cognisant of their responsibilities towards Aboriginal people and that steps were being taken to implement the government's new policy in Aboriginal affairs.[64]

In early October 1939 Cooper sent several letters to Menzies, two of which expressed concern about the delay in hearing the result of the petition to the King 'asking, inter alia, that representation in parliament should be afforded to our race'. Two months later, he again raised the matter with the prime minister. In April the following year, Cooper, finally realising that the federal government was unlikely to forward the petition to the King, took up a suggestion made by Ernest Gribble that he address an appeal to a senior Anglican clergyman, Rev. Albert Victor Baillie, of St George's Chapel in Windsor Castle, to press his case with the royal household. In a covering letter that Gribble sent he remarked: 'Yelgaborrnya, who has taken the British name William Cooper, is an elderly Aboriginal, 80 years of age, self-educated and an earnest Christian, who, for many years, has struggled for justice for his brother[s] … His noble efforts, time after time, continue to fall on deaf ears; yet he has full faith in God that his cry will one day be answered and justice will prevail.'[65]

In August 1940, in a further letter to Menzies that proved to be the last letter he ever sent to government, Cooper concluded in this fashion: 'I would point to the fact that no answer has been given to the petition of my League for an aboriginal representative in Parliament. Trusting you will find time to deal with this important matter.' Once again, his request was ignored and the original of the petition with its long list of signatures might have already been consigned to a wastepaper bin by the condescending Carrodus.[66]

9

THE CUMEROOGUNGA WALK-OFF

WHILE THE FOCUS of Cooper's and the Australian Aborigines' League's work was broader than that of other contemporary Aboriginal political organisations, much of it was intensely local. This reflected the nature of the League's membership. Most of those who belonged to it had a connection with Cumeroogunga. For example, one of its vice-presidents, Doug Nicholls, was born and had grown up there.

Most of the League's members continued to regard Cumeroogunga as home, despite or because of the fact that they had left the reserve. Like Cooper, they carried a historical tradition that maintained that their people had won and farmed the land there only to lose it and have their independence undermined and their families and community broken up by a repressive Aborigines Protection Board and be forced into exile. Shadrach James had told this history when he raised his voice in 1929–30 and Anna Morgan had done the same in 1934–35. So too did Cooper in the course of a statement he prepared for the deputation that waited upon Thomas Paterson in Melbourne in January 1935: 'I ... [have] had 60 years' experience of a fruitless task and waste of good energy on an Aboriginal settlement.'[1]

The League's concern with the conditions of Aboriginal people in the most colonised parts of Australia, especially but not only at

Cumeroogunga, was reflected in the program it drew up in October 1935. Most of this focused upon land. In the League's constitution the first demand for 'civilised people' was for '[t]he provision of allotments of land for agriculture or other farming'. (Arthur Burdeu might have drawn the term *allotments* from the 1934 United States Indian Reorganization Act, which had been introduced to develop Native American lands, but it was probably adopted by the League's members because it was commonly used in colonial Australia and resonated with the term 'farm blocks' that they had used in reference to the land at Cumeroogunga.) The League also called for machinery and other equipment so they could work the land on reserves. Finally, it requested that these allotments be the 'unalienable property of the native concerned, and to be disposable by will to the next of kin of the native concerned'. Each of these demands echoed those that Cooper and his fellow petitioners had made in 1887 and that he and his brother Johnny Atkinson had repeated the same year in their approaches to their local member of the Legislative Assembly, John Chanter.[2]

In the course of 1936 and 1937 Cooper repeatedly appealed to government, especially the Government of New South Wales, to provide Aboriginal people with land and capital so that they could develop the land for their communities and thereby uplift themselves and become self-sufficient. He argued that Cumeroogunga was an ideal place for what he characterised as an experiment in the development of Aboriginal lands, and contended that if it proved successful it could provide a model for the numerous other Aboriginal reserve communities. In November 1936 he presented the New South Wales premier, Bertram Stevens, with a detailed plan for such development.[3]

Closely connected to these demands were calls for changes in the ways that government managed reserves such as Cumeroogunga so the control that managers and the protection boards exercised would be loosened and the way paved for eventual Aboriginal control. Cooper urged that the services provided on these reserves first be put into the hands of the Aboriginal people themselves; he insisted that all Aboriginal people should have a right to live on and return to the reserves that were set apart for them. He also called for regulations that would ensure that no resident could be expelled from a reserve for a breach of discipline or some such cause without an open inquiry being conducted by a protection board and the resident being provided with legal assistance. Once again, these demands were a product of Cooper and his Aboriginal associates' bitter experience at Cumeroogunga.[4]

In 1936 and 1937 Cooper also made demands in response to the deterioration that had occurred in the social and economic conditions of Aboriginal people as a result of the Great Depression and the increase in racially discriminatory policies and practices. These had reduced many to a state of extreme poverty and caused hunger and disease. Cooper and the League's protests were informed

Cumeroogunga was not the only reserve whose affairs Cooper and the Australian Aborigines' League took up. Cooper paid visits to reserves in Victoria, no doubt assisted by Helen Baillie and her car. Here he is pictured at Framlingham Reserve, near Warrnambool, with (standing, left to right) Henry McRae, William Austin, Jim Rose and Nicholas Couzens, and (seated, left to right) Mary Lancaster, Esther Couzens and Lucy McDonald. The photograph was probably taken late in 1937.

by the current plight of their family and kin on Cumeroogunga. Cooper called for the restoration of rations to able-bodied men living on reserves; the granting of sustenance to Aboriginal people on the same terms as it was given to unemployed white men; and the award of old age and invalid pensions and the maternity bonus to Aboriginal people.[5]

By May 1937 it appeared that the New South Wales Government had committed itself to implementing some of Cooper's recommendations for Cumeroogunga. But by the end of that year or shortly afterwards, his expectations of reform had been dashed. For a moment it had seemed that the pressure that the Aborigines Progressive Association and its allies in Sydney had brought to bear on the government was going to result in some change. In November 1937 it had been forced to agree, by the barest of majorities, to the establishment of a select committee inquiry into Aboriginal affairs in the state that allowed for Aboriginal testimony to be presented, and Bill Ferguson had taken the opportunity to question the Protection Board's officers. But most of the members of the committee withdrew their support and the inquiry lapsed in February 1938 without producing a report.[6]

At the same time Cooper wrote again to Stevens about the decline in the living conditions at Cumeroogunga. He complained that new houses were being built that were scarcely better than those constructed fifty years previously, and bemoaned the awful sanitary system. In all probability he recalled the suffering he and his family and kin had endured at the time of their move from Maloga to Cumeroogunga, which almost certainly had played a role in the death of his first wife and infant son. He became angrier and angrier about these conditions.[7]

Yet what pained Cooper most was the way in which his kith and kin were being treated by the officers of the Protection Board. 'We were being encouraged to expect something decent,' he complained, 'but it appears that we are to be dehumanised.' Earlier, in terms reminiscent of the protests by James and Morgan, Cooper had told the New South Wales Government that the board was their biggest problem. Most of its officers regarded Aboriginal people as inferior and were never sympathetic towards them. 'We are very disappointed at the departmental attitude in every way', Cooper told Stevens in March 1938. '[T]he last ones to be considered are the natives themselves and their feelings are not considered at all.'[8]

In July 1937 the board had transferred the manager of Cumeroogunga, JG Danvers, whom the people held in high regard, to another reserve and appointed Arthur McQuiggan in his place, even though there had been repeated complaints about the brutal beatings this officer had administered to his young charges when he was the superintendent of the Kinchela Aboriginal Boys' Home. Conflict broke out on Cumeroogunga soon after the authoritarian McQuiggan took over. Some of the people made preparations to walk off the reserve but were prevented from doing so after he arranged for a medical inspection and several policemen to enforce a state of quarantine. Those who had been prepared to leave the reserve appealed to the League to protest further on their behalf. Consequently, Cooper went to Cumeroogunga in May 1938 to investigate. He might have been reminded of the typhoid epidemic that had taken the lives of his first wife and their son fifty years earlier. Certainly he was appalled by what he saw. On returning to Melbourne he addressed four letters to Stevens, each devoted to a particular problem. But by July he had not even received an acknowledgement of them.[9]

Another Cumeroogunga petition

In early November 1938 a petition was drawn up at Cumeroogunga that called on the New South Wales Aborigines Protection Board to remove Arthur McQuiggan as manager and his wife as matron of the reserve. Many of those who would sign it were related to Cooper as well as Nicholls and Margaret Tucker. Cooper probably knew it was being circulated. At any rate he wrote at this time to Stevens after he had seen a newspaper report that the New South Wales Government was planning to reorganise its administration of Aboriginal affairs. '[T]here is one factor which we regard of supreme importance, and that is "representation of aboriginal interests", to which there is no reference [in your plans]', he remarked. 'It will be calamitous if provision is not made for this.' He called for representation on both the Protection Board and each of its reserves. In regard to the latter, he suggested that a council of Aboriginal people be elected by the people themselves and that the responsibility of overseeing the reserve be devolved to it. In calling for these changes Cumeroogunga was undoubtedly on Cooper's mind. On the same day he wrote to Stevens he told his fellow septuagenarian Rev. William Morley that the plans of the New South Wales Government to abolish the Protection Board and appoint a new form of administration would not suffice. '[A] more real reform would remove the power of the managers and matrons, who in some cases, are ruthlessly persecuting our people. I can assure you that our natives are boiling over with indignity at the way the managers and matrons are oppressing us … Did you know the full story your blood would boil.'[10]

About two weeks after the petition had begun to circulate at Cumeroogunga, 33-year-old Jack Patten, who had been born and grown up there, paid the first of several visits he would make to the reserve in the course of the next few months. Since the early 1930s he had been living in the highly politically conscious Aboriginal camp at Salt Pan Creek, surrounded by angry and assertive refugees from Aboriginal reserves on the state's north and south coasts. In mid-1938, in his capacity as the president of the Aborigines Progressive Association, he had made a long trip along the north and south coasts of New South Wales to inform Aboriginal reserve communities about the government's new plans and to share information about the oppressive conditions Aboriginal people were suffering throughout the state. A fiery orator, Patten was determined to rouse his people to revolt. During a visit he made to Cumeroogunga in the middle of November he held a meeting at which he urged the people to call for an inquiry into the management of the reserve. He also encouraged many of the women to draw up a list of the deaths that had occurred since a particular white woman had assumed the role of nurse on the reserve and sign a report calling for an inquiry that would investigate her conduct and consider whether she should be dismissed. A few days later Patten sent McQuiggan two letters in which he complained about his treatment of the people, especially his bullying, and threatened to report his conduct to the board. On returning to Sydney Patten sent the list of recent deaths and the report to the secretary of the Protection Board and informed him that the people at Cumeroogunga and Moonahcullah reserve (near Deniliquin) claimed that the managers and matrons of both reserves used methods of intimidation and forced the women to work for rations, that the rations were quite inadequate, and that overcrowding in the houses was causing illness. At the same time, he made a series of dramatic claims about the conditions on Cumeroogunga to the press. A large number of infants were 'dying of malnutrition'; poor rations were 'slowly exterminating the aborigines'; and those in charge were inflicting 'mental and physical cruelty' on the people. He also raised a long-held grievance at Cumeroogunga, namely the fact that the board had leased most of the reserve's land to white farmers. Finally, he drew attention to the association's program, which closely resembled the League's with its calls for the abolition of the Protection Board, the repeal of the Aborigines Act, citizenship rights, and capital to develop the reserves.[11]

In late November Cooper submitted to the chairman of the Protection Board the petition that had been drawn up and signed at Cumeroogunga. In a covering letter he informed the board that he had been receiving complaints about the conditions at Cumeroogunga for a long time, that he took them seriously as they were made by people of fine character, and that there was good evidence for the allegations they had made. Cooper set out the complaints he had received. Most concerned the matters he had repeatedly raised with the government—small houses, lack of sanitation and poor rations—but he gave most attention to the McQuiggans' harsh treatment of the people, especially the women. On behalf of the League, Cooper expressed support for the petition's claim for 'a full, free and impartial investigation' and made it clear that an inquiry undertaken by an officer or a member of the board would not suffice as this had never been satisfactory in the past.[12]

Soon after sending this letter Cooper paid another visit to Cumeroogunga and then wrote to the board's chairman again. He had been led to believe that there was going to be an inquiry but

was concerned it would not be conducted properly. 'There is just
this[.] The Board, its officers and the manager will be present, and,
I expect, the police. The people with their genuine grievances will
not feel able to present their case for fear of reprisal in the way
of expulsion.' Cooper asked permission to attend as the secretary
of the League in order to represent the people. But the board had
no interest in mounting an inquiry. In parliament in the second
week of December the Labor Party leader, Jack Lang, had asked
the colonial secretary, GC Gollan, whether he would make arrange-
ments for an open inquiry into the reserves to be held, but several
days later the board's secretary informed Gollan that it had not even
considered the matter. Instead, the board had sent the petition back
to Cumeroogunga, where McQuiggan posted it up and invited
the petitioners to remove their names from it. This enraged both
Cooper and Burdeu.[13]

In the closing weeks of December Patten gave three talks on the
radio and at the end of the month he sought to rally the people of
Cumeroogunga, writing to one of their number, Selwyn Briggs, to
tell them that he was now 'ready for action' and would come to the
reserve in the new year to set out his plan and outline what was
required to implement it. He also expressed the opinion that they
should not involve the League in this action as he was suspicious of
Burdeu's influence in its affairs. 'Remember what I have told you.
Don't trust a white man in this fight[;] he is either getting something
out of it or else he is a bit silly. The black does not blend with the
white. There is a demarcation at all times.'[14]

Cooper got wind of Patten's views about the League, which
was hardly surprising given that Briggs was one of his grand-
nephews. Patten's sentiments would have reminded him of some
of the differences between his organisation and the Aborigines
Progressive Association a year earlier at the Day of Mourning.
In a letter he now sent to the editor of the Melbourne Catholic
newspaper, Cooper remarked: 'I have been very concerned since
the advent of the Aborigines Progressive Association because those
in control of the movement have shown no desire to co-operate
with the League, which has been in effective operation for years.

The attitude of the new organisation has rather been to ignore the league altogether.' Cooper had tried to avoid any conflict with the Aborigines Progressive Association because he realised that want of unity among Aboriginal campaigners could damage their people's cause among white supporters. However, he felt compelled to speak out now because Patten had recently called the missionaries 'the aborigines' greatest enemies' and he could not tolerate such an attack. Cooper was probably also anxious about Patten's plans for action at Cumeroogunga.[15]

The walk-off

Patten arrived at Cumeroogunga on 26 January 1939 and two days later addressed a gathering of the people in the church there. He told them that the New South Wales Government was planning a new act of parliament that would see Aboriginal people herded onto compounds and denied the right to leave; that they would be forced to work and all the money they earned placed in a trust fund over which they would have no control; and that their children would be taken away from them. He urged them to act immediately: 'You can do something if you act quickly but if you wait you will be lost.' On 1 February two families left the reserve, crossing the Murray River into Victoria and camping on its banks at Barmah. Two days later Patten and his brother George were arrested at Cumeroogunga by the local police and taken to the Moama police station, where they were charged with enticing Aborigines to leave an Aboriginal reserve. But before he was bundled into a police car Patten shouted to a group of some sixty of the people: 'Now's your chance to leave. All of you leave the reserve at once, go to it boys.' Shortly afterwards many of the people began leaving.[16] Patten had already arranged for the sending of a telegram to the premier of New South Wales, the board's secretary, and several New South Wales parliamentarians. It read: 'Aboriginal men women Leaving Reserve Cummeragunja Cause Intimidation Starvation Victimisation Demand Inquiry Immediately'. After he was arrested Patten told the police: 'We had to use every means we can to get publicity and get [the people] to leave so that there will be an inquiry.'[17]

Upon Patten's release on bail, he travelled to Melbourne to meet with Cooper. The two men seem to have patched up their differences[18] and so were able to send a joint telegram to newspapers that repeated Patten's of a few days earlier. Cooper also issued a statement on behalf of the League claiming that the people who had left the reserve were starving and needed help. Yet both he and Burdeu were cautious, careful to attribute the decision to walk off to those on the reserve. They were actually rather ambivalent about the protest. The League had long had a preference for forms of political action that comprised representations of one kind or another, whether addressing appeals to government, penning letters to the editors of newspapers, making statements to the press, holding public meetings or staging concerts. Consequently, they eschewed the kind of methods Patten used, apprehensive that they would alienate the League's white supporters. They also feared that the walk-off would cause hardship, especially for the women and children. Burdeu was particularly pained by the difficult position of his fellow Church of Christ member Eddy Atkinson as pastor to the people at Cumeroogunga, torn between competing demands for his loyalty.[19]

Very soon after, Cooper and Burdeu espied a particular role for the League in the walk-off—that of explaining to the Protection Board, governments on both sides of the border, the press and members of the public the reasons for it. This task was vital. McQuiggan and the board's chairman had been quick to deny the claims Patten had made about conditions on the reserve, dismiss his allegations that the people were starving, declare that the suggestion that the board wanted to turn the reserve into a compound and remove the children was groundless, damn the whole thing as a publicity stunt by one man, and predict that it would all blow over in a week and that the people would return once they had overcome the fear Patten had aroused in them. Most of the broadsheets in Melbourne and Sydney accepted this characterisation of the walk-off or reported the claims made by the board's officials at considerable length, while one newspaper sought to discredit the protest by alleging that it had been fomented by Nazi Germany (to further Germany's claims for the return of its colony in New Guinea).[20]

A week after the walk-off began, Cooper told a newspaper
that at no point since Cumeroogunga had been founded had the
conditions been so bad. He observed that the people had sent him
complaints some time ago, remarked that they had been talking for
years of walking off the reserve in order to bring their plight to the
attention of white people, and repeated some of the claims he had
made in support of the petition of November the previous year.
A few days later Burdeu spoke in a similarly historical vein, focusing
on an incident that had occurred on the reserve in 1919: one day
the manager had sent the men away on a rabbiting expedition and as
soon as they were out of the way board officers had arrived and taken
several girls, sending some to the Cootamundra Aboriginal Girls'
Home and the rest into domestic service.[21] Margaret Tucker and
one of her sisters were among those taken from the nearby reserve,
Moonahcullah, to the Girls' Home, and she would soon tell this
story to the press as well.[22]

Cooper and Burdeu soon realised that more was required of the
League. The protestors could not expect much support from the
Aborigines Progressive Association. Patten and Ferguson had fallen
out after the Day of Mourning—they could not get on personally
and disagreed over the best political means to use and the most suitable white allies to work with—and the organisation had split into
two bodies that shared the same name. Ferguson now made known
his opinion that Patten had stirred up trouble at Cumeroogunga for
his own purposes. He also declared his organisation's preference for bringing about change by 'constitutional reforms' and
refused to make any statements in support of the walk-off. To
make matters worse, the support Patten had previously received
from PR Stephensen's radical right-wing nationalist organisation,
Australia First, collapsed and another Sydney organisation, the Committee of Aboriginal Citizen Rights, claimed that Patten represented
no known Aboriginal organisation and disassociated itself from
his methods.[23]

At the same time many socialists, communists and Labor supporters in Melbourne were keen to back what they characterised as
a strike, and joined forces with the League to appeal for moral and

material support for the people who had walked off. The Victorian
branch of the Communist Party of Australia started to run a series
of articles in its bi-weekly newspaper about what it called a mass
strike. In mid-February Nicholls, George Patten, Tucker and Caleb
Morgan addressed a protest meeting on the Yarra Bank alongside
Percy Laidlaw (a well-known Melbourne socialist), Helen Baillie,
John Cain (the leader of the state Labor Party) and a Labor senator,
and the money they collected was forwarded to 'the strikers'.[24]

For the time being the League was most concerned to persuade
the New South Wales Government to agree to an inquiry so that the
people could return to the reserve. In mid-February Burdeu made
a statement to the press that the people would not return until the
government promised an inquiry and better conditions. Three days
later he sent a telegram on the League's behalf to a New South Wales
member of the Legislative Assembly, Mark ('Mat') Davidson, who
had been instrumental in the appointment of the select committee
inquiry the previous year, asking him to lobby the government for
an inquiry. On the same day Burdeu made a statement to the press
in which he complained that the New South Wales Government
had yet to acknowledge, let alone reply to, the letter the League had
sent with the petition asking for the removal of the McQuiggans
and an independent inquiry into the reserve. He also organised for
supplies of food to be sent to the people who had walked off in
order to supplement the fish and rabbits they had been catching,
and would soon arrange for money to be sent as well (as would
Morley in Sydney on behalf of the Association for the Protection of
Native Races).[25]

Cooper, after making a visit to the protest camp at Barmah, sent
two letters to Stevens. The first, a short one, called on the government to appoint Davidson to conduct an inquiry into the present
troubles and allow the people to give evidence to it. The second, a
much longer one, concluded with a request for the inquiry so that it
was possible for the people to return to the reserve. In the same letter
he was at pains to argue that the League's grievances did not focus
on the government or even the Protection Board but the board's
rogue employees, and to point out that Aboriginal people had long

been making their representations in the right quarters, and thus to ask why they should be treated as though they were 'an enemy people'. In the same measured terms he sought to explain what he called the present exodus from the station: 'This is our only way of protesting and of directing attention to the wrongs we are compelled to endure. It has had the effect of doing this and now that we have been able to bring the matter to the notice of the government I trust we can expect that fair deal we seek.' He went on to argue in the same fashion that had long informed his political work: 'This is no ordinary strike, seeking conditions that employers will not concede. It is merely drawing attention to conditions which neither government, parliament nor public would suffer, if they but knew them, and to seek the conditions which we believe all three above mentioned would be glad to accede to.' Likewise, while Cooper was undoubtedly angered by the fact that the board had never even acknowledged his letter covering the petition and infuriated by the fact that the reserve's manager had called on its signatories to remove their names from it, he merely pointed out that this was not 'in accordance with British tradition and would not be done for a fully white community'.[26]

Nonetheless, he did not resile from setting out a series of facts in the same manner as the short, clipped sentences in which he always spoke. The treatment by the manager was very bad. The rations were inadequate. The housing was unsatisfactory. The education was poor. And so on. Yet in regard to the first of these matters he elaborated, revealing the degree to which his protest was informed by his people's racial memory: '[The manager] uses vile language … and is very abusive. The people are frightened of him at any time, for we have been cowed down so long, but the fact that he carries a rifle about with him makes matters worse. We have been decimated with the rifle among other things and fear the result of one being carried now.'[27]

By the end of February the protestors were starting to experience a good deal of hardship, but despite the increasingly miserable conditions in the camp they were determined to remain there. By this time Cooper's health was failing—reports had been circulating to this effect for six months or more—and so Nicholls and Tucker travelled to Barmah with Helen Baillie to lend the League's support to the protestors. At a meeting held at their camp Nicholls, Shadrach James and Eddy Atkinson sought to explain to several white folk, including a local journalist, the grievances that had provoked the walk-off, and called on the government to hold an inquiry. Two days later the League's executive agreed to a proposal, which was probably put to it by Burdeu, that it seek an assurance from Stevens that the children would not be taken from their parents at Cumeroogunga and that an inquiry be held, after which he informed the press that he believed the people would return to the reserve if these assurances were given. For his part Cooper made representations to the Victorian premier, Albert Dunstan.[28]

At much the same time, Atkinson appealed to the secretary of the Conference of Churches of Christ for Victoria, William Gale, for advice. Gale suggested that the people return to the reserve and then appeal to the authorities for a hearing of their case. Two local Church of Christ pastors, WB Payne and H Hargreaves, who were well known by some of the people at Cumeroogunga as they had established a church for them, expressed the same opinion and promised that the Church of Christ would try to persuade the New South Wales Government to conduct an inquiry. On this basis the people agreed to return to the reserve. However, news of this leaked out and two days later a message was broadcast on a Sydney radio station declaring that the people had been misled by the Church of Christ. This stirred a spirit of rebellion in the camp and the protestors resolved to remain where they were, determined to suffer rather than submit to any more humiliation.[29]

The people at Barmah were now in dire need of food, but they resolved to stay put until the Patten brothers had stood trial. However, after a police magistrate at the Moama Court dismissed the charges against George and found Jack guilty only to place him on a good behaviour bond for three months, Burdeu advised the protestors to return to the reserve, claiming this would strengthen the hands of the League in pressing the New South Wales Government for an inquiry. He believed that Chief Secretary Gollan was a good man who wanted to do what was right and so would overrule the board, and wrote him a personal letter begging him to intervene. Yet Gollan's response to a question Davidson had asked him a week earlier in parliament, as to whether he would order an independent inquiry, reveals that he saw no need to act. Moreover, the board itself soon made clear that this was also its position. During a visit its vice-chairman, SL Anderson, and a newly appointed superintendent, AWG Lipscombe, made to Cumeroogunga in mid-March to induce the protestors to return, they told six representatives of the camp at Barmah whom they had summoned to the reserve that the board wholeheartedly supported McQuiggan.[30] They also put pressure on the protestors by announcing that unless they returned home in the next seventy-two hours their houses would be assigned to other people and they would become ineligible for family endowment. Expectations among the protestors might have been raised a day or so later as Morley had (mistakenly) gained an impression from an interview with Gollan that the government was willing to grant an inquiry. But at this point the people rejected Burdeu's advice to return to Cumeroogunga and began to scatter. Some returned to the reserve, others moved to Mooroopna, and still others went further afield.[31]

At Cumeroogunga those who returned seem to have met with immediate reprisals from McQuiggan. As a result about eighty people walked off the reserve and returned to the camp at Barmah. The board repeatedly made public statements in which it denied that this second walk-off had occurred and ridiculed the claims of the protestors. Nevertheless, the ongoing protest troubled its members and discussions about the reserve dominated its meetings for several months.[32]

In the last week of March the League brought the conditions at Cumeroogunga to the attention of the annual congress of the Australasian Council of Trade Unions. It passed a resolution calling on the New South Wales Government to hold an inquiry and the Victorian Government to provide for people in the camp at Barmah. In the following weeks some unions in Melbourne did the same. Soon the League appealed to the Victorian Council of the

Young Communist League of Australia and the Australian League for Peace and Democracy for help. With this political support, it began to hold regular meetings on Sundays on the Yarra Bank at which Shadrach James and George Patten spoke, while the latter also spoke to workers at the Spotswood railway workshops and students at the University of Melbourne.[33]

But as April drew to a close Cooper was feeling very dispirited. In conveying to Stevens a resolution passed at a recent public meeting convened by the League, he expressed his disappointment that the League's requests for an inquiry had not even been acknowledged. 'No other State fails to respond to our correspondence, whatever their decision may be', he complained. 'In the federal sphere the utmost courtesy and consideration is always shown and this we claim is consistent with the principles of British justice which should be accorded to a persecuted minority.' Cooper claimed that the Cumeroogunga manager's recent conduct was worse than what his people had borne in the past—indeed, that it was practically intolerable. 'If public opinion only knew the nature and extent of the persecution, victimisation, stoppage of rations, there would be a great outcry', he claimed, adding: 'If you knew yourself, it would stop at once.' A few days later, after more families left the reserve, Baillie sent Gollan and Davidson a telegram on behalf of the League stating that it had received a report that the manager of Cumeroogunga was denying rations to people who had returned recently.[34]

Several days later Cooper sought to appeal to what he called his brother unionists by writing a letter to the *Australian Worker*. After describing the poor conditions on Aboriginal reserves he broadened the League's call for an inquiry into Cumeroogunga by demanding a thorough investigation into the situation of all Aboriginal people in New South Wales. '[N]othing short of a Royal Commission is likely to be satisfactory', he declared. But failing such an inquiry being granted, he concluded, the League was calling for a new board and Aboriginal representation on it.[35]

At this point in the walk-off the League started to seek the help of left-wing organisations more than it had done previously. In the past year or so it had made appeals to the Australian Labor Party and the trade union movement, but now some of its younger members, such as Tucker, were keen to accept the support of socialists and communists. At this time Cooper became very ill—so much so that Burdeu expected he would have to relinquish his position as the League's secretary—and Nicholls assumed the role of secretary for several months. Then Burdeu fell ill and had to leave Melbourne in order to recuperate. For the moment the reins of leadership of the League passed to its younger members.[36]

At this time the League and several left-wing groups agreed to form a new organisation, the Aborigines' Assistance Committee, to carry on the struggle over Cumeroogunga.[37] George Patten was chosen as its organiser, Tucker and Bill Onus became the League's representatives on it, and a committed socialist and the general secretary of the Australian Railways Union, JF Chapple, became its general secretary. Burdeu continued to make public statements on behalf of the League, but Patten and the Assistance Committee

Pictured here are some of the Australian Aborigines' League's left-wing supporters on the road from Melbourne to Barmah in order to take supplies to those who had walked off Cumeroogunga the previous month. George Patten is second on the left, standing next to Helen Baillie.

now assumed the leadership of the fight. Patten participated in
radio broadcasts; addressed meetings of trade unionists and women's
organisations; held public meetings; made statements to the press; and
organised a deputation to the Victorian Government. Local branches
of the Australian League for Peace and Freedom passed resolutions
calling for a royal commission to investigate the New South Wales
Aborigines Protection Board, and the Victorian Council of the
League gathered several hundred signatures of left-wingers on a
petition calling for the same.[38]

In August the League and the Assistance Committee launched a
public campaign to draw attention to the crisis at Cumeroogunga
but also the broader set of problems that Aboriginal people faced
on reserves. The Assistance Committee urged the appointment of
a royal commission to investigate Aboriginal affairs in New South
Wales and made a series of demands that closely resembled those
the League had long been making, though its emphasis on some
matters was more an expression of the program of the Communist
Party of Australia (which had been adopted in 1931). It called for a
change in Aboriginal policy in the state in order to secure: the right
of Aboriginal people to all the lands reserved for their use in New
South Wales; the development of cooperative and/or community
life in all economic undertakings on reserves and under the management of boards elected by Aboriginal people; grants of land wherever
the present reserves were too small for communal farming; majority
representation of Aboriginal people on the Aborigines Protection
Board pending its abolition; a requirement that all Protection Board
inspectors be Aboriginal; and education facilities of a kind that was
appropriate for full Australian citizenship. This was endorsed at a
large public meeting in Melbourne in the middle of August. During
the next few months the Committee held several town hall meetings and many smaller meetings, circulated leaflets and provided
monetary assistance to the protestors camped at Barmah.[39]

Yet the New South Wales Government still refused to accede to
the demand for a public inquiry. Soon the protestors suffered yet
another considerable blow. The living conditions of the seventy or
so people who were still camped at Barmah had improved, thanks to

the agreement of the Victorian Government to grant sustenance to the men there. But in the middle of October the Victorian Government announced that it would stop those payments after the New South Wales Government had lent on it. This effectively put an end to the walk-off.[40]

After nine months of hardship and humiliation, the protest had achieved nothing. Some historians have argued that it forced a major change in the administration of Aboriginal affairs in New South Wales.[41] It is true that in the course of 1939 the state government chose to make some administrative changes—creating a new position of superintendent of the board and appointing the undersecretary of the Chief Secretary's Department as the board's chair in place of the

THE FIGHT AT CUMMERAGUNJA

Aborigines In Protest

*Leave Government Supervised Camp
And Set Up STRIKE CAMP At
BARMAH - VICTORIA*
(ON THE BANKS OF THE MURRAY)

Although supposedly reserved for the benefit of the aborigines, Cummerangunja's 3000 acres of fertile land, cleared by the aborigines, have been leased by the Government to squatters and pastoralists, with the exception of 60 acres, upon which are congested the 320 aborigines.

The 320 were forced to live in 35 two-roomed huts and four bag shelters.

Self-respect is undermined by "dole" living.

Starvation follows weekly rations, valued for adults at 3/5, for children 1/8½.

Social, medical and educational services are insufficient and are so mal-administered as to add to the general misery.

THE ABORIGINES' ASSISTANCE COMMITTEE

WORKING IN CONJUNCTION WITH THE NATIVES' ORGANISATION
THE AUSTRALIAN ABORIGINES' LEAGUE

*Is Organising An Immediate Relief Of Distress
And The Creation Of Supporting Public Opinion*

THE HELP OF YOUR MONEY WILL WIN THEIR FIGHT

Industrial Print, 24 Victoria St., Carlton, N.3.   Aborigines' Assistance Committee, 5th Floor (phone   ).
        (40-hour week)   Kurrajong House, Collins St. (near Metro Theatre).

This flyer was distributed by the Aborigines' Assistance Committee in August 1939.

commissioner of police—and that in the following year it replaced
the Protection Board with a new body called the Aborigines
Welfare Board. But these changes had been in the wind for some
time as a result of pressure by Aboriginal and Christian humanitarian advocates. Moreover, the government made no major changes
in Aboriginal policy or practice, though Lipscombe's appointment
as superintendent in February 1939 was touted as the first stage of a
new deal for Aborigines. And while the composition of the board's
membership changed, the government did not provide for any
Aboriginal representation as a matter of course, stipulating instead
that one of the members be an expert in anthropology or sociology.
This indicates the relative power of white and Aboriginal lobbyists
at this time.[42]

It also seems unlikely that the League's principal figures felt
they had influenced any of these outcomes. Tucker made a special
plea for McQuiggan to be dismissed when she was a member of
an Aborigines Progressive Association deputation that sought to
meet the New South Wales chief secretary in the early months of
1940, but all she got was a half-hearted promise that the board's
superintendent would look into the matter. (Later she learned on
the grapevine that McQuiggan had been sacked by the board.)
For his part Nicholls concluded that the costs of the walk-off were
too high and the outcomes so negligible that methods other than
direct action would best serve the interests of Aboriginal people.
The League's failure to secure its goals by supporting the protest
seems to have contributed to a marked tailing-off in its activity in
the following year, though the decline in Cooper's health played a
major role in this, too.[43]

War

By the time the walk-off at Cumeroogunga had run its course,
Australia was becoming embroiled in another overseas war. While
this meant that Minister for the Interior John McEwen's New
Deal for Aborigines was put on hold, it gave the League and other
Aboriginal political organisations the opportunity to press their
demands for citizenship rights. Eighteen months earlier, Burdeu had

suggested, on behalf of the League, the formation of an Aboriginal citizen corps, thereby making a connection between military service and a right to citizenship. (Other Aboriginal political players were also interested in the formation of an Aboriginal force at this time.)[44]

Yet in January 1939 Cooper reversed the League's position on this matter, suggesting that establishing an Aboriginal corps would be akin to Aboriginal people creating a 'mercenary army' rather than forming 'an army of men fighting for all that is dear in life'. Military service was a deeply personal matter for him. As he told McEwen: 'I am father of a soldier who gave his life for his King on the battlefield.' He went on to argue that thousands of Aboriginal men had enlisted in the AIF (Australian Imperial Force) in the Great War but that those who had survived were denied the rights of citizenship on their return home. In one of the letters Cooper had sent after beginning his political work in Melbourne in 1933 he had pointed out that many Aboriginal men had been among the first to enlist in the AIF and suggested that there should have been some quid pro quo. This time he was determined that this should occur. He told McEwen that Aboriginal men had no reason to enlist as they had 'no status [and] no rights'. More pointedly, he argued that they had 'no country and nothing to fight for but the privilege of defending the land which was taken from him by the white race without compensation'. In short Cooper contended it was 'not right' to put Aboriginal men 'in the trenches, until [they had] something to fight for'. In other words, he made it clear that the enlistment of Aboriginal men should be conditional upon their being granted citizenship *before* they went to war. On another occasion he pointedly remarked: 'They were wanted to fight to make Australia safe for those who took it from the native.'[45]

Very soon after the war began, Cooper seized the opportunity to make the case for citizenship rights. He started an appeal to Prime Minister Robert Menzies with these words: 'not merely as an aboriginal but as a war pensioner of the last war who gave a son for the Empire, one of many colored men whose blood mingled with that of their white comrades as they died in the cause of liberty'.

He then proceeded to argue that Australia was involved in a war in which the Empire was fighting for the rights of minorities and that this meant the government needed to make sure that it granted rights to *its* own minority, the Aboriginal people. '[I]t would be disastrous if, in the fight for liberty, we lost what we were fighting for though we won the war', he asserted. 'It will be worse than that if, after the Empire has fought for the liberty of European minorities, Australia should continue to refuse freedom and liberty to her sadly treated minority.' In December he made this point again in another letter to Menzies, arguing that the war was being fought 'by reason of the tyranny over minorities and their cruel discriminating treatment' and so Australia could not 'fight that cause in honesty while still oppressing her minority'. This problem could only be rectified by the government granting citizenship rights to 'civilised' Aborigines.[46]

In June the following year, writing on behalf of the Aborigines' Uplift Society (which he had founded two years previously, primarily in order to provide 'a social service to aborigines', especially in Melbourne), Burdeu called on Menzies to immediately grant the rights of citizenship to all Aboriginal people who had been accepted by the AIF and ensure that they retained those rights on their return from the war. He spelt out what Cooper had implied in one of his earlier letters, namely that these rights should include the rights to military, old age and invalid pensions, and the right to vote.[47]

The Australian military forces, however, soon came to hold that the enlistment of Australians of non-European origin was neither desirable nor necessary and began to bar Aboriginal men (though many had volunteered and were accepted).[48] In July 1940 Burdeu protested against such discrimination on behalf of the League, as would other organisations such as the Association for the Protection of Native Races and the Committee of Aboriginal Citizen Rights in the years that followed.[49] Sometime later, another refugee from Cumeroogunga, Bill Onus, would tell Prime Minister John Curtin that the Commonwealth's failure to grant citizenship, particularly to Aboriginal servicemen, had weakened his people's support for the war effort. Some resented their discriminatory treatment so much, he observed, that they had become quite indifferent, 'their attitude being summed up by one Native who [had] remarked that "the natives are being asked to fight to make Australia safe for those who took it from their people"'.[50]

In August 1940, in the last letter Cooper sent as the secretary of the Australian Aborigines' League, he raised with Menzies the matters he had broached several months earlier. 'If Australia is sincere in her stand for democracy and her desire to free the peoples of other lands from the oppression of Hitlerism,' he asserted, 'her sincerity will be shown by the attitude she adopts towards her own exploited minority. Lip service to democracy and Christianity is not enough. "By their fruits ye shall know them".'[51]

EPILOGUE

B Y NOVEMBER 1940 William Cooper must have known his long life was drawing to a close as he decided to stand down as the secretary of the Australian Aborigines' League, and at a meeting held in his honour the organisation's members presented him with a testimonial for all the work he had done for his people. Shortly afterwards he returned to his own country, where he died a few months later at the Mooroopna hospital. He was buried in the cemetery at Cumeroogunga after a service conducted in the church by Eddy Atkinson and a prayer read at his graveside by Doug Nicholls. Many people came to pay their last respects. Arthur Burdeu, who in the company of Helen Baillie had visited Cooper in hospital shortly before died, told one of the Matthewses' daughters 'that there were never so many cars at Cumeroogunga before'. The Melbourne newspapers remembered Cooper for his petition to the King.[1]

In the wake of Cooper's death the League, not surprisingly, suffered something of a decline. Yet a few years later Nicholls would combine forces with Bill Onus in order to revive the organisation and renew Cooper's calls for rights for Aboriginal people, thereby sustaining his legacy during the postwar years. Nicholls recalled that Cooper would walk all the way from Footscray to Fitzroy and wait outside the football ground for him to appear so that he could try to persuade him to take up the cause. "'You've got through to the whites, Doug", he would say; "they listen to you. Now you have to start wobbling your tongue on behalf of your own people. Lead them to better things."' Nicholls fondly recalled: 'I used to wish I could dodge Uncle William, but he stuck to me ... It was William sticking to me ... that fired me. I can see it now ... Everything comes back to [him] ... he fired me to follow through.' In the following years, Nicholls would often use the term that Cooper had used: *thinking black*. 'A man looking after Aborigines' affairs must think black', he told a Melbourne newspaper on one occasion, 'and only an Aborigine can do that.'[2]

In these postwar years Nicholls pursued Cooper's principal goal: parliamentary representation for Aboriginal people. In July 1949 he asked the federal leaders of all three major political parties to support his call for Aboriginal people to be accorded representation in the Commonwealth parliament on the basis of an electorate comprising Aboriginal people who were already eligible to vote, thereby providing for what he called 'a spokesman for my people in the national parliament of their own native land'. In a letter addressed to these leaders, which Shadrach James probably had a hand in preparing, Nicholls told them: 'We feel that we are not asking more than the minimum to which we are entitled in requesting one spokesman for the native Australian race to sit in the Australian national parliament where the white people of our native country will have 180 representatives in the next parliament.' A month later, at a meeting of Aboriginal people at Mooroopna, a resolution was passed that began in this fashion: 'That, as a first and fundamental step towards securing proper recognition and just treatment for the Australian Aboriginal race, a law should be enacted to provide for a member in the federal parliament as a representative of the Australian Aborigines'. This, it went on to say, would be an 'act of justice'. Nicholls must have felt his grand-uncle was looking over his shoulder and urging him on.[3]

In the late 1960s Cooper's notion of 'thinking black' was taken up by many Aboriginal campaigners with Cumeroogunga roots, such as Onus's brother, Eric. In helping to found the Victorian Tribal Council along the same lines as the League, he paid tribute to Cooper as the founder of the organisation that had 'opened the way for [us] to carry on'. Three decades later, Cooper's work helped inspire another generation of Yorta Yorta people to pursue a claim to native title. As one of their spokespeople, Wayne Atkinson, remarked at the time, '[o]ne can be assured that Uncle William's words will continue to be the driving force of the Yorta Yorta struggle'. He particularly had in mind these words of Cooper's: 'How much compensation have we had? How much of our land has been paid for? Not one iota! Again we state that we are the original owners of the country.'[4]

Most recently, Cooper has been honoured by the country's legal and political establishment. A major building in the Melbourne legal district has been named the William Cooper Justice Centre,[5] as has a federal electorate in one of Melbourne's northern suburbs.[6] But the goals to which he devoted the last years of his life have yet to be realised.

In this book I have endeavoured to recover as much as possible the historical context in which Cooper lived. I have done so in order to make sense of the nature of his political work and dispel the misrepresentations of it that have grown largely because of a particular way in which a fleeting act by his organisation has been commemorated and celebrated in recent years.

I have shown that Cooper's political endeavours cannot be understood properly without reference to the history of Aboriginal people in the areas most ravaged by British colonisation, especially that of his own people, the Yorta Yorta, and the community of Aboriginal people that was forged at Maloga Mission first of all and Cumeroogunga Reserve later on. The dispossession, displacement, decimation, disease and deprivation they suffered across several generations after the white man's invasion propelled his political campaign. But so too did the fact that Cooper's people had been able for some time to remain on their own country and fight for land, family and kin.

We have seen that the means that Cooper adopted for his political work in the 1930s owed a good deal to his people's postcolonial history. His preferred method, that of petitioning, came naturally to him, we might say. Yorta Yorta men, who included Cooper and several of his brothers, had been party to several petitions since the early 1880s, and they knew they had secured some of what they demanded, in good part because they had the support of sympathetic white men like John Chanter.

Cooper's life and political work, we have observed, were profoundly shaped by his missionary mentors: Daniel and Janet Matthews most obviously, perhaps, but also his brother-in-law Thomas Shadrach James. They provided him with a political language to contest the discriminatory policies and practices that his people suffered. In their teachings they helped Cooper and his Aboriginal associates to conceive of themselves as the aboriginal or first peoples of the land, as human beings, as God's people, and as British subjects, and thus to insist that they had rightful claims upon Australian governments and the British Crown.

We have seen that Cooper did not undertake single-handedly the political work in Melbourne that occupied him in the last several years of his life. He was assisted by a group of Aboriginal people. The Australian Aborigines' League largely comprised his fellow countrymen and women who were refugees from Cumeroogunga, most notably Shadrach James, Anna and Caleb Morgan, Doug Nicholls, Margaret Tucker and George Patten. White mediators and advocates, namely Helen Baillie and Arthur Burdeu, also played an important role. They enabled Cooper to sustain the work of campaigning that he would otherwise have been unable to do because he lacked the resources that so many white men (and some white women) in Australia were able to take for granted.

In their political campaign, we have noted, Cooper and his associates framed their claims in several ways. At a time when Aboriginal people's difference was deemed to be the cause of their plight and constituted the grounds upon which they were denied the rights and privileges enjoyed by British subjects, they emphasised their common nature with their fellow Australians and demanded the same rights as Australian citizens had. But in pressing these claims they often made reference to their difference, though the differences they had in mind were primarily rooted in their people's history rather than culture (or civilisation) and race (or biology). Most often, Cooper and the members of his organisation invoked the fact that they were the descendants of this country's first peoples and that the British Crown had given them an undertaking to protect them. At other moments they riffed on their status as a minority and protested against the persecution of other minorities in the world in order to draw attention to the plight of their own people.

Cooper emphasised that Aboriginal people were different in certain respects from white Australians primarily because of the oppression they had experienced at their hands. As he told the journalist Clive Turnbull in 1937 as he prepared to submit his petition to the British king, Aboriginal people were the sufferers, white men the aggressors. Cooper called for this difference—this black history—to be recognised so that the injustices that had occurred could be redressed. But what most distinguished him from other campaigners was the fact that he called for Aboriginal political representation. He realised that historical difference meant that Aboriginal people saw the world differently: they thought black whereas whitefellas could not do this. This meant that in order to hear the Aboriginal voice the federal parliament had to agree to changes being made to the nation's constitution.

ILLUSTRATIONS

William Cooper, Sarah Nelson (nee McRae), Annie Hamilton and children, c. 1908, Esmay Mann Collection
William Cooper and children, c. 1908, Alf (Uncle Boydie) Turner Collection
Daniel Cooper, c. 1916, Esmay Mann Collection
Jessie Mann and children, c. 1922, Esmay Mann Collection
Lynch Cooper, late 1920s, Esmay Mann Collection
Sarah Cooper (nee McRae), undated, Alick Jackomos Collection, Australian Institute of Aboriginal and Torres Strait Island Studies
William Cooper on Nicholson Street, Footscray, undated, Esmay Mann Collection

Chapter 5
Letters in William Cooper's name; ERB Gribble Papers, Australian Institute of Aboriginal and Torres Strait Islander Studies, MS 1515, Box 11, Item 66, and National Archives of Australia, A431, 1949/1591
William Cooper, portrait, c. 1934, Alick Jackomos Collection, Australian Institute of Aboriginal and Torres Strait Islander Studies
William Cooper addressing members of the Australian Aborigines' League, c. 1935, Esmay Mann Collection
Cartoon, 1935, State Library Victoria

Chapter 6
Helen Baillie, 1936, State Library Victoria
William Cooper, Margaret Tucker, Lynch Cooper and Sarah Cooper, State Library Victoria
William Cooper and members of the Australian Aborigines' League, c. 1935, Alf (Uncle Boydie) Turner Collection
Anna Morgan, 1934, State Library Victoria
Arthur Burdeu, c. 1934, Dorothea Fry Collection
Doug Nicholls, 1931, Fairfax Syndication
Letter of William Cooper, National Archives of Australia, A659, 1940/1/858

Chapter 8
Cartoon, 1937, State Library Victoria
Edwin G Adamson, William Cooper and members of the Australian Aborigines' League, undated, Alf (Uncle Boydie) Turner Collection
William Cooper at John Batman's grave, State Library Victoria
Poster for the 1938 Day of Mourning, Weston Library, Oxford University
Bill Ferguson, Jack Patten and others at the 1938 Day of Mourning, Matheson Library, Monash University
William Cooper and Doug Nicholls at the 1938 Day of Mourning meeting, Matheson Library, Monash University

Chapter 9
William Cooper and others at Framlingham, c. 1937, Alick Jackomos Collection, Australian Institute of Aboriginal and Torres Strait Islander Studies
Left-wing supporters of the Australian Aborigines' League, 1939, Alick Jackomos Collection, Australian Institute of Aboriginal and Torres Strait Islander Studies
Aborigines' Assistance League flyer, 1939, New South Wales Archives and Records

ACKNOWLEDGEMENTS

Research for this book was conducted in many libraries, archives and other institutions over the course of several decades. I am grateful for the assistance provided by the staff of the Australian Institute of Aboriginal and Torres Strait Islander Studies; the Australian National University Archives; the Koorie Heritage Trust; the Matheson Library, Monash University; the Mitchell Library, State Library New South Wales; the Mortlock Library, State Library of South Australia; the National Archives of Australia (Canberra and Melbourne); New South Wales Archives and Records; the Noel Butlin Archives Centre, the Australian National University; the Public Record Office Victoria; the Royal Historical Society of Victoria; Screensound (Melbourne); State Library Victoria; the State Records of South Australia; University of Melbourne Archives; University of Sydney Archives; State Records Office of Western Australia; and the Weston Library, Oxford University. I am also grateful for the assistance of the staff at the Local Studies Collection, Dubbo Regional Council; and Research and Archives, Echuca Historical Society. Some of the research I drew upon for this book was made possible by an Australian Research Council grant many years ago. The remainder was funded recently by Gandel Philanthropy; the William Cooper Institute, Monash University; and the School of Philosophical, Historical and International Studies, Monash University.

Several historians—Sam Dalgarno, Fiona Davis, Stephen Foster, Christine Halse, Claire McLisky and Jan Penney—generously helped me with aspects of the research, as did the linguist Heather Bowe and the geneticists Shayne Bellingham and Bastien Llamas. At the National Library of Australia, the Manuscripts Librarian, Andrew Sergeant, patiently helped me source material that would otherwise have been unavailable to me during the pandemic.

Richard Broome, Margaret Burdeu, Robert Burdeu, Dennis Nutt, Sam Furphy, Harold Hayward, Misty Jenkins, Jayne Josem, John Lack, Michael Pearce, Catherine Reichert, Jan Richardson, Diane Singh, Peter Stanley, Anne Twomey and David Yarrow, provided me with advice, contacts or information. Kate Brocker, Graeme Davison, Barbara Gravener, David Jago, Michael McDonogh, Robynne Nelson, Lois Peeler, Clem and Rusty Smith, Jamil Tye and Jack White provided me with copies of photographs or helped me try to identify people and places in them. The Jackomos family gave permission to reproduce photographs from Alick Jackomos' collection, Uncle Boydie Turner, Barbara Gravener and Michael McDonogh, and Dorothea Fry did the same for their personal collections.

At Monash University a reference group, which was chaired by the Pro-Vice Chancellor (Indigenous), Jacinta Elston, and comprised Leonie Drummond, Bob Gerrity, Andrew Markus, Lynette Russell, Kevin Russell and Jamil Tye, was a tower of strength and a fund of sage advice.

I especially wish to thank William Cooper's grandson Uncle Boydie Turner for his enthusiastic support, and two of Cooper's great-grandchildren, Leonie Drummond and Kevin Russell, and one of his great-great-grandchildren, David Jago, all of whom gave hours and hours of their time to discussing this book with me and providing me with a great deal of guidance.

Stephen Foster, Heather Goodall, Andrew Markus, Lynette Russell and Jamil Tye all read a draft of the manuscript and provided invaluable criticism and suggestions, as did anonymous readers for Melbourne University Publishing. Leonie Drummond, David Jago and Claudia Haake read several drafts, or parts thereof, and gave excellent advice, often at very short notice. Needless to say, I alone am responsible for any errors in this account of Cooper's life and work.

At Melbourne University Publishing its director, Nathan Hollier, embraced this book from the outset; Louise Stirling ably oversaw its publication; Katie Purvis was a superb copyeditor; and Pilar Aguilera, the production manager, took meticulous care over the reproduction of the numerous images.

Finally, I wish to give my heartfelt thanks to my partner, Claudia Haake, and our daughter, Katarina, for their love and forbearance as I worked on this book.

NOTES

Prologue

1 *The Herald* (Melbourne), 6 August 1937, p. 2; 7 August 1937, p. 31.

2 *The Herald* (Melbourne), 15 September 1933, p. 2; Peter Ryan, 'Turnbull, Stanley Clive (1906–1975)', *Australian Dictionary of Biography*, http://adb.anu.edu.au/biography/turnbull-stanley-clive-11893/text21301, published first in hardcopy 2002.

3 Clive Turnbull, 'Aborigines Petition the King', *The Herald* (Melbourne), 7 August 1937, p. 31.

4 Petition, National Archives of Australia, A431, 1949/1591; Turnbull, 'Aborigines Petition the King'.

5 Turnbull.

6 After the Second World War, Turnbull would write a book about the extermination of Aboriginal people in Tasmania: *Black War: The Extermination of the Tasmanian Aborigines*, Cheshire, Melbourne, 1948. Once such histories became popular, it was reprinted twice (in 1965 and 1974).

7 Turnbull, 'Aborigines Petition the King'.

8 I am aware that an Aboriginal author and more especially a member of Cooper's own family would provide—and will provide—an account of Cooper's life and times different from mine.

9 Diane Barwick, 'Writing Aboriginal History', *Canberra Anthropology*, 4(2), 1981, pp. 77–78, 83–84.

10 I have discussed this at some length in 'The Founding of *Aboriginal History* and the Forming of Aboriginal History', *Aboriginal History*, 36, 2012, pp. 119–71.

11 For a discussion of these matters, see Allan Megill, *Historical Knowledge, Historical Error: A Contemporary Guide to Practice*, University of Chicago Press, Chicago, 2007, Part I.

12 See my book *Rights for Aborigines*, Allen & Unwin, Sydney, 2003, chapters 2 and 3, and Bain Attwood and Andrew Markus, *Thinking Black: William Cooper and the Australian Aborigines' League*, Aboriginal Studies Press, Canberra, 2004. This book has a wider focus than my previous accounts, which concentrated on Cooper's political work in the 1930s. I have undertaken more research about his life, especially the first seventy or so years, and the political dimensions of it.

13 One of them springs from my reservations about much of the recent historical scholarship on Cooper's political work. For example, it overlooks the role that other people, both Aboriginal and non-Aboriginal, played in it and disregards the influence of powerful historical forces that meant Cooper needed allies.

14 For a discussion of this protest, see pp. 144–6, 241–2, note 29.

Chapter 1: Beginnings

1 Diane Barwick, Draft of the entry for William Cooper, National Centre for Biography, File for William Cooper entry for the Australian Dictionary of Biography, Australian National University Archives, AU ANUA 312-2061; Barwick, 'Cooper, William (1861–1941), *Australian Dictionary of Biography*, Australian National University, http://adb.anu.edu.au/biography/cooper-william-5773/text9787, published first in hardcopy 1981; Tony Swain, *A Place for Strangers: Towards a History of Australian Aboriginal Being*, Cambridge University Press, Melbourne, 1993, pp. 2, 4.

2 During Cooper's lifetime various names were used to refer to his people. Among them were 'Bangerang' (or 'Pangerang') and 'Yorta Yorta'.

3 This is how Cooper or the missionary Ernest Gribble (who preferred to use Aboriginal people's Aboriginal names whenever possible) spelt this name (Rev. Ernest Gribble to Rev. AV Baillie, 15 April 1940, Australian Board of Missions, Further Records, 1873–1978, Mitchell Library, MLMSS 4503, Add-on 1822, Box 11, Folder 17; Christine Halse, personal communication, 2 March 2021). I am indebted to the linguist Heather Bowe for her suggestions about the meaning of Cooper's name (personal communication, 5 March 2021).

4 See Colin Pardoe, 'The Cemetery as Symbol: The Distribution of Prehistoric Burial Grounds in South-Eastern Australia', *Archaeology in Oceania*, 23(1), 1988, pp. 1–16, and 'Bioscapes: The Evolutionary Landscape of Australia', *Archaeology in Oceania*, 29(3), 1994, pp. 182–90.

5 This often saw Aboriginal men and women take the surname of a white man. In this case, Kitty took the name of Lewis for a while. From time to time the Victorian Government similarly (mis)spelt Lewes' name as Lewis. See, for example, the 1858–59 Victorian Legislative Council's Select Committee Report on Aborigines, pp. 27ff.

6 Marriage Certificate of Aaron Atkinson and Louisa Frost, 1 July 1873, New South Wales Registry of Births, Deaths and Marriages, 1873/003032; 'List of Names of Aborigines who Usually or Permanently Reside at Maloga Mission Station', *Fourth Report of the Maloga Aboriginal Mission School*, Riverine Herald, Echuca, 1879, p. 34; *Sydney Mail and New South Wales Advertiser*, 29 December 1883, p. 1223; *Weekly Times*, 8 December 1928, p. 5; Helen Baillie to AP Elkin, 11 June [1933], AP Elkin Papers, University of Sydney Archives, P.130, Series 12, Item 124; William Cooper to Mrs WA Norman, 21 August 1940, Norman Family Papers, Mortlock Library, State Library of South Australia, PRG 422/31.

7 On the certificate for Cooper's first marriage, no information is provided about either of his parents (17 June 1884, New South Wales Registry for Births, Deaths and Marriages, 5992/1884).

8 Certificate of Marriage between William Cooper and Agnes Hamilton, 30 March 1893, Victorian Registry of Births, Deaths and Marriages, 515/1893; Certificate of Marriage between William Cooper and Sarah McRae, 4 August 1928, Victorian

Registry of Births, Deaths and Marriages, 9525/1928; Baillie to Elkin, 11 June [1933]; Death Certificate for William Cooper, 29 March 1941, Victorian Registry of Births, Deaths and Marriages, 1941/5144.

9 Edward Cooper married a white woman in Echuca in 1868 and had ten or more children by her (Edward Freeman Cooper family tree, Ancestry.com).

10 Cooper to Norman, 21 August 1940; Cooper, Letter to the Editor, undated, *Australian Worker*, 10 May 1939, p. 15; Death Certificate for Cooper; Barwick, 'Cooper'.

11 See https://en.wikipedia.org/wiki/William_Cooper_(Aboriginal_Australian), note 3. This entry is incorrect in stating that Cooper's death certificate records his date of birth as 18 December 1861. In fact, this certificate records no date of birth whatsoever.

12 In at least one of his diary entries the missionary Daniel Matthews suggested that the Aboriginal people who had been drawn to Maloga Mission celebrated birthdays whereas those he called 'the blacks' had 'no record of their birthday' (28 February 1877, *Second Report of the Maloga Aboriginal Mission School*, Haverfield and Co., Echuca, 1877, p. 18).

13 This was a common practice among missionaries. For example, as discussed in Chapter 3, Matthews bestowed the name of 'Clarendon' on a young woman who later married Cooper.

14 There is another way of accounting for members of the Cooper family using the surname of Wilberforce for a while. According to one of the family's oral traditions, a grandson of William Wilberforce was sent to the Australian colonies and had a relationship with Cooper's maternal forebear. One cannot rule out this possibility. There are historical records of a white man by the name of James Lishman Wilberforce living in the town of Beechworth, a distance of some 200 kilometres away, from the late 1850s (*Ovens and Murray River Advertiser*, 18 November 1857, p. 2; 15 August 1860, p. 2; 27 April 1861, p. 2; 30 November 1865, p. 2).

15 See, for example, *Riverine Herald*, 2 December 1879, p. 2. In a list of the names of the Aboriginal people living at Maloga in a report in 1879, the names of Kitty Cooper, Jacky Wilberforce, Ada Wilberforce and Bobby Wilberforce appear, while in a mission report in 1884 the names of Kitty Cooper, Jacky Cooper, Ada Cooper and Bobby Cooper are listed (*Fourth Report of Maloga*, p. 34; *Ninth Report of the Maloga Aboriginal Mission School*, Riverine Herald, Echuca, 1884, p. 53).

16 Charles Sturt, Account of Journey, 1838, State Library Victoria, MS 9025; Diane Barwick, 'Changes in the Aboriginal Population of Victoria, 1863–1966', in Jack Golson and DJ Mulvaney (eds), *Aboriginal Man and Environment in Australia*, Australian National University Press, Canberra, 1971, pp. 292–93; NG Butlin, *Economics and the Dreamtime: A Hypothetical History*, Cambridge University Press, Melbourne, 1993, p. 135.

17 Marie Fels, *Good Men and True: The Aboriginal Police of the Port Phillip District 1837–53*, Melbourne University Press, Melbourne, 1988, pp. 158–61, 167–69; Jan Penney, Encounters on the River: Aborigines and Europeans in the Murray Valley 1820–1920, PhD thesis, La Trobe University, 1989, pp. 165, 221; Samuel Furphy, *Edmund M Curr and the Tide of History*, Australian National University E-Press, Canberra, 2013, pp. 58–63. Accounts of a massacre of twenty or more Yorta Yorta men, women and children (by the Port Phillip District's Native Police Force led by white officers) at Barmah in February 1843 need to be treated more sceptically than those

engaged in mapping massacres in Australia appear to have done (Lyndall Ryan et al., *Colonial Frontier Massacres in Australia, 1788–1930*, https://c21ch.newcastle.edu.au/colonialmassacres/detail.php?r=536). See Fels' account, noted above.

18 Penney, pp. 241–42.

19 Ibid., pp. 247–48, 251; Henry Reynolds, *With the White People*, 2nd edn, Penguin, Melbourne, 2000, p. 250.

20 *The Argus*, 15 December 1856, p. 5; *Sydney Morning Herald*, 4 August 1862, p. 2; JJ Westwood, *The Journal of JJ Westwood*, Clarson, Shallard & Co., Melbourne, 1865, entry for 18 February 1864, p. 401; *The Australasian*, 5 November 1864, p. 9; *Illustrated Australian News for Home Readers*, 29 March 1869, Supplement, p. 13; Susan Priestley, *Echuca: A Centenary History*, Jacaranda Press, Brisbane, 1965, p. 46; Penney, pp. 284–85.

21 HWH Smythe, Commissioner of Crown Lands for the Murray District, Report, 10 February 1852, Victoria Legislative Council, *Votes and Proceedings*, 1853–54, vol. 3, Aborigines. Return to Address, Mr Parker, 21 October 1853, p. 24; *The Argus*, 15 December 1856, p. 5; Victoria Legislative Council, *Votes and Proceedings*, 1858–59, Report of the Select Committee on Aborigines, p. 27; Penney, p. 234.

22 *First Report of the Victorian Central Board for the Protection of the Aborigines*, 1861, p. 19; Daniel Matthews, Diary, entries 23 January 1865, 14 January 1868, Maloga from the Diaries and Mission Reports of Daniel Matthews, 1861–1873 (henceforth Matthews, Mitchell Diary), Mitchell Library MS A 3384; Priestley, p. 152; Penney, pp. 244–45; GM Hibbins, *Barmah Chronicles*, Lynedoch Publications, Melbourne, 1991, p. 92; SM Ingham, 'O'Shanassy, Sir John (1818–1883)', *Australian Dictionary of Biography*, National Centre of Biography, Australian National University, https://adb.anu.edu.au/biography/oshanassy-sir-john-4347/text7059, published first in hardcopy 1974.

23 *Fifth Report of the Victorian Central Board for the Protection of the Aborigines, 1866*, p. 18; Penney, pp. 251–52, 301.

24 Matthews, Mitchell Diary, entries 23 January 1865, 14 January 1868, 26 February 1868, 10 April 1869; Matthews, Letter to the Editor, 10 April 1866, *Riverine Herald*, 11 April 1866, p. 2; *Fifth Report of the Victorian Central Board for the Protection of Aborigines*, 1866, pp. 16–17; *Riverine Herald*, 2 March 1867, p. 2, 6 March 1867, p. 2; Matthews, Letter to the Editor, 5 March 1867, *Riverine Herald*, 6 March 1867, p. 2; John Green, Report on the Murray River, April 1869, *Sixth Report of the Victorian Central Board for the Protection of the Aborigines*, 1869, pp. 11–12; Diane Barwick, 'Coranderrk and Cumeroogunga: Pioneers and Policy', in T Scarlett Epstein and David H Penny (eds), *Opportunity and Response: Case Studies in Economic Development*, C Hurst, London, 1972, p. 45.

25 Matthews, Mitchell Diary, entries 26 January 1863, 23 January 1865, 28 February 1868; [APA Burdeu], Episodes of Interest in the Life of the Late William Cooper (Told by Himself), 30 June 1941, Norman Family Papers, Mortlock Library, State Library of South Australia, PRG 422/31; Priestley, p. 77.

26 [Burdeu]; Ingham; Barwick; Andrew Markus, *Blood from a Stone: William Cooper and the Australian Aborigines' League*, Allen & Unwin, Sydney, 1988, p. 7; Alf Turner, personal communication, 21 January 2021.

27 [Burdeu].

28 James Rutherford to Robert Brough Smyth, 23 October 1875, *Twelfth Report of the Victorian Board for the Protection of the Aborigines*, 1876, p. 13; Rutherford to the

Secretary, Victorian Board for the Protection of the Aborigines, 27 May 1878 and 11 July 1878, National Archives of Australia, B313, 41.

29 The most valuable historical source for Maloga Mission is the diaries of Daniel Matthews, so long as one bears in mind that they primarily give his perspective on the events he related. Apparently he carried around with him small pocket diaries in which he scribbled brief notes during the day, after which he would enlarge on them in the evening. Unfortunately, few of his diaries in either of these forms have survived (Nancy Cato, *Mister Maloga: Daniel Matthews and His Mission, Murray River, 1864–1902*, University of Queensland Press, St Lucia, 1976, pp. 95, 176, 360). However, there are typewritten transcripts of three of them and Matthews drew upon his diaries copiously for the annual reports he produced about the mission. While he undoubtedly rewrote many of his original entries for publication, he was often very candid.

30 For a further discussion of this point, see Priestley, p. 38.

31 *Riverine Herald*, undated, reproduced in *Geelong Advertiser*, 6 April 1866, p. 2; Matthews, Notebooks, 1864–74, extracts reproduced in Cato, pp. 50–51; Matthews, Mitchell Diary, entries 27 February 1868, 14 April 1870; Daniel Matthews, *An Appeal on Behalf of the Australian Aboriginals*, Haverfield and Co., Echuca, 1873, p. 3; Cato, pp. 12, 15–16.

32 Matthews, Letter to the Editor, 10 April 1866, *Riverine Herald*, 11 April 1866, p. 2; Matthews, Letter to the Editor of *The Age*, 29 May 1866; reproduced in *Australian News for Home Readers*, 27 June 1866, p. 6; Matthews, Letter to the Editor, 5 March 1867, *Riverine Herald*, 6 March 1867, p. 2.

33 *Riverine Herald*, undated, reproduced in *Geelong Advertiser*, 6 April 1866, p. 6; *Riverine Herald*, 25 April 1866, p. 2; Matthews, Letter to the Editor of *The Age*, 29 May 1866; Matthews, Mitchell Diary, entries 19 and 20 September 1868; John Green to Robert Brough Smyth, 16 July 1870, *Seventh Report of the Victorian Board for the Protection of the Aborigines*, p. 5; Edward Curr and Christian Ogilvie, Report on the Murray River, 20 December 1875, *Twelfth Report of the Victorian Board for the Protection of the Aborigines*, 1876, p. 7; Cato, p. 27.

34 Matthews, Letter to the Editor, 5 March 1867, *Riverine Herald*, 6 March 1867; Matthews, Mitchell Diary, entry 5 September 1867.

35 Matthews, Mitchell Diary, entry 28 February 1868; *Riverine Herald*, 23 April 1870, p. 2, 27 April 1870, p. 2, 20 August 1870, p. 2; Matthews, *An Appeal*, p. 5; *Riverine Herald*, [30] April 1870, transcription in Matthews, Mitchell Diary; *First Report of the Maloga Aboriginal Mission School*, John Lutton, Sydney, 1876, p. 3; Matthews to the Chairman, Victorian Board for Protection of Aborigines, 12 July 1883, National Archives of Australia, B313, 26.

36 For a discussion of the importance of Janet Matthews to Maloga Mission, see Claire McLisky, Settlers on a Mission: Power and Subjectivity in the Lives of Daniel and Janet Matthews, PhD thesis, University of Melbourne, 2008, and 'From Missionary Wife to Superintendent: Janet Matthews on Three Independent Murray River Missions', *Journal of Australian Studies*, 39(1), 2015, pp. 33–35.

37 Matthews to Janet Johnson, 4 April 1872, cited in McLisky, Settlers on a Mission, p. 110; Matthews, *An Appeal*, p. 4.

38 Matthews, *An Appeal*, pp. 4–6; *Riverine Herald*, 4 June 1873, p. 2; Matthews, Mitchell Diary, entry 21 July 1874.

39 Matthews, *An Appeal*, p. 5; Cato, pp. 18, 28; Heather Goodall, 'Land in Our Own Country: The Aboriginal Lands Rights Movement in South-Eastern Australia, 1860 to 1914', *Aboriginal History*, 14(1), 1990, especially pp. 3–9.

40 Matthews, Mitchell Diary, entries 27 June 1874, 6 August 1874.

41 Matthews, Letter to the Editor, 2 September 1874, *Riverine Herald*, 5 September 1874, p. 2; Robert Kenny, *The Lamb Enters the Dreaming: Nathanael Pepper & the Ruptured World*, Scribe, Melbourne, 2007, pp. 24, 26.

42 Matthews, Mitchell Diary, entries 21 June 1874, 27 June 1874, 11 July 1874, 22 July 1874, 3 August 1874, 4 August 1874, 7 September 1874, 2 November 1874.

43 Matthews, Mitchell Diary, entries 16 August 1874, 2 September 1874, 12 September 1874, 27 September 1874, 4 October 1874, 18 October 1874, 1 November 1874; *First Report of Maloga*, p. 3, Matthews, Mitchell Diary, entry 25 October 1874, *First Report of Maloga*, p. 9.

44 Matthews, Mitchell Diary, entries 27 June 1874, 11 July 1874, 22 July 1874, 25 July 1874, 4 August 1874, 23 August 1874; 2 September 1874, 4 September 1874, 7 September 1874, 18 September 1874, 29 September 1874; 30 September 1874, 4 October 1874; 'A Friend to the Outcast', Letter to the Editor, undated, *Riverine Herald*, 26 August 1874, p. 2; 'An Observer', Letter to the Editor, 11 September 1874, *Riverine Herald*, 12 September 1874, p. 2; *Second Report of Maloga*, p. 5.

45 Matthews, Mitchell Diary, entry 7 September 1874.

46 Matthews, Letter to the Editor, 2 September 1874, *Riverine Herald*, 5 September 1874, p. 2; Matthews, Mitchell Diary, entry 29 September 1874.

47 It is difficult to recover some of the particulars of this incident as the only extant copy of Matthews' diary for this period is a transcript and two pages appear to be missing and the names of the white men involved have been censored by turning their surnames into initials.

48 Matthews, Mitchell Diary, entries 1 November 1874, 2 November 1874, 5 November 1874, 6 November 1874; Statement of Billy (Half-Caste Lad), undated [2 November 1874], Matthews, Mitchell Diary; Matthews, Mitchell Diary, entry 3 November 1874, *First Report of Maloga*, p. 10.

49 For a discussion of this matter, see Nancy E Wright, 'The Problem of Aboriginal Evidence in Early Colonial New South Wales', in Diane Kirkby and Catharine Colebourne (eds), *Law, History, Colonialism: The Reach of Empire*, Manchester University Press, Manchester, 2001, especially pp. 140–45.

50 Matthews, Mitchell Diary, entry 5 November 1874, *First Report of Maloga*, pp. 10–11; Matthews, Mitchell Diary, entries 6 and 7 November 1874.

51 Matthews, Letter to the Editor, 2 September 1874, *Riverine Herald*, 5 September 1874, p. 2; Matthews, Mitchell Diary, entry [4] November 1874; *Riverine Herald*, 18 August 1877, p. 3.

Chapter 2: Conversion

1 For this period in Cooper's life the contemporary historical record is very thin. I have come across only a couple of references to him between November 1874 and January 1882.

2 *Southland Times*, 23 November 1876, p. 2; Helen Baillie to AP Elkin, 11 June [1933], AP Elkin Papers, University of Sydney Archives, P.130, Series 12, Item 124.

3 Daniel Matthews, Diary, entries 15 February 1877, 20 March 1877, *Second Report of the Maloga Aboriginal Mission School*, Haverfield and Co., Echuca, 1877, pp. 16, 20;

Matthews, Diary, entry 23 March 1880, *Fifth Report of the Maloga Aboriginal Mission School*, Riverine Herald, Echuca, 1880, p. 31; *Report of the New South Wales Aborigines Protection Association, June 30 1881*, s.n., Sydney, 1881, p. 4; William Cooper to ERB Gribble, 10 July 1933, ERB Gribble Papers, Australian Institute of Aboriginal and Torres Strait Islander Studies, MS 1515, Box 11, Item 66; Clive Turnbull, 'Aborigines Petition the King', *The Herald* (Melbourne), 7 August 1937, p. 31.

4 Matthews, Diary, entries 26 October 1876, 29 October 1876, 30 October 1876, 12 March 1877, *Second Report of Maloga*, p. 8–9, 19, 23; Matthews, Diary, entries 18 June 1877, 25 December 1877, 31 March 1878, *Third Report of the Maloga Aboriginal Mission School*, Riverine Herald, Echuca, 1878, pp. 9, 33; Victorian Board for the Protection of the Aborigines to Matthews, 23 July 1878, National Archives of Australia, B313, 26; *Fourth Report of the Maloga Aboriginal Mission School*, Riverine Herald, Echuca, 1879, p. 5; *Goulburn Herald and Chronicle*, 7 June 1879, p. 6.

5 Matthews, Diary, entries 25 October 1876, 2 November 1876, 23 November 1876, 11 December 1876, *Second Report of Maloga*, pp. 8, 12; *Third Report of Maloga*, p. 1; Matthews, Diary, entries 2 April 1877, 11 May 1877, 3 October 1877, 7 November 1877, 29 November 1877, 15 January 1878, 5 February 1878, 11 February 1878, 24 March 1878, 25 March 1878, *Third Report of Maloga*, pp. 3, 6, 21, 25–26, 28, 34–36, 42; Matthews, Diary, entries 16 April 1878, 26 May 1878, 24 July 1878, 28 October 1878, 4 November 1878, 29 November 1878, 4 March 1879, *Fourth Report of Maloga*, pp. 6, 10, 12, 18, 20, 25; Addenda, *Fourth Report of Maloga*, p. 28; *Fifth Report of Maloga*, p. 5; Matthews, Diary, entries 4 April 1879, 3 June 1879, 2 July 1879, 16 July 1879, 28 December 1879, *Fifth Report of Maloga*, pp. 7, 11, 13–14, 26; Report of the New South Wales Aborigines Protection Association, 30 June 1881, New South Wales Legislative Assembly, *Votes and Proceedings*, 1883, Protection of the Aborigines (Minute of Colonial Secretary, Together with Reports), p. 10, https://aiatsis.gov.au/sites/default/files/docs/digitised_collections/remove/91930.pdf.

6 Matthews, Diary, entries 30 October 1876, 12 March 1877, *Second Report of Maloga*, pp. 9, 18–19; *Bendigo Advertiser*, 21 December 1878, p. 1; Secretary to the Protector of the Aborigines to the Principal Under-Secretary of New South Wales, 12 September 1882, New South Wales Legislative Assembly, *Votes and Proceedings*, Report of the Protector of Aborigines to 31 December 1882, p. 14; Diane Barwick, 'Coranderrk and Cumeroogunga: Pioneers and Policy', in T Scarlett Epstein and David H Penny (eds), *Opportunity and Response: Case Studies in Economic Development*, C Hurst, London, 1972, pp. 45–46.

7 John Green, Report on the Murray River, April 1869, *Sixth Report of the Victorian Central Board for the Protection of the Aborigines*, 1869, p. 11; James Rutherford to Robert Brough Smyth, 23 October 1875, *Twelfth Report of the Victorian Board for the Protection of the Aborigines*, 1876, p. 13; Report on the Murray River by Edmund Curr and Christian Oglivie, 20 December 1875, *Twelfth Report of the Victorian Board for the Protection of the Aborigines*, 1876, p. 7; John McKenzie to the Secretary, Victorian Board for the Protection of the Aborigines, 17 May 1876, 12 April 1878, 8 May 1878, 11 August 1878, 4 July 1879, 29 July 1879, National Archives of Australia, B313, 47; Matthews, Diary, entries 15 November 1876, 23 December 1876, 26 January 1877, *Second Report of Maloga*, pp. 11, 13, 14–15; Victorian Legislative Assembly, *Votes and Proceedings*, 1877–78, vol. 3, Royal Commission on the Aborigines, p. 114; Matthews, Diary, entry 23 July 1877, *Third Report of Maloga*,

p. 13; *Bendigo Advertiser*, 21 December 1878, p. 1; Rutherford to the Secretary, Victorian Board for the Protection of the Aborigines, 27 May 1878, National Archives of Australia, B313, 41; Matthews to McKenzie, 4 April 1881, National Archives of Australia, B313, 47; Jan Penney, Encounters on the River: Aborigines and Europeans in the Murray Valley 1820–1920, PhD thesis, La Trobe University, 1989, p. 305.

8　Matthews, Diary, entry 16 September [sic, i.e. October] 1878, *Fourth Report of Maloga*, p. 15; *Sydney Morning Herald*, 15 October 1878, p. 3; Matthews, Diary, entries 28 December 1879, 16 January 1880, 3 March 1880, *Fifth Report of Maloga*, pp. 26–27, 29; Matthews, Diary, entries 23 April 1880, 11 June 1880, 27 June 1880, *Sixth Report of Maloga*, pp. 4–5; *Sydney Morning Herald*, 17 February 1880, p. 6; Edward GW Palmer, Honorary Secretary of the Aborigines Protection Association of New South Wales, to Colonial Secretary, 23 February 1880, New South Wales Legislative Assembly, *Votes and Proceedings*, 1883, Protection of the Aborigines (Minute of Colonial Secretary, Together with Reports), p. 4; Matthews, Diary, entry 1 April 1881, *Seventh Report of the Maloga Aboriginal Mission Station*, Colonial Publishing Society, Sydney, 1882, p. 6; *Seventh Report of Maloga*, p. 23; Ann Curthoys, 'Good Christians and Useful Workers: Aborigines, Church and State in NSW 1870–1883', in Sydney Labour History Group (eds), *What Rough Beast? The State and Social Order in Australian History*, George Allen & Unwin, Sydney, 1982, pp. 42–46.

9　Addenda, *Fourth Report of Maloga*, p. 28; Matthews, Diary, entries 14 April 1879, 16 August 1879, 10 November 1879, *Fifth Report of Maloga*, pp. 7, 19.

10　Matthews, Diary, entry 18 September [sic, i.e. October] 1878, *Fourth Report of Maloga*, p. 15; *Bendigo Advertiser*, 28 December 1878, p. 1; Palmer to Colonial Secretary, 23 February 1880, New South Wales Legislative Assembly, *Votes and Proceedings*, 1883, Protection of the Aborigines (Minute of Colonial Secretary, Together with Reports), p. 4, https://aiatsis.gov.au/sites/default/files/docs/digitised_collections/remove/91930.pdf; *Sydney Morning Herald*, 25 February 1880, pp. 5, 6.

11　Several of these people died at Maloga in the course of the next two years, and thirteen of them returned home shortly afterwards (Paul Irish, *Hidden in Plain Sight: The Aboriginal People of Coastal Sydney*, NewSouth, Sydney, 2017, p. 189 note 51).

12　Matthews, Diary, entries 19 April 1879, 10 August 1879, *Fifth Report of Maloga*, pp. 7, 17; Matthews, Letter to the Editor undated, *Sydney Morning Herald*, 25 June 1881, p. 7; Matthews, Diary, entry, 6 August 1881, *Seventh Report of Maloga*, p. 6; Barwick, 'Coranderrk and Cumeroogunga', p. 45; Diane E Barwick, *Rebellion at Coranderrk*, edited Laura E and Richard E Barwick, Aboriginal History Inc., Canberra, 1998, pp. 225, 255; Irish, pp. 111–16, 120.

13　George E Nelson, 'James, Thomas Shadrach (1859–1946)', *Australian Dictionary of Biography*, http://adb.anu.edu.au/biography/james-thomas-shadrach-10610/text18855, published first in hardcopy 1996; George Nelson and Robynne Nelson, *Dharmalan Dana: An Australian Aboriginal Man's 73-Year Search for the Story of his Aboriginal and Indian Ancestors*, Australian National University Press, Canberra, 2014, pp. 210, 249, 252–54, 256–58, 279.

14　Matthews, Diary, entry 3 January 1881, *Sixth Report of Maloga*, p. 12; *The Age*, 15 January 1881, p. 6; Warrack, 'The Cummeragunja Aboriginal Station',

Numurkah Standard, 19 August 1892, p. 2; Thomas James, 'Baimai', *Australasian Anthropological Journal*, 1(4), 1897, pp. 87–89; Nelson and Nelson, pp. 144–45.

15 Nelson and Nelson, p. 148.

16 Maloga Petition, *Daily Telegraph* (Sydney), 5 July 1881, p. 3; Christopher Leslie Brown, *Moral Capital: Foundations of British Abolitionism*, University of North Carolina Press, Chapel Hill, NC, 2006, p. 448.

17 Maloga Petition.

18 William Thomas, Guardian of Aborigines, Victoria, to Charles Duffy, Commissioner of Lands and Survey, Victoria, 4 March 1859, *The Herald* (Melbourne), 8 March 1859, reproduced in Bain Attwood and Andrew Markus (eds), *The Struggle for Aboriginal Rights: A Documentary History*, Allen & Unwin, Sydney, 1999, pp. 41–42; Henry Palmer, Superintendent of Police, Echuca, Telegram to AWA Page, Secretary of the Victorian Board for the Protection of the Aborigines, 16 May 1881, National Archives of Australia, B313, 26; Barwick, 'Coranderrk and Cumeroogunga', pp. 45, 47.

19 Matthews, *An Appeal on Behalf of the Australian Aboriginals*, Haverfield and Co., Echuca, 1873, p. 3; Matthews, Letter to the Editor, 21 August 1874, *Bendigo Advertiser*, 24 August 1874; *First Report of the Maloga Mission* School, John Lutton, Sydney, 1876, pp. 2–3; Matthews, Diary, entry 17 June 1881, Diaries and Papers of Daniel Matthews, 1866–1909, National Library of Australia, MS 2195/5/1.

20 *Sydney Morning Herald*, 2 July 1881, p. 8, 11 July 1881, p. 6; Palmer to Under Secretary, Department of Lands, 17 May 1881, New South Wales Archives Office, NRS 7953, Item No. [2/1745]; McKenzie to the Secretary, Victorian Board for the Protection of the Aborigines, 16 July 1881, National Archives of Australia, B313, 47; *Riverine Herald*, 21 July 1881, p. 2; *Ninth Report of the Maloga Aboriginal Mission School*, Riverine Herald, Echuca, 1884, p. 4.

21 *Sydney Morning Herald*, 11 July 1881, p. 6, 2 August 1881, p. 6, 29 August 1881, p. 7, 2 January 1882, p. 3, 4 March 1882, p. 7; Matthews to Page, 9 December 1881, National Archives of Australia, B313, 26; *Riverine Herald*, 17 February 1882, p. 3; Menzies to the Secretary, Victorian Board for the Protection of the Aborigines, 22 February 1882, National Archives of Australia, B313, 47; Principal Under-Secretary to Philip Gidley King, 23 June 1882, New South Wales Legislative Assembly, *Votes and Proceedings*, 1883, Aboriginal Mission Stations at Warangesda and Maloga, p. 1, https://aiatsis.gov.au/sites/default/files/docs/digitised_collections/remove/91936.pdf; *Sydney Morning Herald*, 3 February 1883, p. 5.

22 Secretary of the Protector of the Aborigines to the Principal Under-Secretary of New South Wales, 12 September 1882, New South Wales Legislative Assembly, *Votes and Proceedings*, Report of the Protector of Aborigines to 31 December 1882, p. 15, https://aiatsis.gov.au/sites/default/files/docs/digitised_collections/remove/91912.pdf; George Thornton, Report to Principal Under-Secretary, 22 January 1883, New South Wales Legislative Assembly, *Votes and Proceedings*, Report of the Protector of Aborigines to 31 December 1882, pp. 2–3; Minute of Colonial Secretary, 26 February 1883, New South Wales Legislative Assembly, *Votes and Proceedings*, 1883, Protection of the Aborigines (Minute of Colonial Secretary, Together with Reports), p. 3, https://aiatsis.gov.au/sites/default/files/docs/digitised_collections/remove/91930.pdf; *Sydney Morning Herald*, 3 March 1883, p. 3; *New South Wales Government Gazette*, 9 April 1883, p. 1873; Curthoys, pp. 46, 50–51; Irish, pp. 111–19.

23 Palmer to the Colonial Secretary, 23 February 1880, New South Wales Legislative Assembly, *Votes and Proceedings*, 1883, Protection of the Aborigines (Minute of Colonial Secretary, Together with Reports), p. 4, https://aiatsis.gov.au/sites/default/files/docs/digitised_collections/remove/91930.pdf; Matthews, Diary, entries 9 April 1883, 15 April 1883, 18 April 1883, *Ninth Report of Maloga*, pp. 6–7; Matthews to Page, 20 April 1883, National Archives of Australia, B313, 26; Claire McLisky, Settlers on a Mission: Power and Subjectivity in the Lives of Daniel and Janet Matthews, PhD thesis, University of Melbourne, 2008, p. 167.

24 In the 'Names of Aborigines and Half-Castes who Usually or Habitually Reside at Maloga Station' that appears in the mission's ninth report, Cooper is listed for 22 January 1882 (*Ninth Report of Maloga*, p. 54).

25 Matthews, Diary, entry 6 January 1884, *Ninth Report of Maloga*, pp. 27–28; McLisky, Settlers on a Mission, Chapter 5, and 'The Location of Faith: Power, Gender and Spirituality in the 1883–84 Maloga Religious Revival', *History Australia*, 7(1), 2010, pp. 08.1–20.

26 Matthews, Diary, entries 15 April 1883, 8 May 1883, 1 June 1883, 5 August 1883, 21 October 1883, 2 December 1883, 23 December 1883, 24 December 1883, 1 January 1884, 13 January 1884, 16 January 1884, 20 January 1884, 29 February 1884, 10 March 1884, 21 March 1884, *Ninth Report of Maloga*, pp. 6, 8 10, 12–13, 18, 20, 23–24, 26–27, 29–30, 32, 34, 36–37.

27 Matthews, Diary, 2 December 1883, 17 December 1883, 23 December 1883, 28 December 1883, *Ninth Report of Maloga*, pp. 20–21, 23, 25.

28 Matthews, Diary, entries 24 December 1883, 3 January 1884, 13 January 1884, 16 January 1884, *Ninth Report of Maloga*, pp. 24, 27–29, 32; McLisky, 'Location of Faith', pp. 08.9–10.

29 Matthews, Diary, entries 6 January 1884, 13 January 1884, 16 January 1884, *Ninth Report of Maloga*, pp. 27–30, 32; McLisky, 'Location of Faith', p. 08.9.

30 Maloga Petition, *Daily Telegraph* (Sydney), 5 July 1881, p. 3; McLisky, 'Location of Faith', p. 08.12.

31 William Cooper to Mrs WA Norman, 21 August 1940, Norman Family Papers, Mortlock Library, State Library of South Australia, PRG 422/31; Cooper, 'Victory', Norman Family Papers, Mortlock Library, State Library of South Australia, PRG 422/31; Nancy Cato, *Mister Maloga: Daniel Matthews and His Mission, Murray River, 1864–1902*, University of Queensland Press, St Lucia, 1976, p. 347.

32 Matthews, Diary, entries 23 December 1883, 24 December 1883, 3 January 1884, 6 January 1884, 13 January 1884, 29 February 1884, 9 March 1884, *Ninth Report of Maloga*, pp. 23–4, 27, 29, 31, 34, 36, 38.

33 Matthews, Diary, entries 4 April 1883, 8 May 1883, 22 August 1883, *Ninth Report of Maloga*, pp. 5, 8, 14; Robert Kenny, *The Lamb Enters the Dreaming: Nathanael Pepper & the Ruptured World*, Scribe, Melbourne, 2007, p. 192.

34 Matthews, Diary, entry 29 February 1884, *Ninth Report of Maloga*, p. 35; Alf Turner, personal communication, 14 November 2020.

Chapter 3: Crisis at Maloga

1 'Names of Children Supported', *Fourth Report of the Maloga Aboriginal Mission School*, Riverine Herald, 1879, p. 33.

2 'Names of Aborigines and Half-Castes who Usually or Habitually Reside at Maloga Station', *Ninth Report of the Maloga Aboriginal Mission School*, Riverine

Herald, Echuca, 1884, p. 53; Daniel Matthews, Diary, entry 29 February 1884, *Ninth Report of Maloga*, p. 35; Marriage Certificate for William Cooper and Annie Murrie, 17 June 1884, New South Wales Registry of Births, Marriages and Deaths, 5992/1884; Matthews, Diary, entry 17 June 1884, *Tenth Report of the Maloga Aboriginal Mission Station*, Riverine Herald, Echuca, 1885, p. 13; 'Names of Aborigines and Half-Castes who Generally or Permanently Reside at Maloga', Maloga Aboriginal Mission School (registering Emily's birth on 25 July 1885), *Eleventh Report of the Maloga Aboriginal Mission Station*, Mackay & Foyster, Echuca, 1886, p. 35; Death Certificate for Bartlett Cooper, 10 January 1889, New South Wales Registry of Births, Marriages and Deaths, 11720/1889; Diane Barwick, 'Cooper, William (1861–1941)', *Australian Dictionary of Biography*, Australian National University, http://adb.anu.edu.au/biography/cooper-william-5773/text9787, published first in hardcopy 1981.

3 Matthews, Diary, entries 15 December 1883, 17 December 1883, *Ninth Report of Maloga*, p. 21; Matthews, Diary, entries 6 July 1884, 28 August 1884, 1 October 1884, 23 October 1884, *Tenth Report of Maloga*, pp. 13, 19, 24; Matthews, Diary, entries 21 September 1885, 4 November 1885, 14 December 1885, *Eleventh Report of Maloga*, pp. 15, 19, 21; Matthews, Diary, entry 18 October 1886, *Twelfth Report of the Maloga Aboriginal Mission Station*, Mackay & Foyster, Echuca, 1888, p. 11.

4 Matthews, Diary, entry 1 April 1885, *Eleventh Report of Maloga*, p. 5; Keighley Goodchild, 'A Week at Maloga', *Riverine Herald*, 16 November 1886, p. 2, 17 November 1886, p. 2, 19 November 1886, p. 2; Claire McLisky, Settlers on a Mission: Power and Subjectivity in the Lives of Daniel and Janet Matthews, PhD thesis, University of Melbourne, 2008, pp. 213, 227.

5 McLisky, pp. 211, 215.

6 *Riverine Herald*, 28 December 1883, p. 2; Matthews, Diary, entries 3 April 1885, 10 April 1885, 25 May 1885, 1 March 1886, *Eleventh Report of Maloga*, pp. 6, 11, 25; Matthews, Diary, entries 26 April 1886, 23 August 1886, *Twelfth Report of Maloga*, pp. 5, 8; *The Sportsman*, 16 June 1886, p. 8, 23 June 1886, p. 8; *Riverine Herald*, 28 March 1892, p. 2; *Sporting Globe*, 10 April 1926, p. 3; *Riverine Herald*, 7 April 1941, p. 3.

7 Matthews, Diary, entries 2 June 1884, 21 July 1884, 31 March 1885, *Tenth Report of Maloga*, pp. 11, 15, 35; Matthews, Diary entries 15 April 1885 and 24 June 1885, *Eleventh Report of Maloga*, pp. 7, 12; Matthews, Diary, entry 1 October 1886, *Twelfth Report of Maloga*, p. 10.

8 Matthews, Diary, entry 16 August 1874, Maloga from the Diaries and Mission Reports of Daniel Matthews, 1861–1873, Mitchell Library, MS A 3384; *Empire*, 26 August 1874, p. 3; *Second Report of the Maloga Aboriginal Mission School*, Haverfield and Co., Echuca, 1877, p. 3; *Bendigo Advertiser*, 28 December 1878, p. 1; *Fifth Report of Maloga*, pp. 5–6; *The Leader*, 13 August 1881, p. 2; Matthews, Diary, entry 18 February 1882, *Seventh Report of the Maloga Aboriginal Mission Station*, Colonial Publishing Society, Sydney, 1882, p. 7; Matthews to the Secretary, Victorian Board for the Protection of the Aborigines, AWA Page, 5 December 1884, National Archives of Australia, B313, 27; Matthews, Diary, entry 15 November 1887, *Thirteenth Report of the Maloga Aboriginal Mission*, Mackay & Foyster, Echuca, 1888, p. 17; McLisky, p. 267.

9 For a scrapbook containing advertisements, programs and reports of their concerts during this tour, held by the Beinecke Rare Book and Manuscript Library, Yale University Library, see https://brbl-zoom.library.yale.edu/viewer/16026937.

10 Doug Seroff, 'A Voice in the Wilderness: The Fisk Jubilee Singers' Civil Rights Tours of 1879–1882', *Popular Music and Society*, 25(1–2), 2001, pp. 131–32, 136, 141, 171–72.

11 Matthews, Diary, entry, 27 August 1886, *Twelfth Report of Maloga*, p. 8; *Riverine Herald*, 30 August 1886, p. 7; Frederick Loudin, 'From the Antipodes', 11 June 1888, quoted in Lynn Abbott and Doug Seroff, *Out of Sight: The Rise of African American Popular Music, 1889–1895*, University Press of Mississippi, Jackson, MS, 2002, p. 7; Seroff, p. 158.

12 Matthews, Diary, entries, 27 August 1886, 23 September 1886, *Twelfth Report of Maloga*, pp. 8–9; Goodchild, 'A Week at Maloga', *Riverine Herald*, 16 November 1886, p. 2; *The Argus*, 15 January 1887, p. 13; *Ovens and Murray Advertiser*, 26 February 1887, p. 4; Matthews, Diary, entry 15 November 1887, *Thirteenth Report of Maloga*, p. 17; Warrack, 'The Cummeragunja Aboriginal Station', *Numurkah Standard*, 19 August 1892, p. 2; Heather Bowe et al., *Yorta Yorta Language Heritage*, Department of Linguistics, Monash University, Melbourne, 1997, pp. 19–21; Seroff, p. 146; McLisky, p. 237.

13 McLisky provides a list of these employees in her thesis (p. 316).

14 McLisky, p. 239.

15 Matthews to Page, 20 April 1883, 2 May 1884, National Archives of Australia, B313, 26; Account Showing Income and Expenditure for the Year Ending 31 March 1885, *Tenth Report of Maloga*, p. 34; Matthews, Diary, entries 1 April 1885, 3 April 1885, 26 April 1885, 28 September 1885, 1 October 1885, 4 November 1885, 31 March 1886, *Eleventh Report of Maloga*, pp. 4–7, 16–17, 19, 27; Matthews, Diary, entry 23 September 1886, *Twelfth Report of Maloga*, p. 10; McLisky, pp. 242–43.

16 Matthews, Diary, entries 23 September 1886, 1 October 1886, *Twelfth Report of Maloga*, pp. 10–11; Thomas James to John Duncan St Clair MacLardy, Assistant Inspector of Schools, New South Wales, 11 October 1886, Cummeragunja (Aboriginal) School Administrative File, 1889–1910, New South Wales State Archives and Records, NRS 3829, Item No. [5/15619.2]; *Sydney Morning Herald*, 13 November 1886, p. 9; Andrew Menzies, Honorary Secretary, Aborigines Protection Association, to the Editor, 19 November 1886, *Sydney Morning Herald*, 23 November 1886, p. 9.

17 Matthews, Diary, entries 18 October 1886, 1 November 1886, 12 November 1886, *Twelfth Report of Maloga*, p. 11.

18 Other visitors at much the same time described Maloga in similar terms. See, for example, Splodger Astray, 'Twenty Years After', *Footscray Advertiser*, 2 April 1887, p. 2.

19 Goodchild, 'A Week at Maloga', *Riverine Herald*, 16 November 1886, p. 2, 17 November 1886, p. 2, 19 November 1886, p. 2; Keighley Goodchild (1851–88), https://echucahistoricalsociety.org.au/poetry-trail/keighley-goodchild/.

20 *Bendigo Advertiser*, 28 December 1878, p. 1; Goodchild, 'A Week at Maloga', *Riverine Herald*, 17 November 1886, p. 2, 19 November 1886, p. 2.

21 Goodchild, 'A Week at Maloga', 17 November 1886, p. 2.

22 Goodchild, 'A Week at Maloga', 19 November 1886, p. 2.

23 Matthews, Diary, entries 2 December 1886, 17 January 1887, 20 January 1887, 21 February 1887, *Twelfth Report of Maloga*, pp. 12–13.

24 *Sydney Morning Herald*, 31 March 1887, p. 7; Matthews, Diary, entries 1 April 1887, 6 April 1887, 10 May 1887, *Thirteenth Report of Maloga*, pp. 4, 7.

25 Matthews, Diary, entries 15 April 1887, 10 May 1887, 4 June 1887, 1 July 1887, *Thirteenth Report of Maloga*, pp. 5, 7, 9–10.

26 Petition, undated, *Riverine Herald*, 20 July 1887, p. 2.

27 *Riverine Herald*, 20 July 1887, p. 2. In his account of this occasion Matthews reckoned Jack Cooper, rather than Thomas James, had presented the address (Diary, entry 19 July 1887, *Thirteenth Report of Maloga*, p. 11).

28 Matthews, Diary, entries 22 August 1887, 26 September 1887, 26 October 1887, *Thirteenth Report of Maloga*, pp. 12–13, 15, 17.

29 John Atkinson to JM Chanter, 4 November 1887, and William Cooper to Chanter, 16 November 1887, Colonial Secretary's Correspondence, New South Wales State Archives and Records, NRS 905, Item No. [1/2667].

30 Cooper to Chanter, 16 November 1887; Heather Goodall, *Invasion to Embassy: Land in Aboriginal Politics in New South Wales, 1770–1972*, Black Books/Allen & Unwin, Sydney, 1996, p. 78.

31 *Sydney Morning Herald*, 5 November 1887, p. 7 (this occurred in question time, which was not reported in the parliamentary debates); W Wilson, Under-Secretary of New South Wales, to Chanter, 20 March 1888, reproduced in *Riverine Herald*, 26 March 1888, p. 2.

32 Matthews, Diary, entries 2 January 1888, 15 January 1888, *Thirteenth Report of Maloga*, p. 19; J Hay, undated minute on Edmund Fosbery, Chairman, New South Wales Aborigines Protection Board, to Under-Secretary, New South Wales Department of Public Education, 6 February 1888, Cummeragunja (Aboriginal) School Administrative File, 1889–1910, New South Wales State Archives and Records, NRS 3829, Item No. [5/15619.2].

33 Matthews, Diary, entries 15 January 1888, 3 February 1888, 6 February 1888, 8 March 1888, *Thirteenth Report of Maloga*, pp. 19–22.

34 Matthews, Diary, entries 18 February 1888, 20 March 1888, *Thirteenth Report of Maloga*, pp. 22–23.

35 Wilson to Chanter, 20 March 1888; *Riverine Herald*, 26 March 1888, p. 2; Matthews, Diary, entry 30 March 1888, *Thirteenth Report of Maloga*, pp. 23–24.

36 The reserve's name was spelt in several different ways, for example Cumeroogunja, Cumerogunja, Cumeroogunga and Cummeragunja. I have adopted the spelling that Cooper most often used.

37 *Riverine Herald*, 20 April 1888, p. 2; Matthews, Diary, entry 21 April 1888, *Fourteenth Report of the Maloga Aboriginal Mission*, Woodford Fawcett, London, [1889], p. 10; Cooper to Mrs WA Norman, 31 August 1940, Norman Family Papers, Mortlock Library, State Library of South Australia, PRG 422/31.

38 Matthews, Diary, entries 6 May 1888, 13 May 1888, 20 May 1888, 3 June 1888, *Fourteenth Report of Maloga*, pp. 11, 15, 17–18.

39 George Bellenger, Letter to the Editor, undated, *The Age*, 31 May 1888, p. 6; Matthews, Diary, entries 6 May 1888, 13 May 1888, 20 May 1888, 3 June 1888, 4 June 1888, 18 June 1888, 1 September 1888, *Fourteenth Report of Maloga*, pp. 11, 15, 18, 20, 23; Bellenger to Matthews, 4 June 1888, reproduced in *Fourteenth Report of Maloga*, p. 19.

Chapter 4: Cumeroogunga

1 His cause of death was recorded as inflammation, but he died before it was realised that there were cases of typhoid fever on the reserve (Death Certificate for Bartlett

Cooper, 10 January 1889, Victorian Registry of Births, Marriages and Deaths, 11720/1889).

2 *Australasian Sketcher with Pen and Pencil*, 11 February 1885, p. 17; *The Age*, 15 January 1887, p. 13, 17 December 1888, p. 2, 21 December 1888, p. 4, 24 December 1888, p. 5, 7 January 1889, p. 4; Death Certificate for Annie Cooper, 19 January 1889, New South Wales Registry of Births, Marriages and Deaths, 4852/1889; Hugh Anderson, Letter to the Editor, 25 January 1889, *Riverine Herald*, 29 January 1889, p. 2.

3 Dr George Eakins, Government Medical Officer, Moama and District, to the New South Wales Government Medical Adviser, Telegram, 25 January 1889, HN McLaurin, Medical Adviser, New South Wales Board of Health, Telegram to Eakins, 26 January 1899, Eakins to the New South Wales Chief Medical Adviser, 27 January 1889, New South Wales Legislative Assembly, *Votes and Proceedings*, 1889, vol. 5, Medical Attendants to Aborigines at Cumeroogunga Mission Station (Further Correspondence Respecting), p. 2; *Riverine Herald*, 28 January 1889, p. 2.

4 McLaurin to Secretary, New South Wales Aborigines Protection Board, 30 January 1889, A Berckelman, Secretary, New South Wales Aborigines Protection Board, to Superintendent of Police, Deniliquin, Telegram, 30 January 1889, Alfred Comber, Senior Sergeant of Police, Deniliquin, to Secretary of the Board of Health, Telegram, 31 January 1889, James Robertson, Senior Constable of Police, Moama, to Superintendent of Police, Deniliquin, 31 January 1889, Eakins to Secretary, New South Wales Board of Health, 1 February 1889, New South Wales Legislative Assembly, *Votes and Proceedings*, 1889, vol. 5, Medical Attendants to Aborigines at Cumeroogunga Mission Station (Further Correspondence Respecting), pp. 2–3; Eakins to Secretary, New South Wales Aborigines Protection Board, 1 February 1889, New South Wales Legislative Assembly, *Votes and Proceedings*, 1889, vol. 5, Medical Attendants to Aborigines at Cumeroogunga Mission Station (Correspondence &c., Relating to Appointment of), pp. 1–2.

5 Anderson, Letter to the Editor, 25 January 1889.

6 Superintendent of Police, Deniliquin, J Dowling Brown, to Chairman, New South Wales Aborigines Protection Board, 2 February 1889, Medical Attendants to Aborigines at Cumeroogunga Mission Station (Further Correspondence Respecting), p. 4; Anderson, Letter to the Editor, undated, *Riverine Herald*, 2 February 1889, p. 2.

7 George Bellenger, Letter to the Editor, 1 February 1889, *Riverine Herald*, 4 February 1889, p. 2; William Warren, Letter to the Editor, 2 February 1889, *Riverine Herald*, 4 February 1889, p. 2; Edmund Fosbery, Chairman of the New South Wales Aborigines Protection Board, Telegram to the Officer in charge of Police, Moama, 4 February 1889, Medical Attendants to Aborigines at Cumeroogunga Mission Station (Further Correspondence Respecting), p. 4; Eakins to the Aborigines Protection Board, 5 February 1889, Medical Attendants to Aborigines at Cumeroogunga Mission Station (Correspondence &c, Relating to Appointment of), p. 2; GE Ardill, Secretary, Aborigines Protection Association, to Berckelman, 9 February 1889, Medical Attendants to Aborigines at Cumeroogunga Mission Station (Correspondence &c, Relating to Appointment of), p. 2; James Robertson, Senior Constable of Police, Moama, to the Superintendent of Police, Deniliquin, 14 February 1889, Medical Attendants to Aborigines at Cumeroogunga Mission Station (Further Correspondence Respecting), p. 4.

8 Eakins to New South Wales Aborigines Protection Board, 10 February 1889, Medical Attendants to Aborigines at Cumeroogunga Mission Station (Correspondence &c, Relating to Appointment of), p. 2; Fosbery, Telegram to the Superintendent of Police, Deniliquin, 12 February 1889; Berckelman, Telegram to Bellenger, 13 February 1889, Medical Attendants to Aborigines at Cumeroogunga Mission Station (Correspondence &c, Relating to Appointment of), p. 3.

9 *Riverine Herald*, 13 February 1889, p. 2.

10 Bellenger, Letter to the Editor, undated [c. 15 February 1889], *Riverine Herald*, 19 February 1889, p. 2; Petition, 16 February 1889, Medical Attendants to Aborigines at Cumeroogunga Mission Station (Further Correspondence Respecting), p. 5.

11 Petition, 16 February 1889, Medical Attendants to Aborigines at Cumeroogunga Mission Station (Further Correspondence Respecting), p. 5.

12 Berckelman, Minute re the Petition, undated, Medical Attendants to Aborigines at Cumeroogunga Mission Station (Further Correspondence Respecting), p. 5.

13 Eakins to the Chairman of the New South Wales Aborigines Protection Board, 12 April 1889, Medical Attendants to Aborigines at Cumeroogunga Mission Station (Correspondence &c, Relating to Appointment of), pp. 3–4.

14 Medical Attendants to Aborigines at Cumeroogunga Mission Station (Correspondence &c, Relating to Appointment of), p. 1; Medical Attendants to Aborigines at Cumeroogunga Mission Station (Further Correspondence Respecting), p. 1; *Riverine Herald*, 10 April 1889, p. 2; Nancy Cato, *Mister Maloga: Daniel Matthews and His Mission, Murray River, 1864–1902*, University of Queensland Press, St Lucia, 1976, p. 251.

15 Among those who were to leave Cumeroogunga at this time, eventually for good, was Whyman McLean, whose wife was one of those Matthews had persuaded to leave Sydney and come to Maloga in 1881. McLean became a police tracker. For this period in his life, see the chapter devoted to him in Michael Bennett, *Pathfinders: A History of Aboriginal Trackers in NSW*, NewSouth, Sydney, 2020, pp. 119–42.

16 GW Carpenter, Chairman of the Council of the Aborigines Protection Association, and GE Ardill, General Secretary of the Aborigines Protection Association, to the Editor of *The Argus*, 26 May 1890, *The Argus*, 29 May 1890, p. 8; Bellenger, Manager's Report for Cumeroogunga, 1890, New South Wales Aborigines Protection Association, *The Rightful Owners, Our Duty to Them, Being the Annual Report of the Aborigines Protection Association for 1890*, p. 6; John G Treseder, Report of a Visit to the Aborigines Mission Stations at Coomeragunga and Warangesda, 13 July 1891, Australian Institute of Aborigines and Torres Strait Islander Studies Library, PMS 4606; Ardill, Report, 10 December 1891, New South Wales Aborigines Protection Association, *Our Black Brethren: Their Past, Present, and Future: Being the Annual Report of the Aborigines Protection Association for 1891*, p. 13; Report on Cumeroogunga, New South Wales Aborigines Protection Association, *Our Black Brethren*, pp. 4–6; *New South Wales Parliamentary Debates*, 18 February 1892, p. 5466; Warrack, 'The Cummeragunja Aboriginal Station', *Numurkah Standard*, 19 August 1892, p. 2; Daniel Matthews, *The Story of the Maloga Mission*, Rae Bros, Melbourne, 1893, pp. 13, 15; Diane Barwick, 'Coranderrk and Cumeroogunga: Pioneers and Policy', in T Scarlett Epstein and David H Penny (eds), *Opportunity and Response: Case Studies in Economic Development*, C Hurst, London, 1972, p. 50.

17 Treseder, Report; Suggestions, New South Wales Aborigines Protection Association, *Our Black Brethren*, pp. 10–11.
18 *New South Wales Parliamentary Debates*, 18 February 1892, pp. 5455–56.
19 New South Wales Aborigines Protection Association, *'The Heathen at Our Doors': Being the Annual Report of the New South Wales Aborigines Protection Association for 1893*, p. 4, and Supplement; Bruce Ferguson, Manager's Report for Cumeroogunga, New South Wales Aborigines Protection Association, *The Australian Aboriginal, Being the Annual Report of the New South Wales Aborigines Protection Association for 1894*, p. 12; Barwick, 'Coranderrk and Cumeroogunga', p. 52.
20 New South Wales Legislative Assembly, *Votes and Proceedings*, 1894–95, Aborigines Protection Board to the Principal Under Secretary of New South Wales, 1 March 1895, New South Wales Aborigines Protection Board, Report for 1894, p. 3, https://aiatsis.gov.au/sites/default/files/docs/digitised_collections/remove/22879.pdf.
21 Barwick, 'Coranderrk and Cumeroogunga', pp. 50–51; Cato, p. 309.
22 His place of residence was registered as Cumeroogunga on the certificate for his second marriage and the certificates for all but one of the children born of that marriage (see note 25 below) between 1893 and 1905. Newspaper reports also document his presence there in December 1894 and December 1900 (Cooper to the Editor, 28 December 1894, *Riverine Herald*, 31 December 1894, p. 2; *Riverine Herald*, 18 December 1900, p. 2).
23 On the birth certificates of his children Cooper's profession was described variously as shearer, fisherman and labourer, but mostly as the last of these.
24 Cooper, Letter to the Editor, undated, *Australian Worker*, 10 May 1939, p. 15; APA Burdeu to William Morley, 2 July 1939, Association for the Protection of Native Races Papers, University of Sydney Archives, Series 55, item 7; Diane Barwick, 'Cooper, William (1861–1941), *Australian Dictionary of Biography*, Australian National University, http://adb.anu.edu.au/biography/cooper-william-5773/text9787, published first in hardcopy 1981.
25 Death Certificate for Agnes Cooper, 8 April 1893, Victorian Registry of Births, Deaths and Marriages, 4211/1893; Birth Certificate for Jessie Cooper, 30 December 1893, New South Wales Registry of Births, Deaths and Marriages, 21237/1894; Birth Certificate for Ultimore Cooper, 8 March 1895, New South Wales Registry of Births, Deaths and Marriages, 14542/1895; Birth Certificate for Daniel Cooper, 15 April 1896, New South Wales Registry of Births, Deaths and Marriages, 14218/1896; Birth Certificate for Gillison Cooper, 2 July 1898, New South Wales Registry of Births, Deaths and Marriages, 23093/1898; Birth Certificate for Amy Cooper, 21 November 1900, New South Wales Registry of Births, Deaths and Marriages, 33118/1900; Birth Certificate for Lynch Cooper, 1 February 1905, New South Wales Registry of Births, Deaths and Marriages, 5318/1905; Birth Certificate for Maria Sarah (Sally) Cooper, 23 March 1907, Victorian Registry of Births, Deaths and Marriages, 8279/1907. Death Certificate for Ultimore Cooper, 9 May 1895, New South Wales Registry of Births, Deaths and Marriages, 5413/1895; Death Certificate for Kitty Cooper, 6 January 1900, New South Wales Registry of Births, Deaths and Marriages, 2342/1900; Barwick, 'Cooper'; Diane E Barwick, *Rebellion at Coranderrk*, edited by Laura E and Richard E Barwick, Aboriginal History Inc., Canberra, 1998, pp. 80, 161, 201 note 30.
26 Cooper to the Editor, 28 December 1894, *Riverine Herald*, 31 December 1894, p. 2; *Riverine Herald*, 18 December 1900, p. 2; *Riverine Herald*, 27 March 1905,

p. 3; Ronald Morgan, *Reminiscences of the Aboriginal Station at Cummeragunga and its Aboriginal People*, s.n., Melbourne, 1952, p. 3; Barwick, *Rebellion at Coranderrk*, p. 303; Giordano Nanni and Andrea James, *Coranderrk: We Will Show the Country*, Aboriginal Studies Press, Canberra, 2013, p. 106.

27 *Report of the New South Wales Board for the Protection of Aborigines for 1904*, p. 8; Barwick, 'Coranderrk and Cumeroogunga', p. 52; Heather Goodall, 'Land in Our Own Country: The Aboriginal Lands Rights Movement in South-Eastern Australia, 1860 to 1914', *Aboriginal History*, 14(1), 1990, p. 16.

28 *Report of the New South Wales Board for the Protection of Aborigines for 1903*, p. 5, *Report of the New South Wales Board for the Protection of Aborigines for 1905*, p. 6; *Report of the New South Wales Board for the Protection of Aborigines for 1906*, p. 7; *Report of the New South Wales Board for the Protection of Aborigines for 1907*, p. 9; New South Wales Board for the Protection of Aborigines to George Harris, 4 April 1908, quoted in *Riverine Herald*, 24 April 1908, p. 3; Barwick, 'Coranderrk and Cumeroogunga', p. 52; Heather Goodall, *Invasion to Embassy: Land in Aboriginal Politics in New South Wales, 1770–1972*, Black Books/Allen & Unwin, Sydney, 1996, p. 117.

29 *Daily Telegraph* (Sydney), 31 August 1904, p. 10; Letter to the Editor by 'Resident', undated, *Riverine Herald*, 12 July 1904, p. 2; *Riverine Herald*, 8 November 1905, p. 2, 15 March 1906, p. 3; *Report of the Board for the New South Wales Protection of Aborigines for 1906*, p. 3; *Riverine Herald*, 24 April 1908, p. 3; Letter to the Editor by 'Residents', undated, *Riverine Herald*, 4 May 1908, p. 2; Letter to the Editor by 'Your Reporter', 4 May 1908, *Riverine Herald*, 5 May 1908, p. 3; *Riverine Herald*, 17 June 1908, p. 2; *Report of the New South Wales Board for the Protection of Aborigines for 1908*, pp. 7–8.

30 Letter to the Editor by 'Several Sufferers', 13 March 1909, *Riverine Herald*, 17 March 1909, p. 2. The previous month the relationship between Thomas James and George Harris had begun to fray badly. This can largely be attributed to Harris's resentment of the influence James had among the people and his attempt to counter it by undermining Thomas's role as the principal teacher at the mission. For a discussion of this matter, see George Nelson and Robynne Nelson, *Dharmalan Dana: An Australian Aboriginal Man's 73-Year Search for the Story of his Aboriginal and Indian Ancestors*, Australian National University Press, Canberra, 2014, pp. 169–80, and Fiona Davis, *Australian Settler Colonialism and the Cummeragunja Aboriginal Station: Redrawing Boundaries*, Sussex Academic Press, Brighton, 2014, pp. 24–35.

31 Letter to the Editor by John Lewis, undated, *Riverine Herald*, 19 March 1909, p. 2; Letter to the Editor by 'One Sufferer', 20 March 1909, *Riverine Herald*, 23 March 1909, p. 2; AE Kinsey, Letter to the Editor, 10 April 1909, *Riverine Herald*, 15 April 1909, p. 3.

32 On the birth certificate for William and Agnes's last-born child in March 1907, the family is registered as living at Barmah. However, a newspaper report in May 1908 suggests he had returned to Cumeroogunga (*Riverine Herald*, 30 May 1908, p. 3), as did one two years later (*Riverine Herald*, 11 June 1910, p. 2).

33 Death Certificate for Agnes Cooper, 8 April 1909, Victoria Registry of Births, Deaths and Marriages, 1909/4211; *Riverine Herald*, Wednesday 14 April 1909, p. 2; *New South Wales Parliamentary Debates*, 15 December 1909, p. 4547; *Report of the New South Wales Board for the Protection of Aborigines for 1909*, p. 8; *Report of the New South Wales Board for the Protection of Aborigines for 1910*, p. 3; Goodall, *Invasion to Embassy*, p. 126.

34 'One Who Suffers' to the Editor, undated, *Riverine Herald*, 30 April 1910, p. 3.

35 New South Wales Aborigines Protection Act, 1909, https://aiatsis.gov.au/sites/default/files/docs/digitised_collections/remove/52303.pdf.

36 Goodall, *Invasion to Embassy*, pp. 118–19.

37 Report to the New South Wales Aborigines Protection Board, 3 August 1910, quoted in Nelson and Nelson, p. 177; *Riverine Herald*, 5 August 1910, p. 3.

38 *Report of the New South Wales Board for the Protection of Aborigines for 1911*, p. 9.

39 *Riverine Herald*, 14 May 1912, p. 3; JT Jenkins, Report for the New South Wales Aborigines Protection Board, 28 May 1912, New South Wales Archives and Records, NRS 905, Item No. [5/7204]; Thomas Garvin to the New South Wales Aborigines Protection Board, June 1912, New South Wales Archives and Records, NRS 905, Item No. [5/7165]; Aborigines Protection Amending Act 1915, https://aiatsis.gov.au/sites/default/files/docs/digitised_collections/remove/52290.pdf.

40 Goodall, *Invasion to Embassy*, pp. 122–23, 127.

41 Ibid., pp. 128–31.

42 *Riverine Herald*, 27 December 1910, p. 2; Death Certificate for Emma Dunolly, nee Cooper, 11 August 1913, New South Wales Registry of Births, Deaths and Marriages, 12763/1913; Attestation Paper for Person Enlisted for Service Abroad for Daniel Cooper, 8 February 1916, and Casualty Form—Active Service for Daniel Cooper, 31 May 1916 to 29 September 1917, National Archives of Australia, Series B2455, Cooper, Daniel, https://recordsearch.naa.gov.au/SearchNRetrieve/Interface/ViewImage.aspx?B=3409020; Death Certificate for Jessie Mann, nee Cooper, 7 December 1922, New South Wales Registry of Births, Deaths and Marriages, 15143/1922; JJ Maher, 'Failing at Stawell and Bendigo, Cooper Triumphs at Warracknabeal', *Sporting Globe*, 14 April 1926, p. 9; Helen Baillie to AP Elkin, 11 June [1933], AP Elkin Papers, University of Sydney Archives, P.130, Series 12, Item 134; Cooper to Mrs WA Norman, 30 July 1940, Norman Family Papers, Mortlock Library, State Library of South Australia, PRG 422/31; [APA Burdeu], Episodes of Interest in the Life of the Late William Cooper (Told by Himself), 30 June 1941, Norman Family Papers, Mortlock Library, State Library of South Australia, PRG 422/31); Alf Turner, personal communication, 14 November 2020.

43 Early in his career the *Riverine Herald* remarked: 'Lynch Cooper … comes from a native family that, during the last half century, established a reputation for prowess on the running track. His father and uncle were brilliant performers, who in their day put up many a record' (22 December 1926, p. 2).

44 *Sporting Globe*, 10 April 1926, p. 3; Maher, 'Failing'; *Referee*, 11 April 1928, p. 15; Maher, 'Gift Winner: Cooper's Pluck Tells', *Sporting Globe*, 11 April 1928, p. 1; *Weekly Times*, 2 March 1929, p. 66; Richard Broome, *Aboriginal Victorians: A History Since 1800*, Allen & Unwin, Sydney, 2005, pp. 269–70.

45 Marriage Certificate for William Cooper and Sarah Nelson, 4 August 1928, Victorian Registry of Births, Deaths and Marriages, 9525/1928; Baillie to Elkin, 11 June [1933]; Barwick, 'Cooper'; Diane Barwick, 'Aunty Ellen: The Pastor's Wife', in Isobel White et al. (eds), *Fighters and Singers: The Lives of Some Aboriginal Women*, George Allen & Unwin, Sydney, 1985, p. 187; Andrew Sayers, 'McRae, Tommy (1835–1901)', *Australian Dictionary of Biography*, http://adb.anu.edu.au/biography/mcrae-tommy-13074/text23649, published first in hardcopy 2005; Turner.

46 In 1940 Cooper recalled that he had moved to Melbourne in 1931 (Cooper to Norman, 30 July 1940), but the other historical evidence available suggests that this occurred two years later (Secretary of the Victorian Board for the Protection of the Aborigines, to AO Neville, 19 October 1933, State Records Office of Western Australia, AU WA S2030—cons993 1933/0368).

47 For a discussion of this matter, see John Murphy, 'Conditional Inclusion: Aborigines and Welfare Rights in Australia, 1900–47', *Australian Historical Studies*, 44(2), 2013, pp. 206–26.

48 Baillie to Elkin, 11 June [1933]; Barwick, 'Aunty Ellen', p. 189; Andrew Markus, *Blood from a Stone: William Cooper and the Australian Aborigines' League*, Allen & Unwin, Sydney, 1988, p. 9; Goodall, *Invasion to Embassy*, p. 186; Bain Attwood and Andrew Markus, *Thinking Black: William Cooper and the Australian Aborigines' League*, Aboriginal Studies Press, Canberra, 2004, p. 4.

49 They shifted several times during these years. According to the historical record, between July 1933 and November 1934 they were living at 120 Ballarat Road, Footscray (which seems to have been a boarding house); by March 1935 they had moved to 27 Federal Street, Footscray; in May 1937 they were living at 111 Ballarat Road, Footscray, but in the following month they moved to 43 Mackay Street, Yarraville, and remained there until January 1938; at this point they moved to 73 Southampton Street, Footscray, where they stayed until they left Melbourne in late 1940. At both 27 Federal Street and 111 Ballarat Road they might have been sharing a house with Cooper's daughter Sally and her husband (see David Rhodes Taryn Debney and Mark Grist, Maribyrnong Aboriginal Heritage Study: Report for City of Maribyrnong, December 1999, p. 106.

50 Marriage Certificate for Gillison Cooper and Elizabeth Young, 20 February 1930, Victorian Registry of Births, Deaths and Marriages, 416/1930; *Census of the Commonwealth of Australia 30 June 1933*, 1, p. 908; *The Herald* (Melbourne), 15 March 1937, p. 3; Inspector Roland S Browne to the Director, Commonwealth Investigation Branch, 5 January 1938, National Archives of Australia, A431, 1949/1591; Mavis Thorpe Clark, *Pastor Doug: The Story of Sir Douglas Nicholls, Aboriginal Leader*, Lansdowne Press, Melbourne, 1965, pp. 87–88; Rhodes, Debney and Grist, p. 106.

51 At the point Cooper began receiving the war pension in December 1917, it amounted to 14 shillings a fortnight (War Pension Statement for William Cooper, 14 December 1917, National Archives of Australia, Series B2455, Cooper, Daniel, https://recordsearch.naa.gov.au/SearchNRetrieve/Interface/ViewImage. aspx?B=3409020), while the old age pension in the period 1933–41 averaged less than £1 a week (https://guides.dss.gov.au/guide-social-security-law/5/2/2/10).

52 Baillie to Elkin, 11 June [1933]; Browne to the Director, 5 January 1938; [Burdeu], Episodes; Clark, p. 87; Turner; David Jago, personal communication, 17 January 2021.

Chapter 5: Petitioning the King

1 *Riverine Herald*, 10 October 1919, p. 2; George E Nelson, 'James, Thomas Shadrach (1859–1946)', *Australian Dictionary of Biography*, National Centre of Biography, Australian National University, http://adb.anu.edu.au/biography/james-thomas-shadrach-10610/text18855, published first in hardcopy 1996; Fiona Davis,

Colouring within the Lines: Settler Colonialism and the Cummeragunja Aboriginal Station, 1888–1960s, PhD thesis, University of Melbourne, 2010, pp. 90–91, 95.

2 *The Sun* (Melbourne), 22 February 1929, p. 8; Shadrach James, Letter to the Editor, undated, *Australian Worker*, 10 July 1929, p. 2.

3 *The Sun* (Melbourne), 12 April 1929, p. 18; James, 'The Wrongs of the Australian Aboriginal', *Australian Intercollegian,* 1 May 1929, pp. 64–65; James, Letter to *Australian Worker*.

4 *The Sun* (Melbourne), 12 April 1929, p. 18; James, 'The Wrongs', p. 64.

5 *The Sun* (Melbourne), 12 April 1929, p. 18; *The Herald* (Melbourne), 12 April 1929, p. 25; James, 'The Wrongs', p. 63; James, Letter to *Australian Worker*.

6 *The Sun* (Melbourne), 12 April 1929, p. 18; James, 'The Wrongs', p. 64; James, Letter to *Australian Worker*. It is apparent that James was drawing here on his own experience: see his letters to the Secretary of the Victorian Board for the Protection of the Aborigines, AE Parker, 16 February 1929, 29 April 1929, National Archives of Australia, B337, 362.

7 *The Sun* (Melbourne), 12 April 1929, p. 18; James, 'The Wrongs', p. 63; James, Letter to *Australian Worker*.

8 Enclosure [1911] in Memorandum of 30 March 1928, National Archives of Australia, A1, 1936/6595; Archdeacon CEC Lefroy, Evidence, Report of the Royal Commission on the Constitution, Together with Appendices and Index, Government Printer, Canberra, 1929, pp. 478–81; James, 'The Wrongs'; James, Letter to *Australian Worker*; *The Herald*, 13 February 1930, p. 17.

9 James, 'The Wrongs'; James, Letter to *Australian Worker*.

10 Shadrach James, 'Help My People! Native Preacher's Strong Plea: Case for the Aborigines', *The Herald* (Melbourne), 24 March 1930, p. 3.

11 *The Sun* (Melbourne), 12 April 1929, p. 18; James, 'Help My People'; Andrew Markus, *Governing Savages*, Allen & Unwin, Sydney, 1990, pp. 161–63.

12 *The Sun* (Melbourne), 12 April 1929, p. 18.

13 *The Herald* (Melbourne), 12 April 1929, p. 25; James, 'The Wrongs'; James, Letter to *Australian Worker*; James, 'Help My People'.

14 *The Age*, 3 February 1933, p. 10; William Cooper, Letter to the Editor, undated, *The Age*, 16 March 1933, p. 10; Cooper to Rev. Ernest Gribble, 10 July 1933, ERB Gribble Papers, Australian Institute of Aboriginal and Torres Strait Islander Studies, MS 1515, Box 11, Item 66 (henceforth Gribble Papers); Gribble to Cooper, 30 December 1933, Australian Board of Missions, Further Records, 1873–1978, Mitchell Library, MLMSS 4503, Add-on 1822, Box 9, Folder 2. For a splendid biography of Ernest Gribble, see Christine Halse, *A Terribly Wild Man*, Allen & Unwin, Sydney, 2002.

15 My contention here rests on the differences between the grammar in this letter and that in letters Cooper wrote in his own hand to Gribble in the next few months.

16 Cooper, Letter, *The Age,* 16 March 1933.

17 In making this argument Cooper might have recalled the visits of more than one phrenologist to Maloga and Cumeroogunga, who measured the heads of several of his kin (see, for example, *Riverine Herald*, 16 June 1892, p. 2).

18 Cooper, Letter, *The Age,* 16 March 1933.

19 Ibid.

20 Helen Baillie to Father Farnham Maynard, 27 April 1933, St Peter's Eastern Hill
    Papers, State Library Victoria, MS 15811, Box 19, Folder 1; Cooper to Gribble,
    10 July 1933.
21 Baillie to Maynard, 27 April 1933, 1 October [1933], 7 October [1933], St Peter's
    Eastern Hill Papers, State Library Victoria, MS 15811, Box 19, Folder 1; Baillie
    to AP Elkin, 2 June 193[3], AP Elkin Papers, University of Sydney Archives,
    P.130 (henceforth Elkin Papers), Series 12, Item 146; Baillie to Elkin, 11 June
    [1933], Elkin Papers, Series 12, Item 124; Rev. William Morley to Sir John
    Harris, Secretary, Anti-Slavery Society, 1 April 1935, Papers of the Anti-Slavery
    Society, Weston Library, University of Oxford, MSS. Brit. Emp. s. 22 (henceforth
    Papers of the Anti-Slavery Society), G379; APA Burdeu to Harris, 11 March
    1936, Papers of the Anti-Slavery Society, G378; *The Aborigines' Protector*, 1(2),
    1936, p. 22; Morley to Rev. LH Purnell, 14 July 1938, Elkin Papers, Series 12,
    Item 149.
22 I say *seems* because the relevant page of the source I am relying upon here is
    missing.
23 Cooper to Gribble, 10 July 1933.
24 For this organisation, see Heather Goodall, *Invasion to Embassy: Land in Aboriginal
    Politics in New South Wales, 1770–1972*, Black Books/Allen & Unwin, Sydney,
    1996, Chapter 12, and John Maynard, *Fight for Liberty and Freedom: The Origins of
    Australian Aboriginal Activism*, Aboriginal Studies Press, Canberra, 2007.
25 This organisation awaits a thorough study, but see Anna Haebich, *For Their
    Own Good: Aborigines and Government in the Southwest of Western Australia,
    1900–1940*, University of Western Australia Press, Perth, 1988, pp. 269–76,
    and George Ganitis, 'Early Aboriginal Civil Resistance: The Untold Story of
    William Harris', *Overland*, 1 November 2018, https://overland.org.au/2018/11/
    early-aboriginal-civil-resistance-in-wa-the-untold-story-of-william-harris/.
26 For an overview of this earlier protest, see the introduction to Bain Attwood and
    Andrew Markus, *The Struggle for Aboriginal Rights: A Documentary History*, Allen &
    Unwin, Sydney, 1999, and Part I.
27 See Markus, *Governing Savages*, Chapter 11, and my *Rights for Aborigines*, Allen &
    Unwin, Sydney, 2003, Chapter 4.
28 At least one historian, Russell McGregor, has argued that the petition was later
    overshadowed in Cooper's political work by what he calls 'the grander issues of
    the uplift of the Aboriginal race and the granting of citizenship rights' ('Protest and
    Progress: Aboriginal Activism in the 1930s', *Australian Historical Studies*, 25(101),
    1993, p. 567). But this overlooks the fact that it continued to occupy a significant
    place in Cooper's heart and mind—indeed, we might say it preoccupied him—
    and that he pressed its main claim repeatedly throughout the remainder of his
    life. In Chapter 8 I argue that McGregor has misunderstood the nature of the
    parliamentary representation that Cooper was seeking.
29 Petition, National Archives of Australia, A431, 1949/1591; *The Herald* (Melbourne),
    15 September 1933, p. 2.
30 In January 1938, shortly before the Day of Mourning, Mannix expressed the
    opinion that 'Australia was beginning to make reparation to the aborigines for all
    the wrongs, wittingly or unwittingly, they had inflicted upon them' (*The Argus*,
    24 January 1938, p. 4; Brenda Niall, *Mannix*, Text Publishing, Melbourne, 2015,
    pp. 303–04, 400 note 29).

31 Baillie to Elkin, 11 June [1933]; Burdeu to Mrs WA Norman, 23 September 1940, Norman Family Papers, Mortlock Library, State Library of South Australia, PRG 422/31.

32 None of these letters seems to have survived, but there appears to be little doubt that Cooper wrote them as newspapers in cities other than Melbourne ran articles about the petition on the same day as the Melbourne *Herald* did.

33 *The Herald* (Melbourne), 15 September 1933, p. 2.

34 Baillie to Elkin, 11 June [1933]; *The Herald* (Melbourne), 15 September 1933, p. 2; Cooper to the Victorian Board of Protection for the Aborigines, undated [19 September 1933], National Archives of Australia, B337, 187; Cooper to Prime Minister Joseph Lyons, 25 July 1934, National Archives of Australia, A461, A 300/1 Part 2.

35 Cooper's use of this notion probably owed something to a famous 1912 book, *Thinking Black*, which was written by a Scottish evangelical missionary, Daniel Crawford, who worked in Central Africa. Crawford made a lecture tour of Australasia in 1914 and received considerable attention (see, for example, *The Leader* [Melbourne], 29 August 1914, p. 25), and his notion was picked up by a Methodist missionary in northern Australia and used in an article he wrote for the Melbourne *Herald* in 1933 (HE Read, 'Thinking Black with the Abos', 30 September 1933, p. 21). For a discussion of Crawford's book, see Mark S Sweetnam, 'Dan Crawford, *Thinking Black*, and the Challenge of a Missionary Canon', *Journal of Ecclesiastical History*, 38(4), 2007, pp. 705–25.

36 Cooper to the Premier, New South Wales, Bertram Stevens, 19 February 1936, New South Wales Archives and Records, NRS 12060, File No. [12/8749]; Cooper to the Minister for the Interior, Thomas Paterson, 18 February 1937, National Archives of Australia, A659, 1940/1/858; Cooper to Paterson, 25 June 1937, National Archives of Australia, A659, 1940/1/858; Cooper to the Minister of the Interior, John McEwen, 26 July 1938, National Archives of Australia, A659, 1940/1/858; Cooper to McEwen, 17 December 1938, National Archives of Australia, A659, 1940/1/858.

37 This petition is reproduced in Chiara Gamboz, Australian Indigenous Petitions: Emergence and Negotiations of Indigenous Authorship and Writings, PhD thesis, University of New South Wales, 2012, http://unsworks.unsw.edu.au/fapi/datastream/unsworks:10983/SOURCE01, p. 181; Gamboz provides an analysis of it and an account of its reception at pp. 179–82.

38 The sources we have for Cooper's political work are almost exclusively official, consisting of the letters he wrote to government, missionaries and newspapers. He undoubtedly wrote to his fellow Aboriginal advocates, but barely any of those letters have survived.

39 During this period Anderson preached and lectured from time to time in towns such as Benalla. His account of the history of Aboriginal people since contact and their rights to land echoed that of other Maloga men such as Cooper. For example, in March 1905 he stated: 'When the white man came first to Australia he did not knock on the blackfellow's door. He simply pushed it open and gave old Billy and Jimmy—short names for the black man—a kick and told them to move along … As a result the blacks to-day have nothing to call their own … The blackfellow was contented till the white man disturbed him. God placed the black people in this land and gave it to them as their own possession … This land is their possession, by

right. It was given to them by the great God in all' (*North Eastern Ensign* [Benalla], 24 March 1905, p. 3).

40 *Goulburn Herald*, 21 November 1889, p. 2; *Sydney Morning Herald*, 15 November 1927, p. 11; *Cinesound Review*, 100, 29 September 1933, 'Australian Royalty Pleads for His People: Burraga, chief of Aboriginal Thirroul tribe, to petition the King for blacks' representation in Federal Parliament', Screensound (Melbourne), transcript in Bain Attwood and Andrew Markus, *Thinking Black: William Cooper and the Australian Aborigines' League*, Aboriginal Studies Press, Canberra, 2004, p. 36 (the newsreel itself can be viewed at https://www.burraga.org/about); Maynard, *Fight for Liberty*, pp. 97–98; Heather Goodall and Alison Cadzow, *Rivers and Resilience: Aboriginal People on Sydney's Georges River*, UNSW Press, Sydney, 2009, pp. 1, 3–4, 109–10, 113–15, 122, 137, 139.

41 *Daily Telegraph* (Sydney), 25 July 1924, p. 5; John A Williams, *Politics of the New Zealand Maori: Protest and Cooperation, 1891–1909*, Auckland University Press, Auckland, 1969, Chapter 4; Angela Ballara, 'Rātana, Tahupōtiki Wiremu', *Dictionary of New Zealand Biography*, first published in 1996; Te Ara: The Encyclopedia of New Zealand, https://teara.govt.nz/en/biographies/3r4/ratana-tahupotiki-wiremu; Jim Miller, 'Petitioning the Great White Mother: First Nations Organizations and Lobbying in London', in his *Reflections on Native–Newcomer Relations: Selected Essays*, University of Toronto Press, Toronto, 2004, pp. 217–41; Michael Belgrave, '"We rejoice to honour the Queen, for she is a good woman, who cares for the Māori race": Loyalty and Protest in Māori Politics in Nineteenth-Century New Zealand', in Sarah Carter and Maria Nugent (eds), *Mistress of Everything: Queen Victoria in Indigenous Worlds*, Manchester University Press, Manchester, 2016, pp. 54–77.

42 The central text of this petition can be found in Michael Roe, 'A Model Aboriginal State', *Aboriginal History*, 10(1), 1986, pp. 40–42.

43 *The Sun* (Melbourne), 22 February 1929, p. 8; Robert Foster, 'Contested Destinies: Aboriginal Advocacy in South Australia's Interwar Years', *Aboriginal History*, 42, 2018, p. 74.

44 Edmund S Morgan, *Inventing the People: The Rise of Popular Sovereignty in England and America*, WW Norton & Company, New York, 1988, p. 223; Ravi de Costa, 'Identity, Authority and the Moral Worlds of Indigenous Petitions', *Comparative Studies in Society and History*, 48(3), 2006, pp. 669–70.

45 *Labor Daily*, 16 September 1933, p. 9; *Australian Worker*, 20 September 1933, p. 10; Cooper to Gribble, 31 October 1933, Gribble Papers; *The Herald* (Melbourne), 28 November 1933, p. 4; Cooper to Norman Makin, 19 March 1934, National Archives of Australia, A431, 1949/1591; Notes of Deputation representing Aborigines and various associations interested in Aboriginal welfare to the Minister for the Interior, Thomas Paterson, Melbourne, 23 January 1935, National Archives of Australia, A1, 1935/3951; Ravi de Costa, *A Higher Authority: Indigenous Transnationalism and Australia*, UNSW Press, Sydney, 2006, pp. 49, 60.

46 Cooper to Paterson, 16 June 1937, National Archives of Australia, A659, 1940/1/858.

47 There was a similarly widespread belief among Indigenous people in New Zealand, Canada, the Cape Colony and other British colonies that the key agreements struck with them during the colonisation of their territories had been made by Queen Victoria herself: Maria Nugent and Sarah Carter, 'Introduction: Indigenous

Histories, Settler Colonies and Queen Victoria', in Carter and Nugent (eds), *Mistress of Everything*, p. 1.

48 Joe Anderson to Elkin, 16 January 1936, Elkin Papers, Series 12, Item 144; Cooper to Norman, 21 August 1940, Norman Family Papers, Mortlock Library, State Library of South Australia, PRG 422/31; Goodall, *Invasion to Embassy*, p. 103; Bain Attwood, *Rights for Aborigines*, Allen & Unwin, Sydney, 2003, pp. 15–17; Maria Nugent, 'The Politics of Memory and the Memory of Politics: Australian Aboriginal Interpretations of Queen Victoria, 1881–2011', in Carter and Nugent (eds), *Mistress of Everything*, pp. 100–07.

49 de Costa, 'Identity', p. 674.

50 *Australian Worker*, 20 September 1933, p. 10.

51 Cooper to the Victorian Board of Protection for Aborigines, undated [19 September 1933]; Cooper to the Western Australian Board for the Protection of Aborigines, undated [19 September 1933], State Records Office of Western Australia, AU WA S2030—cons993 1933/0368; Constable FR Grinter to Chief Commissioner of Police, 13 October 1933, National Archives of Australia, B337, 187; AO Neville to the Secretary of the Victorian Board for the Protection of the Aborigines, 27 September 1933, AU WA S2030—cons993 1933/0368; Cooper to the Western Australian Board for the Protection of Aborigines, 16 October 1933, State Records Office of Western Australia, AU WA S2030—cons993 1933/0368; Secretary of the Victorian Board for the Protection of the Aborigines to Neville, 19 October 1933, State Records Office of Western Australia, AU WA S2030—cons993 1933/0368; Cooper to Lyons, 23 October 1933 (two letters), National Archives of Australia, A431, 1949/1591; JA Carrodus to JW Bleakley, 21 February 1934, National Archives of Australia, A431, 1949/1591; Victorian Under Secretary to Chief Protector of Aboriginals, South Australia, 11 June 1936, Public Record Office, VPRS 3992/P, unit 2557, item L3734.

52 Cooper to Gribble, 26 October 1933, Gribble Papers; Cooper to the Minister for the Interior, JA Perkins, 21 November 1933, National Archives of Australia, A431, 1949/1591; Makin to Cooper, 4 December 1933, Gribble Papers; Cooper to Gribble, 17 December 1933, Gribble Papers; Bleakley to Neville, 15 January 1934, State Records Office of Western Australia, AU WA S2030—cons993 1933/0368; Cooper to Makin, 19 March 1934; Minutes of the Meetings of the New South Wales Aborigines Protection Board, 13 April 1934, New South Wales Archives and Records, NRS 2, Item No. [4/7126]; David Lowe, 'Makin, Norman John (1889–1982)', *Australian Dictionary of Biography*, http://adb.anu.edu.au/biography/makin-norman-john-14673/text25810, published first in hardcopy 2012; Foster, p. 83.

53 Cooper to Gribble, 26 October 1933; Cooper to Gribble, 31 October 1933; Cooper to Gribble, 17 December 1933; Baillie to Norman Harris, 15 February 1934, Elkin Papers, Series 12, Item 144; Carrodus to Bleakley, 21 February 1934; Minutes of the Meetings of the New South Wales Aborigines Protection Board, 13 March 1935, New South Wales Archives and Records, NRS 2, Item No. [4/7126].

54 Cooper to Gribble, 10 July 1933; Cooper to Gribble, 17 December 1933; Cooper to Gribble, 29 January 1934, Gribble Papers; Cooper to Perkins, 7 May 1934, National Archives of Australia, A431, 1949/1591; Cooper to Lyons, 20 June 1934, National Archives of Australia, A431, 1949/1591; Cooper to Lyons, 25 July 1934; Cooper, Circular Letter, 22 September 1934, Australian Board of Missions,

Further Records, 1873–1978, Mitchell Library, MLMSS 4503, Add-on 1822, Box 8, Folder 4.

55 Cooper, Circular Letter, undated [September or October 1934], Gribble Papers; Cooper, Letter to the Editor, undated, *Argus*, 5 December 1934, p. 10.

56 One press report claimed there were eight (*The Herald* [Melbourne], 23 January 1935, p. 5), while Morley reckoned there were about fourteen (Morley to Harris, 1 April 1935).

57 Notes of Deputation, 23 January 1935; *The Age*, 24 January 1935, p. 10; *The Argus*, 24 January 1935, p. 14; *Labor Daily*, 24 January 1935, p. 8; Morley to Harris, 1 April 1935.

58 Notes of Deputation, 23 January 1935; *Sydney Morning Herald*, 24 January 1935, p. 11; Morley to Harris, 1 April 1935.

59 *The Argus*, 24 January 1935, p. 14; Carrodus, Memorandum on Deputation representing aboriginals, which waited on the Minister on 23 January 1935, 4 April 1935, National Archives of Australia, A1, 1935/3951.

60 Cooper to Paterson, 20 May 1935, National Archives of Australia, A1, 1935/3951; Paterson to Cooper, 29 May 1935, National Archives of Australia, A1, 1935/3951.

61 Cooper to Gribble, 14 June 1935, Australian Board of Missions, Further Records, 1873–1978, Mitchell Library, MLMSS 4503, Add-on 1822, Box 8, Folder 4; *Commonwealth Parliamentary Debates*, 26 September 1935, p. 278, https://parlinfo. aph.gov.au/parlInfo/download/hansard80/hansardr80/1935-09-26/toc_pdf/ 19350926_reps_14_147.pdf;fileType=application%2Fpdf#search=%221930s%20 1935%22.

Chapter 6: The League

1 See, for example, Wayne Atkinson, 'The Schools of Human Experience', in Rachel Perkins and Marcia Langton (eds), *First Australians: An Illustrated History*, Miegunyah Press, Melbourne, 2008, p. 294, who uses both these names in referring to Cooper's organisation.

2 For a brief account of Nicholls' life, see Richard Broome, 'Nicholls, Sir Douglas Ralph (Doug) (1906–1988)', *Australian Dictionary of Biography*, National Centre of Biography, Australian National University, https://adb.anu.edu.au/biography/ nicholls-sir-douglas-ralph-doug-14920/text26109, published first in hardcopy 2012.

3 For a recent history of the Victorian Aborigines Advancement League, see Richard Broome, *Fighting Hard: The Victorian Aborigines Advancement League*, Aboriginal Studies Press, Canberra, 2015.

4 See, for example, Jack Horner and Marcia Langton, 'The Day of Mourning', in Bill Gammage and Peter Spearritt (eds), *Australians 1938*, Fairfax, Syme & Weldon, Sydney, 1987, p. 33, and Bain Attwood and Andrew Markus, *Thinking Black: William Cooper and the Australian Aborigines' League*, Aboriginal Studies Press, Canberra, 2004, p. 11.

5 This was Theresa Clements (the mother of Margaret Tucker, later to become one of the League's vice-presidents), who was protesting against being charged with vagrancy merely because she had been playing in an Aboriginal gumleaf band in the streets of Melbourne (*The Herald* [Melbourne], 5 April 1935, p. 18).

6 William Cooper to Rev. Ernest Gribble, 10 July 1933, ERB Gribble Papers, Australian Institute of Aboriginal and Torres Strait Islander Studies, MS 1515,

Box 11, Item 66 (henceforth Gribble Papers); Cooper to Gribble, 26 October 1933, Gribble Papers; Cooper, Circular letter, November 1934, Gribble Papers; Cooper, Letter to the Editor, 3 December 1934, *The Argus*, 5 December 1934, p. 10; Cooper to Gribble, 21 March 1935, Gribble Papers; William Cooper, Real Australian Aboriginal Association, to the Minister for the Interior, Thomas Paterson, 1 April 1935, National Archives of Australia, A431, 1949/1591; Cooper to Paterson, 8 April 1935, National Archives of Australia, A431, 1949/1591; Cooper to Paterson, 20 May 1935, National Archives of Australia, A1, 1935/3951; Cooper to Paterson, 29 May 1935, National Archives of Australia, A1, 1935/3951; Cooper to Gribble, undated, c. June 1935, Gribble Papers; Cooper to Paterson, June 1935, National Archives of Australia, A1, 1935/3951; Cooper to Paterson, 10 July 1935, National Archives of Australia, A1, 1935/3951.

7 Helen Baillie to JA Perkins, 16 March 1933, 3 April 1933, National Archives of Australia, A659, 1940/1/524; Baillie to Father Farnham Maynard, 29 June [1933], 1 October [1933], 7 October [1933], St Peter's Eastern Hill Papers, State Library Victoria, MS 15811 (henceforth St Peter's Eastern Hill Papers), Box 19, Folder 1; Helen Baillie, *The Call of the Aboriginal*, Fraser & Morphet, Melbourne, 193[3], pp. 2–3; Statement of Aboriginal Fellowship Group, [May 1933], Papers of the Anti-Slavery Society, Weston Library, University of Oxford, MSS. Brit. Emp. s. 22 (henceforth Papers of the Anti-Slavery Society), G382; Baillie to Maynard, 2 February [1935], St Peter's Eastern Hill Papers, Box 20, Folder 1; Baillie to Maynard, 14 April [1936], St Peter's Eastern Hill Papers, Box 21, Folder 8; Baillie to Rev. William Morley, 25 February 1936, AP Elkin Papers, University of Sydney Archives, P.130 (henceforth Elkin Papers), Series 12, Item 148; Claire McLisky, Settlers on a Mission: Power and Subjectivity in the Lives of Daniel and Janet Matthews, PhD thesis, University of Melbourne, 2008, p. 213.

8 Baillie to AP Elkin, 13 May 1933, Elkin Papers, Series 12, Item 124; Travers Buxton, 18 September 1933, Papers of the Anti-Slavery Society, G382; Baillie to Perkins, 4 October 1933, National Archives of Australia, A431, 1948/961; Baillie to Elkin, 17 October 1933, Elkin Papers, Series 12, Item 124; Baillie to Elkin, 2 June 1934, Elkin Papers, Series 12, Item 146; Baillie to Joseph Lyons, 2 December 1937, National Archives of Australia, A659, 1940/1/524.

9 Baillie, *The Call*, pp. 3–4, 10, Baillie, 'The Right to Live: Conditions of Our Native Race', *Woman Today*, 1(1), 1936, p. 13; 1(2), 1936, p. 5.

10 Norman Harris to Baillie, 15 February 1934, Elkin Papers, Series 12, Item 144; Baillie to Morley, 25 February 1936; Baillie, 'The Great Need of Trained Woman Protectors for the Aboriginal and Half-Caste Women and Children of Australia', paper written for British Commonwealth League Conference, February 1937, National Archives of Australia, A659, 1940/1/524; Baillie to Harris, 24 November 1937, Papers of the Anti-Slavery Society, G379; Morley to AN Brown, 14 November 1937, AN Brown Papers, State Library Victoria, MS 9212, Box 3654, Folder 1j.

11 Baillie to Maynard, 27 April 1933, 7 October [1933], St Peter's Eastern Hill Papers, Box 19, Folder 1; Baillie to Elkin, 11 June [1933], Elkin Papers, Series 12, Item 124; NM (Micklem) Morley to Cooper, 6 November 1934, Australian Board of Missions, Further Records, 1873–1978, Mitchell Library, MLMSS 4503, Add-on 1822, Box 8, Folder 4; Baillie to Sir John Harris, 1 May 1935, Papers of the Anti-Slavery Society, G377; Baillie to Maynard, 3 June 1936, St Peter's Eastern Hill Papers, Box 21, Folder 8.

12 Baillie, *The Call*, p. 10; Baillie to Secretary, New South Wales Trades and Labour Council, 27 December 1939, Tom and Mary Wright Papers, Noel Butlin Archives Centre, Australian National University, MS Z267/8.

13 Margaret Tucker, 'My Initiation into What? The Unknown', undated, cited in Jennifer Jones, *Black Writers, White Editors: Episodes of Collaboration and Compromise in Australian Publishing History*, Australian Scholarly Publishing, Melbourne, 2009, p. 140.

14 Joanne Bach, 'Morgan, Anna Euphemia (1874–1935)', Australian Dictionary of Biography, National Centre of Biography, Australian National University, http:// adb.anu.edu.au/biography/morgan-anna-euphemia-13108/text23715, published first in hardcopy 2005.

15 *The Worker*, 27 June 1912, p. 27; Caleb Morgan, Letter to the Editor, undated, *The Worker*, 18 July 1912, p. 23; New South Wales Aborigines Protection Board, Minutes of Meetings, 4 February 1927, New South Wales Archives and Records, NRS-3, Item No. [4/7126]; Helen Baillie, 'Aboriginal Woman Speaks for her Race', *Woman Today*, 1(5), 1936, pp. 6, 24.

16 The story of this period in their lives can be gleaned from these sources: *Healesville and Yarra Glen Guardian*, 30 August 1930, p. 1, 13 September 1930, p. 1, 11 April 1931, p. 1, 9 May 1931, p. 1, 15 April 1933, p. 2; Anna Morgan to Anna White, 17 October 1933, 21 August 1934, AWR Vroland Papers, National Library of Australia, MS 3991, Box 3, Folder 20 (henceforth Vroland Papers); *Herald* (Melbourne), 24 January 1935, p. 10.

17 Anna Morgan, 'Under the Black Flag', *Labor Call*, 20 September 1934, p. 3.

18 This part of Morgan's account is confirmed by a contemporary newspaper report of the court case: *Riverine Herald*, 23 January 1909, p. 2.

19 Morgan, 'Under the Black Flag'.

20 *The Herald* (Melbourne), 23 January 1935, p. 5; *The Age*, 24 January 1935, p. 10.

21 Morgan to White, 13 October 1934, Vroland Papers; *The Herald* (Melbourne), 24 January 1935, p. 10.

22 Morgan to White, 17 October 1933, 21 August 1934, Vroland Papers; Morgan, 'Under the Black Flag'; editor's note, *Labor Call*, 20 September 1934, p. 3; editor's note, *Working Woman*, 5(3), 1934, p. 10; *The Age*, 24 January 1935, p. 10.

23 In August 1940, a few months before he retired as the League's secretary, Cooper reckoned he had spent more than £100 of his own money on the cause, which amounts to approximately $8500 in today's money (Cooper to Mrs WA Norman, 21 August 1940, Norman Family Papers, Mortlock Library, State Library of South Australia, PRG 422/31; https://www.thomblake.com.au/secondary/hisdata/ calculate.php).

24 Cooper to Paterson, 11 June 1935, National Archives of Australia, A1, 1935/3951; Paterson to Cooper, 17 June 1935, National Archives of Australia, A1, 1935/3951.

25 It seems reasonable to conclude, on the basis of its style, that a letter in Cooper's name that appeared in *Labor Call* on 24 October 1935 (p. 10) was written by Burdeu.

26 The Church of Christ has had several Aboriginal pastors over the years. The others include Cecil Grant, Frank Roberts snr and Frank Roberts jnr. This cannot be a coincidence.

27 After Burdeu died (aged only fifty-nine), the Aboriginal people of Melbourne held a memorial service for him, with Nicholls presiding (Death Certificate for Burdeu,

9 August 1942, Victorian Registry of Births, Deaths and Marriages, 1942/27444; *Argus*, 12 August 1942, p. 3).

28 *The Argus*, 12 August 1937, p. 4; APA Burdeu to GC Gollan, Chief Secretary of New South Wales, 19 March 1939, New South Wales Archives and Records, NRS 905, Item No. [12/7584.1]; Burdeu to Elkin, 2 July 1941, 13 August 1941, Elkin Papers, Series 12, Item 134; Baillie, 'Some Recollections of Mr APA Burdeu', undated, Elkin Papers, Series 12, Item 134; Obituary for APA Burdeu, *Australian Christian*, 44(33), 1941, p. 395; Graeme Chapman, *Ballarat Churches of Christ, 1859–1993: A History*, Churches of Christ Theological College, Melbourne, 1994, p. 247.

29 Field Service for Cyril Burdeu, National Archives of Australia, B2455, Burdeu, CA, https://recordsearch.naa.gov.au/SearchNRetrieve/Interface/ViewImage.aspx?B=3167000; *The Herald* (Melbourne), 24 October 1936, p. 5; Baillie, 'Some Recollections'; Obituary for Burdeu; Kenneth Wiltshire, *CR Burdeu: A Living Legend*, Baskerville Printing, Brisbane, 1971, p. 7.

30 Cooper, Letter to the Editor, undated, *Labor Call*, 24 October 1935, p. 10; Baillie to Harris, 16 December 1935, ASS Papers, G377; Cooper to Paterson, 22 February 1936, National Archives of Australia, A659, 1940/1/858; Association for the Protection of Native Races, Minute Book, entry 17 March 1936, University of Sydney Archives, Series 55, Item 1; Inspector Roland S. Browne to the Director, Commonwealth Investigation Branch, 5 January 1938, National Archives of Australia, A431, 1949/1591; *The Herald* (Melbourne), 11 October 1939, p. 10.

31 Constitution of the Australian Aborigines' League, copy attached to Cooper to Paterson, 22 February 1936; Cooper to Paterson, 31 October 1936, National Archives of Australia, A659, 1940/1/858; Agenda of Proposals Submitted by the Australian Aborigines' League for the consideration of the Conference of Chief Protectors and others, attached to Cooper to Lyons, 16 January 1937, National Archives of Australia, A659, 1942/1/8104; Burdeu to Gollan, 19 March 1939.

32 *The Argus*, 15 April 1936, p. 9; *The Herald* (Melbourne), 15 April 1936, p. 2; *The Argus*, 18 April 1936, p. 18; Cooper to the Minister of the Interior, 9 May 1936, National Archives of Australia, A659, 1940/1/858.

33 Constitution of the Australian Aborigines' League; Burdeu to Gollan, 19 March 1939; Burdeu to Alexander Mair, Premier of New South Wales, 7 August 1939, New South Wales Archives and Records, NRS 12060, Item No. [12/8749-8750]; Burdeu to Elkin, 2 July 1941.

34 Bill Ferguson was sceptical about Burdeu's capacity to see things from an Aboriginal point of view and proceed accordingly, telling Elkin: 'I think you should know that there is no such thing as a white man who can think black. And between Miss Baillie and Mr Burdeu they have disorganised the Aborigines of Victoria altogether.' Yet we should probably bear in mind that Ferguson made this remark after Cooper had died and that he might have been projecting onto Baillie and Burdeu the problems his own organisation had had with a white ally, PR Stephensen, who had tried to take over the Aborigines Progressive Association (Bill Ferguson to Elkin, 18 December 1941, Elkin Papers, Series 12, Item 131).

35 Cooper to WG Sprigg, 22 February 1936, Women's International League of Peace and Freedom Papers, State Library of Victoria, MS 9377, Box 1726, Folder 1; Burdeu to Harris, 11 March 1936, Papers of the Anti-Slavery Society, G378; Australian Aborigines' League, Annual Report for 1936, New South Wales

Archives and Records, NRS 12060, Item No. [12/8749-8750]; Burdeu to Ruth Swann, 18 April 1940, Association for the Protection of the Native Races Papers, Item 7; Burdeu to Elkin, 2 July 1941.

36 None of the historians who have written recently about Cooper's political work have dealt with this question. Indeed, they do not even mention Burdeu's name. See Sarah Irving, 'Governing Nature: The Problem of Northern Australia', *Australian Historical Studies*, 45(3), 2014, pp. 388–406; Tim Rowse, 'Genealogies of Self-Determination', in Joy Damousi and Judith Smart (eds), *Contesting Australian History: Essays in Honour of Marilyn Lake*, Monash University Publishing, Melbourne, 2019, pp. 136–51; and Alison Holland, '"Does the British flag mean nothing to us?" British Democratic Traditions and Aboriginal Rights Claims in Interwar Australia', *Australian Historical Studies*, 2019, 50(3), pp. 321–38.

37 [Burdeu], 'Episodes of Interest in the Life of the Late William Cooper (Told by Himself)', 30 June 1941, Norman Family Papers, Mortlock Library, State Library of South Australia, PRG 422/31).

38 Baillie, 'Some Recollections'.

39 Burdeu to Gollan, 19 March 1939; Burdeu to Elkin, 2 July 1941.

Chapter 7: Race and Rights

1 Russell McGregor, 'Protest and Progress: Aboriginal Activism in the 1930s', *Australian Historical Studies*, 25(101), 1993, pp. 556–58.

2 William Cooper to Thomas Paterson, 18 February 1937, National Archives of Australia, A659, 1940/1/858; Cooper to the Secretary of the Anti-Slavery Society, Sir John Harris, 16 March 1937, Papers of the Anti-Slavery Society, Weston Library, Oxford University, MSS. Brit. Emp. s. 22 (henceforth Papers of the Anti-Slavery Society), G378; Cooper to Paterson, 16 June 1937, National Archives of Australia, A659, 1940/1/858; Cooper to Paterson, 25 June 1937, National Archives of Australia, A659, 1940/1/858; Cooper to Paterson, 30 July 1937, National Archives of Australia, A659, 1940/1/858; Cooper to the Prime Minister, Robert Menzies, 19 April 1939, National Archives of Australia, A461, A300/1 Part 3.

3 Constitution of the Australian Aborigines' League, copy attached to Cooper to Paterson, 22 February 1936, National Archives of Australia, A659, 1940/1/858; Cooper to Paterson, 31 October 1936, National Archives of Australia, A659, 1940/1/858; Cooper to Menzies, 3 December 1939, National Archives of Australia, A461, A300/1 Part 3.

4 Cooper to NM Morley, 7 March 1936, AP Elkin Papers, University of Sydney Archives, P.130, Series 12, Item 148; Cooper to the Editor, 5 November 1936, *Ladder*, 1(4), 1937, p. 23; Cooper to Harris, 22 December 1937, Papers of the Anti-Slavery Society, G378.

5 Cooper to the Minister of the Interior, John McEwen, 17 December 1938, National Archives of Australia, A659, 1940/1/858.

6 Constitution of the Australian Aborigines' League; Cooper to Morley, 7 March 1936; Cooper to Paterson, 31 October 1936; Cooper to the Editor, 5 November 1936, *Ladder*, 1(4), 1937, p. 23; Cooper to the Premier of New South Wales, Bertram Stevens, 15 November 1936; New South Wales Archives and Records, NRS 12060, Item No. [12/8749-8750]; Cooper to Harris, 10 January 1937, Papers of the Anti-Slavery Society, G378; Cooper to Joseph Lyons, 16 January 1937, National Archives of Australia, A659, 1942/1/8104; Cooper to Harris,

16 March 1937; Cooper to Paterson, 16 June 1937; Cooper to Menzies, 3 December 1939.

7 Cooper to Stevens, 15 November 1936; Cooper to Harris, 10 January 1937; Cooper to Stevens, 9 May 1937, New South Wales Archives and Records, NRS 12060, Item No. [12/8749-8750]; Cooper to Stevens, 23 May 1938, New South Wales Archives and Records, NRS 12060, Item No. [12/8749-8750]; *The Argus,* 27 November 1939, p. 2; Cooper to Menzies, 3 December 1939; *The Argus,* 1 March 1954, p. 7.

8 Cooper to Stevens, 15 November 1936; Cooper to Stevens, 7 June 1937, New South Wales Archives and Records, NRS 12060, Item No. [12/8749-8750]; Cooper to Paterson, 16 June 1937; Clive Turnbull, 'Aborigines Petition the King', *The Herald* (Melbourne), 7 August 1937, p. 31; Cooper to McEwen, 26 July 1938, National Archives of Australia, A659, 1940/1/858; *The Argus,* 27 November 1939, p. 2; Cooper to McEwen, 17 December 1938.

9 Cooper to Paterson, 11 March 1936; Cooper to Paterson, 31 October 1936; Cooper to the Editor, 5 November 1936, *Ladder,* 1(4), 1937, p. 23; Cooper to Harris, 10 January 1937; Cooper to McEwen, 19 February 1938, National Archives of Australia, A1, 1936/12778.

10 In a letter the British foreign secretary, Arthur Balfour, had sent an English Zionist, Baron Rothschild, on 2 November 1917 he had stated in part: 'His Majesty's Government view with favour the establishment in Palestine of a national home for the Jewish people, and will use their best endeavours to facilitate the achievement of this object, it being clearly understood that nothing shall be done which may prejudice the civil and religious rights of existing non-Jewish communities in Palestine' (https://sourcebooks.fordham.edu/mod/balfour.asp).

11 Turnbull; Cooper to McEwen, 3 January 1939, National Archives of Australia, A659, 1940/1/858.

12 See Russell McGregor, *Indifferent Inclusion: Aboriginal People and the Australian Nation*, Aboriginal Studies Press, Canberra, 2011, pp. 41–47; Sarah Irving, 'Governing Nature: The Problem of Northern Australia', *Australian Historical Studies*, 45(3), 2014, pp. 400, 403; Tim Rowse, *Indigenous and Other Australians Since 1901*, UNSW Press, Sydney, 2017, pp. 191–92, 194; Alison Holland, '"Does the British flag mean nothing to us?" British Democratic Traditions and Aboriginal Rights Claims in Interwar Australia', *Australian Historical Studies*, 2019, 50(3), p. 323.

13 Cooper to Paterson, 31 October 1936; Cooper to Paterson, 18 February 1937; Cooper to Harris, 16 March 1937; Cooper to Paterson, 25 June 1937; Cooper to McEwen, 19 February 1938; Cooper to McEwen, 26 July 1938; APA Burdeu to McEwen, 25 November 1938, National Archives of Australia, A659, 1940/1/858; Cooper, 'From an Educated Aboriginal', 21 January 1939, National Archives of Australia, A659, 1940/1/858; Patricia Seed, *Ceremonies of Possession in Europe's Conquest of the New World, 1492–1640*, Cambridge University Press, Cambridge, 1995, p. 34.

14 Cooper to Paterson, 31 October 1936; Cooper to Paterson, 18 February 1937; Cooper to Paterson, 30 July 1937; *The Argus*, 13 November 1937, p. 1; Cooper to McEwen, 19 February 1938, original emphasis.

15 Cooper to Harris, 16 March 1937; Cooper to Paterson, 18 February 1937; Cooper to Paterson, 25 June 1937; Cooper to Paterson, 30 July 1937; Cooper,

'From an Educated Black', 31 March 1938, National Archives of Australia, A659, 1940/1/858; Cooper to McEwen, 26 July 1938; Cooper to McEwen, 25 November 1938; Cooper, 'From an Educated Aboriginal'.

16 Cooper to Paterson, 9 May 1936; Cooper to Paterson, 31 October 1936; Cooper to the Editor, undated, *Ladder,* 5 November 1936, *Ladder,* 1(4), 1937, p. 23; Cooper to Paterson, 16 June 1937; Cooper to McEwen, 17 December 1938.

17 Cooper to Paterson, 23 March 1936; National Archives of Australia, A659, 1940/1/858; Cooper to Paterson, 9 May 1936; Cooper to Paterson, 31 October 1936; Cooper to the Editor, undated, *Ladder,* 5 November 1936, *Ladder,* 1(4), 1937, p. 23; Australian Aborigines' League, Annual Report for 1936, New South Wales Archives and Records, NRS 12060, Item No. [12/8749-8750]; Cooper to Joseph Lyons, 16 January 1937; Cooper to Paterson, 25 June 1937; Cooper to Lyons, 10 September 1938, National Archives of Australia, A431, 1949/1591.

18 Cooper to Paterson, 23 March 1936; Cooper to the Editor, undated, *Ladder,* 5 November 1936, *Ladder,* 1(4), 1937, pp. 23–24; Australian Aborigines' League, Annual Report for 1936; Cooper to Paterson, 25 June 1937; Cooper to McEwen, 17 December 1938.

19 On the basis of his argument that Cooper, Ferguson and Patten primarily called on government to grant Aboriginal people the same rights as white Australians had, McGregor has contended that the League and the Progressive Association 'advocated an assimilation programme' and 'expressed desire for incorporation into white society' ('Protest and Progress', pp. 556, 559), suggesting that the former necessarily led to the latter. This strikes me as wrong-headed. In a more recent work McGregor seems to have recognised this problem to some extent and so has mounted a somewhat different argument, namely that those such as Cooper sought '*inclusion* in the Australian *nation*' (*Indifferent Inclusion*, pp. 38, 40–1, 46, 48, 183–4; my emphases).

20 Cooper to Paterson, 16 June 1937; Cooper to McEwen, 19 April 1939.

21 Cooper to the Premier of Western Australia, John Willcock, 19 May 1938, State Records Office of Western Australia, AU WA S2030—cons993 1936/0075; Cooper to Lyons, 23 May 1938; Cooper to Lyons, 4 July 1938; Cooper to Willcock, 11 July 1938, State Records Office of Western Australia, AU WA S2030—cons993 1936/0075; Cooper to the Minister of Native Affairs of Western Australia, 17 July 1938, State Records Office of Western Australia, AU WA S2030—cons993 1936/0075; Cooper, Letter to the Editor, undated, *West Australian*, 22 November 1938, p. 9; Cooper to WH Kitson, Chief Secretary of Western Australia, 30 December 1938, State Records Office of Western Australia, AU WA S2030—cons993 1936/0075; Cooper to McEwen, 19 April 1939.

22 For a discussion of this principle at work internationally in the 1920s and 1930s, see Susan Pedersen, *The Guardians: The League of Nations and the Crisis of Empire*, Oxford University Press, New York, 2015, pp. 277–83.

23 *Australian Worker*, 4 May 1938, p. 7; *The Argus*, 28 September 1938, p. 15; Cooper, Letter to the Editor, undated, *West Australian*, 22 November 1938, p. 9.

24 Turnbull; Cooper to Rev. William Morley, 5 November 1938, Association for the Protection of the Native Races Papers, University of Sydney Archives, S55, Item 7.

25 It is difficult to determine the date of this meeting. While two newspapers (*The Age* and *The Argus*) reported it on 3 December 1938, neither provided any information

about when it had taken place. I assume it occurred in late November as a New South Wales newspaper carried a report on 1 December 1938 of a telegram that Bill Ferguson had sent the League on behalf of his organisation, supporting its action in approaching the German consulate to protest against the Nazis' treatment of Jewish people (*Dubbo Liberal and Macquarie Advocate*, 1 December 1938, p. 6).

26 The contemporary historical record does not reveal the membership of this deputation.

27 *The Argus*, 7 December 1938, p. 3; Diane Singh, personal communication, 28 March 2021; Lois Peeler, personal communication, 30 March 2021.

28 One way of placing this protest in a proper historical perspective is by reviewing all of the political campaigns that Cooper undertook between 1933 and 1940. This can be done by examining the documents in the *Archive* of http://williamcooper. monash.edu/, a website dedicated to Cooper and the Australian Aborigines' League once it has been constructed.

29 As an American historian, Paul A Cohen, has pointed out, mythologisation of the past 'achieves its effect typically not through out-and-out falsification but through distortion, oversimplification, and omission of material that does not serve its purpose or runs counter to it' (*History in Three Keys: The Boxers as Event, Experience, and Myth*, Columbia University Press, New York, 1997, p. 214). Like most myths (or what the historian Eric Hobsbawm famously called the invention of tradition), this one has some basis in historical fact but it also misrepresents the past. Moreover, in the course of promulgating it, its principal champions, who are Jewish, have played fast and loose with historical evidence in two ways. First, in the belief (which was widely held) that the League's petition to the consulate had been lost to history, a document headed 'Resolution, Australian Aborigines' League, 5th December 1938, To the Honorary Consul, Dr R. W. Drechsler, German Consulate, 419 Collins Street, Melbourne' was created, though this required a considerable amount of poetic licence. This document has been displayed in at least one Jewish museum around the world, spoken about on radio programs, quoted in numerous media stories, and even presented to the German parliament. As a result, many have concluded that it is an authentic historical document (see, for example, Marea Donnelly, 'Aboriginal Plea to Help Kristallnacht Jews Finally Heard After 79 Years', *Daily Telegraph*, 25 November 2017). It is not. In fact this document only bears some resemblance to what in all likelihood is the actual petition (which can be said to have been hiding in plain sight). After paraphrasing what appears to be the beginning of it—'The deputation presented to the Consulate a petition protesting against the persecution of the Jews, and asked him to convey to his government a request that it be ended'—an article in a New South Wales newspaper in December 1938 (*Dubbo Liberal and Macquarie Advocate*, 1 December 1938, p. 6) quoted what is probably the remainder of the petition, as follows:

> Like the Jews, our people have suffered much cruelty, exploitation and misunderstanding as a minority at the hands of another race, but we are glad to say that in most parts of Australia we have experienced much kindness and co-operation from the white population, particularly the missionaries of all branches of the Christian Church.
>
> We are also glad to say that we are experiencing a great desire on the part of some governments, particularly the Federal Government, to make amends

for the past and to help our people to take their places as equal citizens in the life of Australia.

We are a very small minority, and we are a poor people, but in extending sympathy to the Jewish people we assure them of our support in every way.

Second, this myth-making has claimed that Cooper and members of the League walked from his house in Footscray to the German consulate to present the petition, but there is no contemporary historical evidence that any such protest march occurred. It should be noted, though, that this is one of those occasions, noted in the Prologue, that the accounts provided by academic history and Yorta Yorta oral tradition diverge.

30 *The Argus*, 18 November 1938, p. 11; *Workers' Voice*, 19 November 1938, p. 1; *Australian Worker*, 23 November 1938, p. 14; *Workers' Voice*, 26 November 1938, p. 1; *Workers' Weekly*, 2 December 1938, p. 3; *Workers' Voice*, 3 December 1938, p. 2; *The Age*, 12 December 1938, p. 10; James Waghorne and Stuart Macintyre, *Liberty: A History of Civil Liberties in Australia*, UNSW Press, Sydney, 2011, p. 24. About two weeks later, a conference to discuss government stances towards refugees from European fascism, which the Australian Council for Civil Liberties had been organising since a group of Jewish refugees had initially been refused permission to land in Australia in early October, expressed its wholehearted sympathy for the refugees, called for the formation of a committee to lobby for a less restrictive immigration policy, and agreed to put several questions to the minister for the interior, John McEwen—one of which was whether he would recommend to the federal government that it protest against the Nazi persecution of Jews and Christians (*The Age*, 12 December 1938, p. 10).

31 *Dubbo Liberal and Macquarie Advocate*, 1 December 1938, p. 6.

32 Others in Australia at this time raised concerns about the fate of Indigenous peoples in nearby New Guinea and Samoa because of the nature of Germany's treatment of the Herero people of south-west Africa before the Great War. See, for example, J Y Dixon, Letter to the Editor, 14 November 1938, *Sydney Morning Herald*, 15 November 1938, p. 3.

33 *Dubbo Liberal and Macquarie Advocate*, 1 December 1938, p. 6. Later in December the *Workers' Weekly* quoted a passage from the petition that read a little differently: 'Like the Jews, our people have suffered cruelty and exploitation as a national minority' (20 December 1938, p. 3).

34 Cooper to McEwen, 17 December 1938; *Workers' Weekly*, 20 December 1938, p. 3; Cooper to Menzies, 19 April 1939; Cooper to Menzies, 5 October 1939, National Archives of Australia, A461, A300/1 Part 3. In October 1940 Doug Nicholls followed in Cooper's footsteps in posing this rhetorical question at a church in Melbourne: 'Australians were raving about persecuted minorities in other parts of the world, but were they ready to voice their support for the unjustly treated aboriginal minority in Australia?' (*Courier-Mail*, 21 October 1940, p. 5).

35 Constitution of the Australian Aborigines' League; Cooper to Morley, 7 March 1936; Cooper to Paterson, 15 June 1936; Australian Aborigines' League, Annual Report for 1936; Cooper to Harris, 16 March 1937; Cooper to Paterson, 25 June 1937.

36 Cooper to Harris, 16 March 1937; Burdeu to McEwen, 25 November 1938.

37 Cooper to Isaac Selby, 16 March 1937, Isaac Selby Papers, Royal Historical Society of Victoria, MS 694/226; Cooper to Paterson, 16 June 1937; Turnbull.

Chapter 8: The Petition and the Day of Mourning

1 APA Burdeu to Rev. William Morley, 19 June 1936, Association for the Protection of the Native Races Papers, University of Sydney Archives, Series 55, Item 7.

2 Ibid.; William Cooper to Thomas Paterson, 16 June 1937, National Archives of Australia, A659, 1940/1/858.

3 Australian Aborigines' League, Agenda of proposals submitted for the consideration of the Conference of Chief Protectors and others, attached to Cooper to Joseph Lyons, 16 January 1937, National Archives of Australia, A659, 1942/1/8104; Cooper to the Secretary, Minister for the Interior, 18 April 1937, National Archives of Australia, A659, 1942/1/8104; Cooper to Paterson, 16 June 1937.

4 Cooper to Paterson, 16 June 1937.

5 A year or so later, in a letter to Paterson's successor, John McEwen, Cooper also remarked that the parliamentary representative he was now seeking would have no vote and merely be able to watch over legislation (26 July 1938, National Archives of Australia, A659, 1940/1/858). On the basis of this, Russell McGregor (in his *Indifferent Inclusion: Aboriginal People and the Australian Nation*, Aboriginal Studies Press, Canberra, 2011, p. 49) has suggested that this was the mere sum of what Cooper and the League were seeking in calling for parliamentary representation:

> His 1933 petition requested that Aboriginal people be granted 'power to propose a member of parliament in the person of our own Blood, or White man known to have studied our needs and to be in Sympathy with our Race to represent us in the Federal Parliament'. Cooper's clear preference was for the representative to be a 'person of our own Blood', and even if the alternative were pursued, the sympathetic white person would still be selected and elected by Aboriginal voters. But by allowing the alternative, he intimated that the parliamentary member's role was not so much to ensure a distinctive Aboriginal voice in the parliamentary forum as to guarantee a watchful eye over the legislative process.

This argument ignores the fact that Cooper repeatedly made it clear that he envisaged this parliamentary representative as a means of Aboriginal people expressing their distinctive views, just as it ignores the political context that had prompted Cooper to qualify the League's demand for this MP.

6 Cooper to Paterson, 16 June 1937; Cooper to the Secretary, Australian Aborigines' Amelioration Association, undated [c. June 1937], *Ladder,* 1(5), October 1937, p. 14.

7 Paterson to Cooper, 17 June 1937, National Archives of Australia, A659, 1940/1/858; Cooper to Paterson, 25 June 1937, National Archives of Australia, A659, 1940/1/858, original emphasis.

8 Paterson, undated minutes c. 28 and 29 June 1937, and Paterson to Cooper, 30 June 1937, National Archives of Australia, A659, 1940/1/858; Andrew Markus, *Governing Savages*, Allen & Unwin, Sydney, 1990, pp. 122–23.

9 Clive Turnbull, 'Aborigines Petition the King', *The Herald* (Melbourne), 7 August 1937, p. 31; Burdeu to Lyons, 25 August 1937, National Archives of Australia, A461, A300/1 Part 3; Cooper to Lyons, undated, [13 September 1937], National Archives of Australia, A461, A300/1 Part 3; Secretary, Prime Minister's Office, to Cooper, 15 September 1937, National Archives of Australia, A431, 1949/1591; Burdeu to Rev. ERB Gribble, 20 September 1937, ERB Gribble Papers, Australian Institute of Aboriginal and Torres Strait Islander Studies, MS 1515, Box 11, Item 66; Burdeu to Lyons, 17 October 1937, National Archives of Australia, A461, A300/1 Part 3.

10 JA Carrodus to the Secretary, Prime Minister's Department, 30 September 1937, National Archives of Australia, A432, 1937/1191; Markus, *Governing Savages*, pp. 122–25; McGregor, p. 49.

11 The original of the petition with its roll of signatures seems to have been destroyed. Certainly the National Archives of Australia has never been able to find it.

12 Carrodus to the Secretary, Prime Minister's Department, 30 September 1937; *The Age*, 26 October 1937, p. 10.

13 Carrodus, Memorandum on Deputation representing aboriginals, which waited on the Minister on 23 January 1935, 4 April 1935, National Archives of Australia, A1, 1935/3951; Carrodus to the Secretary, Prime Minister's Department, 30 September 1937.

14 Strahan to Cooper, 17 October 1937, National Archives of Australia, A432, 1937/1191; *Canberra Times*, 18 January 1938, p. 1; Politicus, 'Constitution Precludes Aboriginal Member for Canberra', *Northern Star* (Lismore), 27 January 1938, p. 2; PR Hart and CJ Lloyd, 'Lyons, Joseph Aloysius (Joe) (1879–1939)', *Australian Dictionary of Biography*, National Centre of Biography, Australian National University, https://adb.anu.edu.au/biography/lyons-joseph-aloysius-joe-7278/text12617, published first in hardcopy 1986.

15 Cooper to Lyons, 26 October 1937, National Archives of Australia, A432, 1937/1191.

16 *Aboriginal Welfare: Initial Conference of Commonwealth and State Aboriginal Authorities held at Canberra, 21 to 23 April 1937*, Government Printer, Canberra [1937], p. 3; Cooper to Lyons, 26 October 1937, National Archives of Australia, A432, 1937/1191.

17 Cooper to Lyons, 26 October 1937.

18 Ibid.

19 *The Age*, 26 October 1937, p. 10; *The Argus*, 26 October 1937, p. 10, 27 October 1937, p. 12; *Workers' Star*, 12 November 1937, p. 2; *The Worker*, 23 November 1937, p. 10; *The Times*, 25 November 1937, p. 15; *Courier-Mail*, 20 January 1938, p. 16; *The Age*, 20 January 1938, p. 10; *The Examiner* (Launceston), 20 January 1938, p. 8; WEH Stanner, *White Man Got No Dreaming: Essays 1938–1973*, Australian National University Press, Canberra, 1979, p. viii.

20 *Aboriginal Welfare*, p. 3; *Adelaide Advertiser*, 27 October 1937, p. 25; *The Mirror* (Perth), 30 October 1937, p. 14.

21 Strahan to Carrodus, 6 November 1937, National Archives of Australia, A431, 1949/1591; Carrodus to the Secretary, Attorney-General's Department, 15 November 1937, National Archives of Australia, A431, 1949/1591; Secretary, Attorney-General's Department, Minute to Carrodus, 16 November 1937 on Carrodus to the Secretary, Attorney-General's Department, 15 November 1937, National Archives of Australia, A431, 1949/1591; Carrodus to the Director, Commonwealth Investigation Branch, 22 November 1937, National Archives of Australia, A431, 1949/1591.

22 George S Knowles, Solicitor-General, Opinion on Representation of Aboriginals in Commonwealth Parliament. Constitution—Sections 5, 24, 51 (xxvi), 122 and 127, 14 January 1938, National Archives of Australia, A432, 1937/1191.

23 PA Gourgaud, Acting Secretary, Department of the Interior, Memorandum, 25 January 1938, National Archives of Australia, A431, 1949/1591; John McEwen, Submission to Cabinet, Australian Aborigines' League—Petition to His Majesty

the King, 1 February 1938, National Archives of Australia, A461, A300/1 Part 3.

24 *The Argus*, 13 November 1937, p. 1.

25 Interestingly, in 1836 William Appess, a Pequot preacher who served the Wampanoag community of Mashpee in Massachusetts, declared both Thanksgiving Day and Independence Day in the United States to be 'days of mourning and not joy' for the Indians because of what had been done to them by the whites (David J Silverman, *This Land is their Land: The Wampanoag Indians, Plymouth Colony, and the Troubled History of Thanksgiving*, Bloomsbury Publishing, New York, 2019, p. 12).

26 Australian Aborigines' League, Annual Report for 1936, New South Wales Archives and Records, NRS 12060, Item No. [12/8749-8750]; Cooper to Paterson, 18 February 1937, National Archives of Australia, A659, 1940/1/858; Cooper to the Premier, New South Wales, Bertram Stevens, 7 June 1937, New South Wales Archives and Records, NRS 12060, Item No. [12/8749-8750]; Cooper to Isaac Selby, 1 February 1937, Isaac Selby Papers, Royal Historical Society of Victoria, MS 694 (henceforth Selby Papers), box 226; *The Age*, 11 November 1937; Cooper, Circular Letter, 27 December 1937, PR Stephensen Papers, Mitchell Library, MS 1284; Cooper, 'From an Educated Black', 31 March 1938, National Archives of Australia, A659, 1940/1/858.

27 Souvenir Programme for Grand Pioneer Rally and Historical Service, 24 January 1937, Selby Papers, box 226.

28 Selby had performed a historical pageant in 1934 that included a scene featuring the signing of the treaty and organised an event in 1935 commemorating the hundredth anniversary of the treaty (advertisement for the pageant 'The Birth of Melbourne', Selby Papers, box 226; handbill for Batman anniversary, January 1934, Selby Papers, box 226; *The Age*, 30 May 1935, p. 10).

29 For a discussion of Aboriginal people's attitudes to Batman and his treaty at this time, see my book *Possession: Batman's Treaty and the Matter of History*, Miegunyah Press, Melbourne, 2008, pp. 241, 248.

30 *The Argus*, 25 January 1937, p. 8; *The Age*, 25 January 1937, pp. 1, 11; Cooper to Selby, 1 February 1937.

31 Cooper to Selby, 1 February 1937.

32 Ibid.

33 *The Herald* (Melbourne), 22 February 1937, p. 20; Cooper to Selby, 16 March 1937, Selby Papers, box 226; Frank Strahan, 'Selby, Isaac (1859–1956)', *Australian Dictionary of Biography*, http://adb.anu.edu.au/biography/selby-isaac-11653/text20817, published first in hardcopy 2002.

34 Burdeu to Selby, 26 March 1937, Selby Papers, box 226; Cooper to Selby, 5 April 1937, Selby Papers, box 226; Burdeu to Selby, 6 May 1937, Selby Papers, box 226; flyer for concert by Aboriginal Choir, Melba Theatre, Warracknabeal, 13 April [1937], Selby Papers, box 226; tickets for the concert of 31 May 1937, Selby Papers, box 226, Burdeu to Morley, 22 February 1937, AP Elkin Papers, University of Sydney Archives, P.130, Series 12, Item 148.

35 Burdeu to Selby, 26 March 1937; Cooper to Selby, 5 and 10 April 1937, Selby Papers, box 226.

36 Tickets and programme for the concert, 31 May 1937, Selby Papers, box 226; *The Age*, 1 June 1937, p. 5; 'Stay in Your Own Back Yard', https://egrove.olemiss.edu/sharris_a/58/; Doug Seroff, 'A Voice in the Wilderness: The Fisk Jubilee

Singers' Civil Rights Tours of 1879–1882', *Popular Music and Society*, 25(1–2), 2001, p. 146.

37 But it is unclear how successful these concerts were financially. In December 1937 Burdeu had to appeal to the public for donations to clear a debt of £26 (approximately $2400 in today's money) that the League had incurred in staging the concerts (*The Argus*, 8 December 1937, p. 14).

38 Cooper, Circular Letter, 27 December 1937; Program for 'Grand Pioneers' Day Rally and Concert', *Uplift*, 1(4), 1938, pp. 4, 6–7; *The Herald* (Melbourne), 18 January 1940, p. 30; Flyer, 'Historical Service', 28 January 1940, Selby Papers, box 226; 'Aborigines' Sunday, 1940', *Uplift*, 2(3), 1940, p. 32.

39 Cooper, Circular Letters, 'Petition to His Majesty' and 'Australia Day, 1938', Stephensen Papers.

40 PR Stephensen, Secretary, Aboriginal Citizenship Committee, to Burdeu, 14 December 1937, and its enclosure, the leaflet advertising the 'Day of Mourning and Protest', Stephensen Papers; Cooper, Circular Letter, 'Australia Day, 1938', 27 December 1938; *The Age*, 18 January 1938, p. 14; *The Advertiser* (Adelaide), 19 January 1938, p. 25; Cooper to McEwen, 19 January 1938, National Archives of Australia, A659, 1940/1/858; *The Age*, 22 January 1938, p. 20; Philip Jones, 'Unaipon, David (1872–1967)', *Australian Dictionary of Biography*, National Centre of Biography, Australian National University, https://adb.anu.edu.au/biography/unaipon-david-8898/text15631, published first in hardcopy 1990.

41 Later, Ferguson changed his position and more or less followed in Cooper's footsteps by appealing to the governor-general, Lord Gowrie, on behalf of the Aborigines Progressive Association, for representation for Aboriginal people in the federal parliament (Ferguson to Lord Gowrie, 30 August 1940, National Archives of Australia, A431, 1949/1591).

42 *The Herald* (Melbourne), 22 January 1938, p. 6; *Daily Telegraph* (Sydney), 24 January 1938, p. 2; *Sydney Morning Herald*, 27 January 1938, p. 6; *Sydney Morning Herald*, 1 February 1938, p. 17; *Abo Call*, 1, 1938, pp. 1–2; Jack Horner, *Vote Ferguson for Aboriginal Freedom: A Biography*, Australian and New Zealand Book Company, Sydney, 1974, pp. 63–65; Gavin Souter, 'Skeleton at the Feast', in Bill Gammage and Peter Spearritt (eds), *Australians 1938*, Fairfax, Syme & Weldon, Sydney, 1987, pp. 15–16.

43 It is often claimed that Cooper was part of the deputation that waited on Lyons on 31 January, but there appears to be no evidence that he was. It seems reasonable to assume that he attended instead the Day of Mourning event that was held in Melbourne on that day, given that the press reported that Nicholls spoke at that meeting and Cooper had returned probably with him (and Tucker) from Sydney at the same time.

44 *The Argus*, 1 February 1938, p. 2; *The Age*, 1 February 1938, p. 7; Horner, p. 64.

45 Historians who have previously discussed the government's response, myself included, have failed to register the fact that the government did not actually inform Cooper of the Cabinet decision (see, for example, Jack Horner and Marcia Langton, 'The Day of Mourning', in Gammage and Spearritt (eds), p. 35). Indeed, at least one historian has claimed that it *did* inform him: Andrew Markus, 'William Cooper and the 1937 Petition to the King', *Aboriginal History*, 7(1), 1983, p. 57 note 36.

46 McEwen, Submission to Cabinet, Australian Aborigines' League—Petition to His Majesty the King, 1 February 1938; Minute on McEwen, Submission to Cabinet,

Australian Aborigines' League—Petition to His Majesty the King, 1 February 1938, 8 February 1938, National Archives of Australia, A431, 1949/1591; Carrodus to Strahan, 23 February 1938, National Archives of Australia, A431, 1949/1591; Strahan to Cooper, 2 March 1938, National Archives of Australia, A431, 1949/1591. It also seems that the government—or perhaps Carrodus—misled the press at this time by suggesting that an amendment of the constitution was required in order to make Aboriginal representation in parliament possible (*The Age*, 20 January 1938, p. 10; Politicus, 'Constitution Precludes Aboriginal Member').

47 There can be no doubt that Burdeu played a major role in drawing up this statement, but Shadrach James might also have had a hand in it. Certainly the later formulation of it (see the next note) bears traces of James's writing style.

48 Several months later, the League revised this statement, retitled it 'From an Educated Aboriginal', and sent it to McEwen (21 January 1939, National Archives of Australia, A659, 1940/1/858).

49 Cooper to Lyons, 31 March 1938, National Archives of Australia, A659, 1940/1/858.

50 Cooper, 'From an Educated Black'.

51 Ibid.

52 In fact they were justified by a board of inquiry. See Bill Wilson and Justin O'Brien, '"To Infuse a Universal Terror": A Reappraisal of the Coniston Killings', *Aboriginal History*, 27, 2003, p. 72.

53 Cooper, 'From an Educated Black'.

54 Ibid.

55 Ibid.

56 See Bain Attwood and Andrew Markus, *The 1967 Referendum: Race, Power and the Australian Constitution*, Aboriginal Studies Press, Canberra, 2017, Chapter 6.

57 Cooper, 'From an Educated Black'.

58 Ibid.

59 Ibid.

60 Ibid.

61 Ibid.

62 Cooper to Lyons, 23 May 1938, National Archives of Australia, A461, A300/1 Part 3; Strahan to Cooper, 27 May 1938, National Archives of Australia, A431, 1949/1591; Secretary, Prime Minister's Department to Carrodus, 27 June 1938; National Archives of Australia, A431, 1949/1591; Carrodus, Draft letter to the Secretary, Prime Minister's Department, 29 June 1938, National Archives of Australia, A431, 1949/1591; Carrodus to the Secretary, Prime Minister's Department, 7 July 1938, National Archives of Australia, A431, 1949/1591.

63 Cooper to Lyons, 4 July 1938, National Archives of Australia, A1, 1938/4793; Secretary, Prime Minister's Department, to Cooper, 15 July 1938, National Archives of Australia, A431, 1949/1591; Cooper to McEwen, 26 July 1938, National Archives of Australia, A659, 1940/1/858.

64 Cooper to Robert Menzies, 19 April 1939, National Archives of Australia, A461, A300/1 Part 3; Menzies to Cooper, 4 May 1939, National Archives of Australia, A431, 1949/1591; Menzies to Harry Foll, 10 May 1939, National Archives of Australia, A431, 1949/1591; Foll to Menzies, 11 June 1939, National Archives of Australia, A431, 1949/1591; Mavis Thorpe Clark, *Pastor Doug: The Story of Sir Douglas Nicholls, Aboriginal Leader*, Lansdowne Press, Melbourne, 1965, p. 102.

65 Cooper to Menzies, 5 October 1939 (two letters), National Archives of Australia, A461, A300/1 Part 3; Cooper to Menzies, 3 December 1939, National Archives of Australia, A461, A300/1 Part 3; Gribble to Rev. AV Baillie, 15 April 1940, Australian Board of Missions, Further Records, 1873–1978, Mitchell Library, MLMSS 4503, Add-on 1822, Box 11, Folder 17; Christine M Halse, The Reverend Ernest Gribble and Race Relations in Northern Australia, PhD thesis, University of Queensland, 1992, pp. 422–23.
66 Cooper to Menzies, 31 August 1940, National Archives of Australia, A659, 1940/1/858.

Chapter 9: The Cumeroogunga Walk-off
1 Notes of Deputation representing Aborigines and various associations interested in Aboriginal welfare to the Minister for the Interior, Thomas Paterson, Melbourne, 23 January 1935, National Archives of Australia, A1, 1935/3951.
2 Constitution of the Australian Aborigines' League, copy attached to William Cooper to Paterson, 22 February 1936, National Archives of Australia, A659, 1940/1/858.
3 Cooper to Paterson, 31 October 1936, National Archives of Australia, A659, 1940/1/858; Cooper to the Premier of New South Wales, Bertram Stevens, 15 November 1936, New South Wales Archives and Records, NRS 12060, Item No. [12/8749-8750]; Cooper to Harris, 10 January 1937, Papers of the Anti-Slavery Society Papers, Weston Library, Oxford University, MSS. Brit. Emp. s. 22 (henceforth Papers of the Anti-Slavery Society), G378; Agenda for the Conference of Chief Protectors, attached to Cooper to Joseph Lyons, 16 January 1937, National Archives of Australia, A659, 1942/1/8104; Cooper to Stevens, 7 June 1937, New South Wales Archives and Records, NRS 12060, Item No. [12/8749-8750]; Cooper to the Secretary, Australian Aborigines' Amelioration Association, undated [c. June 1937], Ladder, 1(5), October 1937, p. 13.
4 Cooper to Paterson, 31 October 1936; Cooper to Stevens, 15 November 1936; Cooper to Harris, 10 January 1937; Agenda for the Conference of Chief Protectors.
5 Cooper to Stevens, 19 February 1936, New South Wales Archives and Records, NRS 12060, Item No. [12/8749-8750]; Cooper to Paterson, 31 October 1936; Cooper to Stevens, 15 November 1936; Cooper to Harris, 10 January 1937; Agenda for the Conference of Chief Protectors.
6 Jack Horner, Vote Ferguson for Aboriginal Freedom: A Biography, Australian and New Zealand Book Company, Sydney, 1974, pp. 46, 49–54.
7 Cooper to Stevens, 1 January 1938, New South Wales Archives and Records, NRS 12060, Item No. [12/8749-8750]; Cooper to Stevens, 31 March 1938, New South Wales Archives and Records, NRS 12060, Item No. [12/8749-8750].
8 Cooper to Stevens, 15 November 1936; Cooper to Paterson, 16 June 1937, National Archives of Australia, A659, 1940/1/858; Cooper to Lyons, 26 October 1937, National Archives of Australia, A432, 1937/1191; Cooper to Stevens, 1 January 1938.
9 Cooper to Stevens, 31 March 1937, New South Wales Archives and Records, NRS 12060, Item No. [12/8749-8750]; Cooper to Stevens, 23 May 1938 (four letters), New South Wales Archives and Records, NRS 12060, Item No. [12/8749-8750]; Heather Goodall, Invasion to Embassy: Land in Aboriginal Politics in New South Wales, 1770–1972, Black Books/Allen & Unwin, Sydney, 1996, pp. 192, 247.

10 Petition to the Board of Cumeroogunga Residents, 2 November 1938, New South Wales Archives and Records, NRS 905, Item No. [12/7584.1]; Cooper to Stevens, 5 November 1938, New South Wales Archives and Records, NRS 12060, Item No. [12/8749-8750]; Cooper to Rev. William Morley, 5 November 1938, Association for the Protection of Native Races Papers, University of Sydney Archives, Series 55, Item 7.

11 Arthur McQuiggan, Telegram to the Secretary, New South Wales Aborigines Protection Board, 17 November 1938, New South Wales Archives and Records, NRS 905, Item No. [12/7584.1]; Report of Aboriginal Women at Cumeroogunga, 18 November 1938, New South Wales Archives and Records, NRS 905, Item No. [12/7584.1]; Jack Patten to McQuiggan, 20 November 1938 and 23 November 1938, New South Wales Archives and Records, NRS 905, Item No. [12/7584.1]; *Inverell Times*, 30 November 1938, p. 1; Patten to the Secretary, New South Wales Aborigines Protection Board, 1 December 1938, New South Wales Archives and Records, NRS 905, Item No. [12/7584.1]; *Daily Telegraph* (Sydney), 2 December 1938, p. 8; Horner, pp. 38–39; Goodall, p. 225.

12 Cooper to the Chairman, New South Wales Aborigines Protection Board, 28 November 1938, New South Wales Archives and Records, NRS 12060, NRS 12060, Item No. [12/8749-8750].

13 Cooper to the Chairman, New South Wales Aborigines Protection Board, 4 December 1939 [sic, 1938], New South Wales Archives and Records, NRS 905, Item No. [12/7584.1]; Patten to JT Lang, undated, [c. early December 1938], New South Wales Archives and Records, NRS 905, Item No. [12/7584.1]; *New South Wales Parliamentary Debates*, Legislative Assembly, 8 December 1938, pp. 3494–95; Secretary, Aborigines Protection Board, to Under-Secretary of New South Wales, 13 December 1938, New South Wales Archives and Records, NRS 905, Item No. [12/7584.1]; Chief Secretary's Office, New South Wales, Statement 'Aborigines: Reserves', 16 December 1938, New South Wales Archives and Records, NRS 905, Item No. [12/7584.1]; Cooper to Selwyn Briggs, date undecipherable but January 1939, New South Wales Archives and Records, NRS 905, Item No. [12/7584.1]; McQuiggan, Memorandum to the Secretary, New South Wales Aborigines Protection Board, 21 January 1939, New South Wales Archives and Records, NRS 905, Item No. [12/7584.1].

14 Patten to Briggs, 27 December 1938, New South Wales Archives and Records, NRS 905, Item No. [12/7584.1].

15 Cooper, Letter to the Editor, 3 January 1939, *The Advocate* (Melbourne), 12 January 1939, p. 21.

16 I do not seek to provide a comprehensive account of the walk-off that followed, though a good deal of what happened will be related in order to make sense of how Cooper and the League responded. There have been several scholarly accounts of the walk-off, the most recent of which at the time of writing is Michael Victor Ward, The Cummeragunja Walk-Off: A Study of Black/White Politics and Public Discourse about Race, Ideology and Place on the Eve of the Second World War, Masters of Research thesis, Macquarie University, 2016. For recollections of the strike by members of the League, see, for example, Mavis Thorpe Clark, *Pastor Doug: The Story of Sir Douglas Nicholls, Aboriginal Leader*, Lansdowne Press, Melbourne, 1965, pp. 112–16, and Margaret Tucker, *If Everyone Cared: Autobiography of Margaret Tucker*, Ure Smith, Sydney, 1977, pp. 168–70.

17 Patten, Telegram, 3 February 1939, New South Wales Archives and Records, NRS 905, Item No. [12/7584.1]; Detective-Sergeant of Police, Moama, to the Commissioner of Police, 6 February 1939, New South Wales Archives and Records, NRS 905, Item No. [12/7584.1]; Constable Arthur McAvoy, Statement, 6 February 1939, New South Wales Archives and Records, NRS 905, Item No. [12/7584.1].

18 Perhaps Sarah Cooper played a role in bringing this about. She was the widow of one of Jack Patten's uncles, Jacob Nelson (Marriage Certificate for Sarah McRae and Jacob Nelson, New South Wales Registry of Births, Deaths and Marriages, 4282/1905; Michael Bennett, *Pathfinders: A History of Aboriginal Trackers in NSW*, NewSouth, Sydney, 2020, p. 136).

19 Manus to the New South Wales Commissioner of Police, 5 February 1939, New South Wales Archives and Records, NRS 905, Item No. [12/7584.1]; *Argus*, 6 February 1939, p. 2; Cooper and Patten, Telegram to newspapers, 6 February 1939, *Daily News*, 7 February 1939, p. 1; APA Burdeu to Edwin Atkinson, 21 February 1939, New South Wales Archives and Records, NRS 905, Item No. [12/7584.1].

20 *The Argus*, 6 February 1939, p. 2; *The Herald* (Melbourne), 6 February 1939, p. 2; *Sydney Morning Herald*, 6 February 1939, p. 11; *Daily News*, 7 February 1939, p. 1; *Daily Telegraph* (Sydney), 7 February 1939, p. 2; *The Age*, 7 February 1939, p. 7; *The Argus*, 7 February 1939, p. 3; *Daily Telegraph* (Sydney), 8 February 1939, p. 2; *Daily Telegraph* (Sydney), 10 February 1939, p. 6.

21 For a contemporary report of this incident, see *The Age*, 24 April 1919, p. 8.

22 *The Argus*, 9 February 1939, p. 10; *Daily Telegraph* (Sydney), 13 February 1939, p. 2; Half Caste Aborigine [Margaret Tucker], 'Aborigine Tells of Conditions at Cumeroogunga', *Workers' Voice*, 1 March 1939, p. 2.

23 *Daily News*, 7 February 1939, p. 1, 9 February 1939, p. 2; William Ferguson to Stevens, 26 March 1938, New South Wales Archives and Records, NRS 12060, Item No. [12/8749-8750]; Patten to Ferguson, [June 1938], PR Stephensen Papers, Mitchell Library, State Library of New South Wales, MS 1284; Horner, p. 71–72, 79; Jack Horner and Marcia Langton, 'The Day of Mourning', in Bill Gammage and Peter Spearritt (eds), *Australians 1938*, Fairfax, Syme & Weldon, Sydney, 1987, p. 35.

24 *Workers' Voice*, 8 February 1939, p. 1; 11 February 1939, pp. 1, 4; *The Age*, 13 February 1939, p. 13; *Workers' Voice*, 18 February 1939, p. 4, 22 February 1939, p. 1; *Workers' Weekly*, 28 February 1939, p. 4; *Workers' Voice*, 1 March 1939, p. 2, 4 March 1939, p. 4, 8 March 1939, p. 1, 11 March 1939, p. 1.

25 *The Herald* (Melbourne), 13 February 1939, p. 8; *Border Morning Mail* (Albury), 14 February 1939, p. 6; Australian Aborigines' League to Mark Davidson, 16 February 1939, New South Wales Archives and Records, NRS 905, Item No. [12/7584.1]; *The Herald* (Melbourne), 16 February 1939, p. 2; *The Herald* (Melbourne), 17 February 1939, p. 2.

26 Cooper to Stevens, 20 February 1939, New South Wales Archives and Records, NRS 905, Item No. [12/7584.1]; Cooper to Stevens, 20 February 1939, New South Wales Archives and Records, NRS 12060, Item No. [12/8749-8750].

27 Cooper to Stevens, 20 February 1939, New South Wales Archives and Records, NRS 12060, Item No. [12/8749-8750].

28 Morley to Rev. LH Purnell, 14 July 1938, AP Elkin Papers, University of Sydney Archives, P.130, Series 12, Item 149; Helen Baillie to Harris, undated [October

or November 1938], Papers of the Anti-Slavery Society, G379; *Shepparton News*, 27 February 1939, p. 1; *The Argus*, 1 March 1939, p. 7; *The Age*, 2 March 1939, p. 11.

29 McQuiggan to the Secretary, New South Wales Aborigines Protection Board, 2 March 1939, New South Wales Archives and Records, NRS 905, Item No. [12/7584.1]; *Sydney Morning Herald*, 4 March 1939, p. 17; H Hargreaves to William Gale, 5 March 1939, New South Wales Archives and Records, NRS 905, Item No. [12/7584.1]; Gale to Stevens, 6 March 1939 and 7 March 1939, New South Wales Archives and Records, NRS 12060, Item No. [12/8749-8750]; WB Payne, Letter to the Editor, undated, *Australian Christian*, 8 March 1939, copy in New South Wales Archives and Records, NRS 905, Item No. [12/7584.1].

30 The historian Heather Goodall has argued that Lipscombe and Anderson promised an inquiry on this occasion (*Invasion to Embassy*, p. 254), but I have seen no evidence to support this contention.

31 Hargreaves to Gale, 5 March 1939; *Workers' Voice*, 11 March 1939, p. 1; *Echuca and Moama Advertiser*, 11 March 1939, [p. 2]; McQuiggan to the Secretary, New South Wales Aborigines Protection Board, 13 March 1939, New South Wales Archives and Records, NRS 905, Item No. [12/7584.1]; *Echuca and Moama Advertiser*, 14 March 1939, [p. 2]; *Workers' Voice*, 15 March 1939, p. 1; Morley to GC Gollan, 15 March 1939, Association for the Protection of Native Races Papers, Item 7; Burdeu to Atkinson, 19 March 1939, New South Wales Archives and Records, NRS 905, Item No. [12/7584.1]; Burdeu to Gollan, 19 March 1939, New South Wales Archives and Records, NRS 905, Item No. [12/7584.1]; SL Anderson to the Chief Secretary's Department, 20 March 1939, New South Wales Archives and Records, NRS 905, Item No. [12/7584.1]; Atkinson to Baillie, March 1939, AWR Vroland Papers, National Library of Australia, MS 3991, Box 3, Folder 20; Cooper, Letter to the Editor, undated, *Australian Worker*, 10 May 1939, p. 15; Morley to Gollan, 13 June 1939, Association for the Protection of Native Races Papers, Item 7; Morley to Rev. HF Peak, 4 July 1939, Association for the Protection of Native Races Papers, Item 7.

32 Secretary, New South Wales Aborigines Protection Board, to McQuiggan, 23 March 1939, New South Wales Archives and Records, NRS 905, Item No. [12/7584.1]; *Workers' Voice*, 25 March 1939, p. 4, 1 April 1939, pp. 1, 4; Anderson to Under-Secretary, Premier's Department, 6 April 1939, New South Wales Archives and Records, NRS 12060, Item No. [12/8749-8750]; *Riverine Herald*, 18 May 1939, p. 2, 22 May 1939, p. 2; *The Herald* (Melbourne), 27 June 1939, p. 3; Gollan to Morley, 10 July 1939, Association for the Protection of Native Races Papers, Item 7; *The Age*, 28 July 1939, p. 14; Goodall, p. 254.

33 *Workers' Voice*, 25 March 1939, p. 4; C Crofts, Secretary, Australasian Council of Trade Unions, to Stevens, 22 March 1939, New South Wales Archives and Records, NRS 12060, Item No. [12/8749-8750]; Crofts to Albert Dunstan, 22 March 1939, Public Record Office of Victoria, VPRS 3992/P, Unit 2796, file 52678; President, Victorian Council of the Young Communist League of Australia, to Stevens, 27 March 1939, New South Wales Archives and Records, NRS 12060, Item No. [12/8749-8750]; *Workers' Voice*, 1 April 1939, pp. 1, 4; JF Chapple, General Secretary, Australian Railways Union, to Stevens, 18 April 1939, New South Wales Archives and Records, NRS 12060, Item No. [12/8749-8750]; *The Age*, 18 April 1939, p. 6; Jean Muir, Secretary, University Labour Club, 20 April 1939,

New South Wales Archives and Records, NRS 12060, Item No. [12/8749-8750]; *The Age*, 20 April 1939, p. 10.

34 Cooper to Stevens, 25 April 1939, New South Wales Archives and Records, NRS 12060, Item No. [12/8749-8750]; Baillie to Gollan, 28 April 1939, New South Wales Archives and Records, NRS 905, Item No. [12/7584.1]; *The Argus*, 29 April 1939, p. 2; *Workers' Voice*, 3 May 1939, p. 4.

35 Cooper, Letter to the Editor, undated, *Australian Worker*, 10 May 1939, p. 15.

36 Cooper to Premier, Western Australia, 19 May 1938, State Records Office of Western Australia, AU WA S2030—cons993 1936/0075; Cooper to John Curtin, 9 July 1938, National Archives of Australia, A659, 1940/1/858; *Workers' Voice*, 3 June 1939, p. 2; Doug Nicholls, Acting Secretary, Australian Aborigines' League, to Secretary, Victorian Board for the Protection of the Aborigines, 13 June 1939, Public Record Office of Victoria, VPRS 3992/P, Unit 2811, File R4729; *The Guardian*, 14 June 1939, p. 1; Burdeu to Morley, 2 July 1939, Association for the Protection of Native Races, Item 7; Baillie, 'Some Recollections of Mr. APA Burdeu', undated, Elkin Papers, Series 12, Item 134; *The Herald* [Melbourne], 11 October 1939, p. 10; Tucker, 'My Initiation into What? The Unknown', cited Jennifer Jones, *Black Writers, White Editors: Episodes of Collaboration and Compromise in Australian Publishing History*, Australian Scholarly Publishing, Melbourne, 2009, p. 138; Tucker, *If Everyone Cared*, p. 163; Alec Morgan (director), *Lousy Little Sixpence*, Australian Film Commission, Sixpence Productions and Ronin Films, 1983.

37 The first reference to this organisation I am aware of is a newspaper article that refers to a radio program broadcast on 28 May 1939: *Workers' Voice*, 3 June 1939, p. 2.

38 George Patten, Circular Letter, 16 May 1939, New South Wales Archives and Records, NRS 905, Item No. [12/7584.1]; *The Herald* (Melbourne), 18 May 1939, p. 10; *The Age*, 1 June 1939, p. 17; LP Fox, Secretary, Victorian League for Peace and Democracy, to Stevens, 9 June 1939, New South Wales Archives and Records, NRS 12060, Item No. [12/8749-8750]; HL Whitney, Secretary, Brighton Branch of the Australian League for Peace and Freedom, to Stevens, 10 June 1939, New South Wales Archives and Records, NRS 12060, Item No. [12/8749-8750]; *The Guardian*, 14 June 1939, p. 1; Acting Under-Secretary, Minute on Request for Royal Commission to Investigate the Activities of the Aborigines Protection Board, 23 June 1939, New South Wales Archives and Records, NRS 12060, Item No. [12/8749-8750]; *The Herald* (Melbourne), 28 June 1939, p. 4; *Australian Worker*, 12 July 1939, p. 13; *The Herald* (Melbourne), 24 July 1939, p. 18; *The Herald* (Melbourne), 26 July 1939, p. 12.

39 *The Herald* (Melbourne), 24 July 1939, p. 18; Aborigines' Assistance Committee, The Fight at Cummeragunja (leaflet), undated, August 1939, copy held New South Wales Archives and Records, NRS 12060, Item No. [12/8749-8750]; Aborigines' Assistance Committee, Plea for Native Freedom (pamphlet), copy held New South Wales Archives and Records, NRS 12060, Item No. [12/8749-8750]; Bernice McAuliffe, Secretary, Aborigines' Assistance Committee, to Alexander Muir, Premier of New South Wales, 19 August 1939, New South Wales Archives and Records, NRS 12060, Item No. [12/8749-8750]; Chapple to Muir, 21 August 1939, New South Wales Archives and Records, NRS 12060, Item No. [12/8749-8750]; Aborigines' Assistance Committee, Aboriginal S.O.S. (flyer), 20 January 1940, copy held Elkin Papers, Series 12, Item 126.

40 *The Herald* (Melbourne), 29 September 1939, p. 4; *The Age*, 12 October 1939, p. 12; Acting Under Secretary, Premier's Department, New South Wales, Minute, 12 October 1939, New South Wales Archives and Records, NRS 12060, Item No. [12/8749-8750]; *Victorian Parliamentary Debates*, Legislative Assembly, 18 October 1939, pp. 1630–31; Anderson to Acting Under Secretary, Premier's Department, New South Wales, 20 October 1939, New South Wales Archives and Records, NRS 12060, Item No. [12/8749-8750].

41 See, for example, Goodall, p. 255; Ward, pp. 35, 71, 81, 85.

42 *Daily Telegraph* (Sydney), 12 March 1938, p. 2; New South Wales Aborigines Protection Board, Minutes, 8 November 1939, 30 December 1939, 12 February 1940, 13 March 1940, New South Wales Archives and Records, NRS-3, Item No. [4/7126]; *Daily News*, 9 February 1939, p. 5; *Government Gazette of New South Wales*, 24 February 1939, p. 997; *New South Wales Parliamentary Debates*, Legislative Council, 15 May 1940; *New South Wales Aborigines Protection (Amendment Act)*, 1940, clause 4 (2) (b), https://aiatsis.gov.au/sites/default/files/docs/digitised_collections/remove/52293.pdf.

43 *The Herald* (Melbourne), 11 October 1939, p. 10; Baillie to Edith Jones, 25 December 1940, Papers of the Anti-Slavery Society, G699; President's Report for Aborigines Progressive Association, 31 December 1940, copy held in the Papers of the Anti-Slavery Society, G699.

44 Burdeu to the Minister for the Interior, John McEwen, 27 February 1938, National Archives of Australia, B1535, 929/19/912; Patten to Lyons, 9 December 1938, National Archives of Australia, B1535, 929/19/912; Robert A Hall, *The Black Diggers: Aborigines and Torres Strait Islanders in the Second World War* (1989), Aboriginal Studies Press, Canberra, 1997, p. 9. Ferguson would do the same in July 1940: letters to Menzies, 8 July 1940, National Archives of Australia, MP508/1, 82/712/670.

45 Cooper, Letter to the Editor, undated, *The Age,* 16 March 1933, p. 10; Cooper to McEwen, 3 January 1939, National Archives of Australia, A659, 1940/1/858; [APA Burdeu], Episodes of Interest in the Life of the Late William Cooper (Told by Himself), 30 June 1941, Norman Family Papers, Mortlock Library, State Library of South Australia, PRG 422/31. See also Cooper to NM Morley, 7 March 1936, Elkin Papers, Series 12, Item 148.

46 Cooper to Menzies, 5 October 1939 and 3 December 1939, National Archives of Australia, A461, A300/1 Part 3.

47 *Uplift: The Official Organ of the Aborigines' Uplift Society*, 1(1), 1938, p. 3; Cooper to Menzies, 5 October 1939; Burdeu to Menzies, 30 June 1940, National Archives of Australia, A431, 1949/822.

48 See Hall, pp. 13–26.

49 Burdeu to Menzies, 7 July 1940, National Archives of Australia, MP508/1, 275/750/1310; Bill Onus, Secretary, Committee for Aboriginal Citizenship, to FM Forde, Minister for the Army, undated [7 January 1942], National Archives of Australia, MP508/1, 275/750/1310; Ruth Swann, Secretary, Association for Protection of Native Races, to Forde, 20 April 1942, National Archives of Australia, MP508/1, 275/750/1310; Onus to the Aborigines Advancement League of South Australia, 30 June 1941, Aborigines Advancement League Papers, Mortlock Library, State Library of South Australia, SRG 250/4.

50 In March 1941 Burdeu, writing on behalf of both the League and the Uplift Society, protested once more about Aboriginal men being barred and discharged

from the army. He reported that he knew of men whose loyalty to the British Crown and the Australian nation had been severely weakened, writing: 'I know of some men ... who ... remain seated with hats on while the National Anthem is sung, remarking "We have no king now and no country"' (Burdeu to the Secretary of the Prime Minister, 30 March 1941, National Archives of Australia, MP508/1, 275/750/1310).

51 Cooper to Menzies, 31 August 1940, National Archives of Australia, A659, 1940/1/858.

Epilogue

1 *The Age*, 29 November 1940, p. 8; Death Certificate for William Cooper, 29 March 1941, Victorian Registry of Births, Marriages and Deaths, 1941/5144; *The Herald* (Melbourne), 31 March 1941, p. 7; *Riverine Herald*, 31 March 1941, p. 2; *The Argus*, 1 April 1941, p. 3; *Numurkah Leader*, 1 April 1941, p. 3; APA Burdeu to Mrs WA Norman, 30 June 1941, Norman Family Papers, Mortlock Library, State Library of South Australia, PRG 422/31; Helen Baillie, 'Some Recollections of Mr APA Burdeu', undated, AP Elkin Papers, University of Sydney Archives, P. 130, Series 12, Item 134.

2 *The Herald* (Melbourne), 20 August 1949, p. 13; *The Age*, 28 June 1951, p. 3; *The Argus*, 21 May 1953, p. 3; Mavis Thorpe Clark, *Pastor Doug: The Story of Sir Douglas Nicholls, Aboriginal Leader*, Lansdowne Press, Melbourne, 1965, pp. 89–90.

3 Doug Nicholls to JB Chifley, 1 July 1949, National Archives of Australia, A431, 1949/1591; Nicholls to Chifley, 6 August 1949, National Archives of Australia, A431, 1949/1591; Cooper, Circular Letter, undated [c. August 1949], National Archives of Australia, A431, 1949/1591.

4 *Victorian Aborigines Advancement League Newsletter*, 17, 1969, p. 3; 19, 1969, p. 8; Wayne Atkinson, '"Not One Iota" of Land Justice: Reflections on the Yorta Yorta Native Title Claim 1994–2001', *Indigenous Law Bulletin*, 5(6), 2001, p. 23.

5 This took place in 2010.

6 This occurred in 2018. Previously, the electorate was called Batman. One wonders what Cooper would have thought of his name supplanting John Batman's.

BIBLIOGRAPHY

Primary Sources

Archives

Australian National University Archives
National Centre for Biography, File for William Cooper entry for the Australian Dictionary of Biography, AU ANUA 312-2061.

National Archives of Australia
Aboriginal Unit for AIF, Letter to Prime Minister from President, Aborigines Progressive Association, Dubbo, MP508/1, 82/712/670.

Association for Protection of Native Races—Aboriginal Matters, File No. 1, A1, 1936/6595.

Attorney-General's Department, Correspondence files, Australian Aborigines' League, Petition to the King—Representation in the Commonwealth Parliament, A432, 1937/1191.

Board for the Protection of the Aborigines, Victoria, Aborigines Case Files: Cooper, William, B337, 187.

——Aborigines Case Files: James, Shadrach Livingstone, B337, 362.

——Correspondence Files, B313, 26, 27, 41 and 47.

Burdeu, CA, Military Record, B2455.

Cooper, Daniel, Military Record, B2455.

Department of Defence, Correspondence Files, Military Training for Aboriginal Youth in Australia, B1535, 929/19/912.

Department of the Interior, Correspondence Files, Aboriginal Welfare Conference—Melbourne—1933, A1, 1933/8782.

——Correspondence Files, Welfare of Aboriginals in the Northern Territory: Deputation to Minister, 23.1.35, A1, 1935/3951.

——Correspondence Files, Corroborees at Aboriginal Compound, Darwin, A1, 1936/7014.

——Correspondence Files, EE Kramer Abo. Affairs NT, A1, 1936/12778.

——Correspondence Files, Aboriginals—Right to Vote, A431, 1949/822.

——Correspondence Files, Representation of Aborigines in the Commonwealth Parliament, A431, 1949/1591.

——Correspondence Files, Australian Aborigines League, A659, 1940/1/858.

Prime Minister's Department, Correspondence files, Aboriginals—Policy ..., A461, A300/1 Parts 2 and 3.

New South Wales Archives and Records

Aborigines Protection Board and Aborigines Welfare Board, Minutes, NRS-3, Item No. [4/7126].

Chief Secretary Letters Received, Files relating to Aboriginal Affairs, NRS 905, Item No. [12/7584.1].

Colonial Secretary Main Series of Letters Received, NRS 905, Item No. [1/2667].

——Main Series of Letters Received, NRS 905, Item No. [2/1745].

——Main Series of Letters Received, NRS 905, Item No. [5/7121].

Department of Education, Cummeragunja (Aboriginal) School Administrative File, 1889–1910, NRS 3829, Item No. [5/15619.2].

Premier's Department, New South Wales, Treatment of Aboriginals in New South Wales, 1936–63 part 1, NRS 12060, Item No. [8479–8750].

Public Record Office Victoria

Chief Secretary's Office, Victoria, Correspondence Files, VPRS 3992.

Supplementary Inward Registered Correspondence, Z6070, Aborigines & Coranderrk Inquiry, VPRS 1226, Unit 4.

State Records of South Australia

Chief Secretary's Department, Inwards Correspondence, GRG 52/1, 1936.

State Records Office of Western Australia

Australian Aboriginals League Melbourne, Information and Constitution of Victorian Aboriginal Group, AU WA S2030—cons993 1936/0075.

Petition to HM the King by Aboriginal Natives re (1) Prevention of Extinction of the Aboriginal Race (2) Representation in Federal Parliament, AU WA S2030—cons993 1933/0368.

University of Melbourne Archives

Edwin Adamson Collection, 1980.0135, Studio Registers, 1933–1965.

Manuscripts

Aborigines Advancement League Papers, Mortlock Library, State Library of South Australia, SRG 250.

Anti-Slavery Society, Papers, Weston Library, Oxford University, MSS. Brit. Emp. s. 22.

Association for the Protection of Native Races Papers, University of Sydney Archives, Series 55.

Australian Board of Missions, Further Records, 1873–1978, Mitchell Library, MLMSS 4503, Add-on 1822, Box 8, Folder 4, Box 9, Folder 2, Box 11, Folder 17.

Brown, AN, Papers, State Library Victoria, MS 9212.

Elkin, AP, Papers, University of Sydney Archives, P.130.

Fisk Jubilee Singers, Scrapbook of Tour of Australasia, Beinecke Rare Book and Manuscript Library, Yale University Library, JWJ MSS 60, https://brbl-zoom.library.yale.edu/viewer/16026937.

Gribble, ERB, Papers, Australian Institute of Aboriginal and Torres Strait Islander Studies Library, MS 1515.

Maloga from the Diaries and Mission Reports of Daniel Matthews, 1861–1873, Mitchell Library, MS A 3384.

Matthews, Daniel, Diaries and Papers, 1866–1909, National Library of Australia, MS 2195.

Norman Papers, State Library of South Australia, PRG 422.

St Peter's Eastern Hill, Papers, State Library Victoria, MS 15811.

Selby, Isaac, Papers, Royal Historical Society of Victoria, MS 694.

Stephensen, PR, Papers, Mitchell Library, State Library of New South Wales, MS 1284.

Sturt, Charles, Account of Journey, 1838, State Library Victoria, MS 9025.

Treseder, John G, Report of a Visit to the Aborigines Mission Stations at Coomeragunga and Warangesda, 13 July 1891, Australian Institute of Aborigines and Torres Strait Islander Studies Library, PMS 4606.

Vroland, AWR, Papers, National Library of Australia, MS 3991.

Women's International League of Peace and Freedom Papers, State Library Victoria, MS 9377.

Wright, Tom and Mary, Papers, Noel Butlin Archives Centre, Australian National University, MS Z267.

Printed Parliamentary Papers

Aboriginal Welfare: Initial Conference of Commonwealth and State Aboriginal Authorities held at Canberra, 21 to 23 April 1937, Government Printer, Canberra, [1937].

Census of the Commonwealth of Australia 30 June 1933.

New South Wales Aborigines Protection Board, Reports for 1894, 1903–1911.

New South Wales Legislative Assembly, *Votes and Proceedings*, 1889, vol. 5, Medical Attendants to Aborigines at Cumeroogunga Mission Station (Correspondence &c., Relating to Appointment of).

——*Votes and Proceedings*, 1889, vol. 5, Medical Attendants to Aborigines at Cumeroogunga Mission Station (Further Correspondence Respecting).

——*Votes and Proceedings*, 1883, Aboriginal Mission Stations at Warangesda and Maloga.

——*Votes and Proceedings*, 1883, Report of the Protector of Aborigines to 31 December 1882.

——*Votes and Proceedings*, 1883, Protection of the Aborigines (Minute of Colonial Secretary, Together with Reports).

——*Votes and Proceedings*, 1894–95, Aborigines Protection Board to the Principal Under Secretary of New South Wales, 1 March 1895.

New South Wales Parliamentary Debates.

Report of the Royal Commission on the Constitution, Together with Appendices and Index, Government Printer, Canberra, 1929.

Victorian Board for the Protection of the Aborigines, Annual Reports, 1871, 1876.

Victorian Central Board for the Protection of the Aborigines, Annual Reports, 1861–69.

Victorian Legislative Assembly, *Votes and Proceedings*, 1877–78, vol. 3, Royal Commission on the Aborigines.
——*Votes and Proceedings*, 1882–83, vol. 2, Board Appointed to Inquire into Coranderrk Aboriginal Station.
Victorian Legislative Council, *Votes and Proceedings*, 1853–54, vol. 3, Aborigines. Return to Address, Mr Parker, 21 October 1853.
——*Votes and Proceedings*, 1858–59, vol. 1, Report of the Select Committee of the Legislative Council on the Aborigines.

Newspapers and Magazines
Abo Call
Adelaide Advertiser
The Age
The Argus
The Australasian
Australasian Sketcher with Pen and Pencil
Australian Christian
Australian Intercollegian
Australian News for Home Readers
Australian Worker
Bendigo Advertiser
Border Morning Mail (Albury)
Canberra Times
Clarence and Richmond Examiner and New England Advertiser
The Courier (Brisbane)
Courier-Mail
Daily News (Sydney)
Daily Telegraph (Sydney)
Dawn
Echuca and Moama Advertiser
Empire
The Examiner (Launceston)
Footscray Advertiser
Geelong Advertiser
Goulburn Herald
Goulburn Herald and Chronicle
Healesville and Yarra Glen Guardian
The Herald (Melbourne)
Illustrated Australian News
Inverell Times
Labor Call
Labor Daily
Ladder
The Leader
The Mirror (Perth)
New South Wales Government Gazette
North Eastern Ensign (Benalla)
Northern Star (Lismore)

Numurkah Leader
Numurkah Standard
Ovens and Murray Advertiser
Riverine Herald
Shepparton News
Southland Times
Sporting Globe
The Sun (Melbourne)
Sydney Mail and New South Wales Advertiser
Sydney Morning Herald
The Times (London)
Uplift: The Official Organ of the Aborigines' Uplift Society
Victorian Aborigines Advancement League Newsletter
Weekly Times
West Australian
Woman Today
The Worker
Workers' Voice
Working Woman Today

Books, Pamphlets and Reports

Baillie, Helen, *The Call of the Aboriginal*, Fraser & Morphet, Melbourne, 193[3].

Clements, Theresa, *From Old Maloga: The Memoirs of an Aboriginal Woman*, Fraser & Morphet, Melbourne, n.d.

Curr, Edward M, *Recollections of Squatting in Victoria* (1883), Melbourne University Press, Melbourne, 1965.

Fletcher, JJ, *Documents in the History of Aboriginal Education in New South Wales*, Carlton, Sydney, 1989.

Hibbins, GM, *Barmah Chronicles*, Lynedoch Publications, Melbourne, 1991.

Jackomos, Alick and Derek Fowell, *Living Aboriginal History of Victoria: Stories in the Oral Tradition*, Cambridge University Press, Melbourne, 1991.

Maloga Aboriginal Mission School, *Reports*, nos 1–6, 1876–1881.

Maloga Aboriginal Mission Station, *Reports*, nos 7–14, 1882–89.

Markus, Andrew, *Blood from a Stone: William Cooper and the Australian Aborigines' League*, Allen & Unwin, Sydney, 1988.

Matthews, Daniel, *An Appeal on Behalf of the Australian Aboriginals*, Haverfield and Co., Echuca, 1873.

——*The Story of the Maloga Mission*, Rae Bros, Melbourne, 1893.

Morgan, Ronald, *Reminiscences of the Aboriginal Station at Cummeragunga and its Aboriginal People*, s.n., Melbourne, 1952.

New South Wales Aborigines Protection Association, *The Australian Aboriginal, Being the Annual Report of the New South Wales Aborigines Protection Association for 1894*.

——'The Heathen at Our Doors': Being the Annual Report of the New South Wales Aborigines Protection Association for 1893*.

——*Our Black Brethren: Their Past, Present, and Future: Being the Annual Report of the Aborigines Protection Association for 1891*.

——*The Rightful Owners, Our Duty to Them, Being the Annual Report of the Aborigines Protection Association for 1890*.

Report of the New South Wales Aborigines Protection Association, June 30 1881, s.n., Sydney, 1881.

Stanner, WEH, *White Man Got No Dreaming: Essays 1938–1973*, Australian National University Press, Canberra, 1979.

Tucker, Margaret, *If Everyone Cared: Autobiography of Margaret Tucker*, Ure Smith, Sydney, 1977.

Turnbull, Clive, *Black War: The Extermination of the Tasmanian Aborigines*, Cheshire, Melbourne, 1948.

Westwood, JJ, *The Journal of JJ Westwood*, Clarson, Shallard and Co., Melbourne, 1865.

Journal articles

Atkinson, Wayne, "'Not One Iota" of Land Justice: Reflections on the Yorta Yorta Native Title Claim 1994–2001', *Indigenous Law Bulletin*, 5(6), 2001, pp. 19–23.

James, Thomas, 'Baimai', *Australasian Anthropological Journal*, 1(4), 1897, pp. 87–89.

Film

Morgan, Alec (director), *Lousy Little Sixpence*, Australian Film Commission, Sixpence Productions and Ronin Films, 1983.

Secondary Sources

Books

Abbott, Lynn and Doug Seroff, *Out of Sight: The Rise of African American Popular Music, 1889–1895*, University Press of Mississippi, Jackson, Miss., 2002.

Attwood, Bain, Possession: *Batman's Treaty and the Matter of History*, Miegunyah Press, Melbourne, 2008.

——*Rights for Aborigines*, Allen & Unwin, Sydney, 2003.

Attwood, Bain and Andrew Markus, *The 1967 Referendum: Race, Power and the Australian Constitution*, Aboriginal Studies Press, Canberra, 2017.

——*The Struggle for Aboriginal Rights: A Documentary History*, Allen & Unwin, Sydney, 1999.

——*Thinking Black: William Cooper and the Australian Aborigines' League*, Aboriginal Studies Press, Canberra, 2004.

Attwood, Bain et al., *A Life Together, a Life Apart: A History of Relations Between Europeans and Aborigines*, Melbourne University Press, Melbourne, 1994.

Barwick, Diane E, *Rebellion at Coranderrk*, edited by Laura E and Richard E Barwick, Aboriginal History Inc., Canberra, 1998.

Bennett, Michael, *Pathfinders: A History of Aboriginal Trackers in NSW*, NewSouth, Sydney, 2020.

Bowe, Heather et al., *Yorta Yorta Language Heritage*, Department of Linguistics, Monash University, Melbourne, 1997.

Broome, Richard, *Aboriginal Victorians: A History since 1800*, Allen & Unwin, Sydney, 2005.

——*Fighting Hard: The Victorian Aborigines Advancement League*, Aboriginal Studies Press, Canberra, 2015.

Brown, Christopher Leslie, *Moral Capital: Foundations of British Abolitionism*, University of North Carolina Press, Chapel Hill, NC, 2006.

Butlin, NG, *Economics and the Dreamtime: A Hypothetical History*, Cambridge University Press, Melbourne, 1993.

Caine, Barbara, *Biography and History*, Palgrave Macmillan, London, 2010.

Cato, Nancy, *Mister Maloga: Daniel Matthews and his Mission, Murray River, 1864–1902*, University of Queensland Press, St Lucia, 1976.

Chapman, Graeme, *Ballarat Churches of Christ, 1859–1993: A History*, Churches of Christ Theological College, Melbourne, 1994.

Clark, Mavis Thorpe, *Pastor Doug: The Story of Sir Douglas Nicholls, Aboriginal Leader*, Lansdowne Press, Melbourne, 1965.

Davis, Fiona, *Australian Settler Colonialism and the Cummeragunja Aboriginal Station: Redrawing Boundaries*, Sussex Academic Press, Brighton, UK, 2014.

de Costa, Ravi, *A Higher Authority: Indigenous Transnationalism and Australia*, UNSW Press, Sydney, 2006.

Fels, Marie, *Good Men and True: The Aboriginal Police of the Port Phillip District 1837–53*, Melbourne University Press, Melbourne, 1988.

Fletcher, JJ, Clean, *Clad and Courteous: A History of Aboriginal Education in New South Wales*, Carlton, Sydney, 1989.

Furphy, Samuel, *Edmund M Curr and the Tide of History*, Australian National University E-Press, Canberra, 2013.

Goodall, Heather, *Invasion to Embassy: Land in Aboriginal Politics in New South Wales, 1770–1972*, Black Books/Allen & Unwin, Sydney, 1996.

Goodall, Heather and Alison Cadzow, *Rivers and Resilience: Aboriginal People on Sydney's Georges River*, UNSW Press, Sydney, 2009.

Haebich, Anna, *For Their Own Good: Aborigines and Government in the Southwest of Western Australia, 1900–1940*, University of Western Australia Press, Perth, 1988.

Hall, Robert A, *The Black Diggers: Aborigines and Torres Strait Islanders in the Second World War* (1989), Aboriginal Studies Press, Canberra, 1997.

Harris, John, *One Blood: 200 Years of Aboriginal Encounter with Christianity: A Story of Hope*, Albatross Books, Sydney, 1990.

Hay, Roy, *Aboriginal People and Australian Football in the Nineteenth Century: They Did Not Come from Nowhere*, Cambridge Scholars Publishing, Newcastle upon Tyne, 2019.

Holland, Alison, *Breaking the Silence: Aboriginal Defenders and the Settler State, 1905–1939*, Melbourne University Press, Melbourne, 2019.

Horner, Jack, *Vote Ferguson for Aboriginal Freedom: A Biography*, Australian and New Zealand Book Company, Sydney, 1974.

Inglis, Amirah, *Australians in the Spanish Civil War*, Allen & Unwin, Sydney, 1987.

Irish, Paul, *Hidden in Plain Sight: The Aboriginal People of Coastal Sydney*, NewSouth, Sydney, 2017.

Jones, Jennifer, *Black Writers, White Editors: Episodes of Collaboration and Compromise in Australian Publishing History*, Australian Scholarly Publishing, Melbourne, 2009.

Kenny, Robert, *The Lamb Enters the Dreaming: Nathanael Pepper & the Ruptured World*, Scribe, Melbourne, 2007.

Lack, John, *A History of Footscray*, Hargreen Publishing in conjunction with the City of Footscray, Melbourne, 1991.

Lake, Meredith, *The Bible in Australia: A Cultural History*, NewSouth, Sydney, 2018.

Lydon, Jane, *Eye Contact: Photographing Indigenous Australians*, Duke University Press, Durham, NC, 2005.

McGregor, Russell, *Imagined Destinies: Aboriginal Australians and the Doomed Race Theory, 1880–1939*, Melbourne University Press, Melbourne, 1997.

——*Indifferent Inclusion: Aboriginal People and the Australian Nation*, Aboriginal Studies Press, Canberra, 2011.

Markus, Andrew, *Governing Savages*, Allen & Unwin, Sydney, 1990.

Maynard, John, *Fight for Liberty and Freedom: The Origins of Australian Aboriginal Activism*, Aboriginal Studies Press, Canberra, 2007.

Morgan, Edmund S, *Inventing the People: The Rise of Popular Sovereignty in England and America*, WW Norton & Company, New York, 1988.

Nanni, Giordano and Andrea James, *Coranderrk: We Will Show the Country*, Aboriginal Studies Press, Canberra, 2013.

Nelson, George and Robynne Nelson, *Dharmalan Dana: An Australian Aboriginal Man's 73-Year Search for the Story of His Aboriginal and Indian Ancestors*, Australian National University Press, Canberra, 2014.

Niall, Brenda, *Mannix*, Text Publishing, Melbourne, 2015.

O'Brien, Karen, *Petitioning for Land: The Petitions of First Peoples of Early Modern British Colonies*, Bloomsbury Academic, London, 2019.

Paisley, Fiona, *The Lone Protestor: AM Fernando in Australia and Europe*, Aboriginal Studies Press, Canberra, 2012.

——*Loving Protection? Australian Feminism and Aboriginal Women's Rights 1919–1939*, Melbourne University Press, Melbourne, 2000.

Pedersen, Susan, *The Guardians: The League of Nations and the Crisis of Empire*, Oxford University Press, New York, 2015.

Pitkethly, Anne and Don, *NJ Caire: Landscape Photographer*, Anne and Don Pitkethly with assistance from Kodak (Australasia), Melbourne, 1988.

Priestley, Susan, *Echuca: A Centenary History*, Jacaranda Press, Brisbane, 1965.

——*Echuca: A History*, Australian Scholarly Press, Melbourne, 2009.

Read, Peter, *A Hundred Years War: The Wiradjuri People and the State*, Australian National University Press, Canberra, 1988.

Reynolds, Henry, *With the White People*, 2nd edn, Penguin Books, Melbourne, 2000.

Rowse, Tim, *Indigenous and Other Australians Since 1901*, UNSW Press, Sydney, 2017.

Seed, Patricia, *Ceremonies of Possession in Europe's Conquest of the New World, 1492–1640*, Cambridge University Press, Cambridge, 1995.

Silverman, David J, *This Land is Their Land: The Wampanoag Indians, Plymouth Colony, and the Troubled History of Thanksgiving*, Bloomsbury Publishing, New York, 2019.

Swain, Tony, *A Place for Strangers: Towards a History of Australian Aboriginal Being*, Cambridge University Press, Melbourne, 1993.

Taffe, Sue, *A White Hot Flame: Mary Montgomerie Bennett—Author, Educator, Activist for Indigenous Justice*, Monash University Publishing, Melbourne, 2018.

Tindale, Norman B, *Aboriginal Tribes of Australia: Their Terrain, Environmental Controls, Distribution, Limits and Proper Names*, 2 vols, Australian National University Press, 1974.

Waghorne, James and Stuart Macintyre, *Liberty: A History of Civil Liberties in Australia*, UNSW Press, Sydney, 2011.

Williams, John A, *Politics of the New Zealand Maori: Protest and Cooperation, 1891–1909*, Auckland University Press, Auckland, 1969.

Wiltshire, Kenneth, *CR Burdeu: A Living Legend*, Baskerville Printing, Brisbane, 1971.

Website

Ryan, Lyndall et al., Colonial Frontier Massacres in Australia, 1788–1930, https://c21ch.newcastle.edu.au/colonialmassacres/.

Journal articles

Attwood, Bain, 'Denial in a Settler Society: The Australian Case', *History Workshop Journal*, 84, 2017, pp. 24–43.

——'The Founding of *Aboriginal History* and the Forming of Aboriginal History', *Aboriginal History*, 36, 2012, pp. 119–71.

Barwick, Diane, 'Writing Aboriginal History', *Canberra Anthropology*, 4(2), 1981, pp. 74–86.

Blackburn, Kevin, 'White Agitation for an Aboriginal State in Australia (1925–1929)', *Australian Journal of Politics and History*, 45(2), 1999, pp. 157–80.

Broome, Richard, 'Aboriginal Workers on South-Eastern Frontiers', *Australian Historical Studies*, 26(103), 1994, pp. 202–20.

Campbell, Judy, 'Smallpox in Aboriginal Australia, 1829–31', *Historical Studies*, 20(81), 1983, pp. 536–56.

de Costa, Ravi, 'Identity, Authority and the Moral Worlds of Indigenous Petitions', *Comparative Studies in Society and History*, 48(3), 2006, pp. 669–98.

Foster, Robert, 'Contested Destinies: Aboriginal Advocacy in South Australia's Interwar Years', *Aboriginal History*, 42, 2018, pp. 73–95.

Ganitis, George, 'Early Aboriginal Civil Resistance: The Untold Story of William Harris', *Overland*, 1 November 2018, https://overland.org.au/2018/11/early-aboriginal-civil-resistance-in-wa-the-untold-story-of-william-harris/.

Goodall, Heather, 'Land in Our Own Country: The Aboriginal Lands Rights Movement in South-Eastern Australia, 1860 to 1914', *Aboriginal History*, 14(1), 1990, pp. 1–24.

Goodall, Heather et al., 'Jumping Ship, Skirting Empire: Indians, Aborigines and Australians Across the Indian Ocean', *Transforming Cultures eJournal*, 3(1), 2008, pp. 44–74.

Gunson, Niel, 'Proud Shoes: Black Family History in Australia', *Aboriginal History*, 5(2), 1981, pp. 147–52.

Holland, Alison, '"Does the British flag mean nothing to us?" British Democratic Traditions and Aboriginal Rights Claims in Interwar Australia', *Australian Historical Studies*, 2019, 50(3), pp. 321–38.

Irving, Sarah, 'Governing Nature: The Problem of Northern Australia', *Australian Historical Studies*, 45(3), 2014, pp. 388–406.

Kleinert, Sylvia, 'Aboriginality in the City: Re-Reading Koorie Photographs', *Aboriginal History*, 30, 2006, pp. 70–94.

McGregor, Russell, 'Protest and Progress: Aboriginal Activism in the 1930s', *Australian Historical Studies*, 25(101), 1993, pp. 555–68.

McLisky, Claire, 'From Missionary Wife to Superintendent: Janet Matthews on Three Independent Murray River Missions', *Journal of Australian Studies*, 39(1), 2015, pp. 32–43.

——'The Location of Faith: Power, Gender and Spirituality in the 1883–84 Maloga Mission Revival', *History Australia*, 7(1), 2010, pp. 08.1–20.

Markus, Andrew, 'William Cooper and the 1937 Petition to the King', *Aboriginal History*, 7(1), 1983, pp. 46–60.

Maynard, John, 'Vision, Voice and Influence: The Rise of the Australian Aboriginal Progressive Association', *Australian Historical Studies*, 34(11), 2003, pp. 91–105.

Murphy, John, 'Conditional Inclusion: Aborigines and Welfare Rights in Australia, 1900–47', *Australian Historical Studies*, 44(2), 2013, pp. 206–26.

Nasaw, David, 'Introduction: AHR Roundtable: Historians and Biography', *American Historical Review*, 114(3), 2009, pp. 573–78.

Painter, Nell Irvin, 'Sojourner Truth in Life and Memory: Writing the Biography of an American Exotic', *Gender and History*, 2(1), 1990, pp. 3–16.

Pardoe, Colin, 'Bioscapes: The Evolutionary Landscape of Australia', *Archaeology in Oceania*, 29(3), 1994, pp. 182–90.

——'The Cemetery as Symbol: The Distribution of Prehistoric Burial Grounds in South-Eastern Australia', *Archaeology in Oceania*, 23(1), 1988, pp. 1–16.

Peck, Julia, 'Performing Aboriginality: Desiring Pre-Contact Aboriginality in Victoria, 1886–1901', *History of Photography*, 34(3), 2010, pp. 214–33.

Roe, Michael, 'A Model Aboriginal State', *Aboriginal History*, 10(1), 1986, pp. 40–44.

Roginski, Alexandra, 'Talking Heads on a Murray River Mission: Phrenological Lecturers and their Aboriginal Receptions Decoded', *History Australia*, 16(4), 2019, pp. 714–32.

Rutland, Suzanne, 'Australian Responses to Jewish Refugee Migration Before and After World War II', *Australian Journal of Politics and History*, 32(1), 1985, pp. 29–48.

Seroff, Doug, 'A Voice in the Wilderness: The Fisk Jubilee Singers' Civil Rights Tours of 1879–1882', *Popular Music and Society*, 25(1–2), 2001, pp. 131–77.

Stallard, Matthew and Jerome de Groot, '"Things Are Coming Out that Are Questionable, We Never Knew About": DNA and the New Family History', *Journal of Family History*, 45(3), 2020, pp. 274–94.

Sweetnam, Mark S, 'Dan Crawford, *Thinking Black*, and the Challenge of a Missionary Canon', *Journal of Ecclesiastical History*, 38(4), 2007, pp. 705–25.

Wilson, Bill and Justin O'Brien, '"To Infuse a Universal Terror": A Reappraisal of the Coniston Killings', *Aboriginal History*, 27, 2003, pp. 59–78.

Chapters and Essays

Atkinson, Wayne, 'The Schools of Human Experience', in Rachel Perkins and Marcia Langton (eds), *First Australians: An Illustrated History*, Miegunyah Press, Melbourne, 2008, pp. 287–329.

Bach, Joanne, 'Morgan, Anna Euphemia (1874–1935)', *Australian Dictionary of Biography*, National Centre of Biography, Australian National University, http://adb.anu.edu.au/biography/morgan-anna-euphemia-13108/text23715, published first in hardcopy 2005.

Ballara, Angela, 'Rātana, Tahupōtiki Wiremu', *Dictionary of New Zealand Biography*, first published in 1996. Te Ara: The Encyclopedia of New Zealand, https://teara.govt.nz/en/biographies/3r4/ratana-tahupotiki-wiremu.

Barwick, Diane, 'Aunty Ellen: The Pastor's Wife', in Isobel White et al. (eds), *Fighters and Singers: The Lives of Some Aboriginal Women*, George Allen & Unwin, Sydney, 1985, pp. 175–99.

——'Changes in the Aboriginal Population of Victoria, 1863–1966', in Jack Golson and DJ Mulvaney (eds), *Aboriginal Man and Environment in Australia*, Australian National University Press, Canberra, 1971, pp. 288–315.

——'Cooper, William (1861–1941)', *Australian Dictionary of Biography*, Australian National University, http://adb.anu.edu.au/biography/cooper-william-5773/text9787, published first in hardcopy 1981.

——'Coranderrk and Cumeroogunga: Pioneers and Policy', in T Scarlett Epstein and David H Penny (eds), *Opportunity and Response: Case Studies in Economic Development*, C Hurst, London, 1972, pp. 11–68.

Belgrave, Michael, '"We rejoice to honour the Queen, for she is a good woman, who cares for the Māori race": Loyalty and Protest in Māori Politics in Nineteenth-Century New Zealand', in Sarah Carter and Maria Nugent (eds), *Mistress of Everything: Queen Victoria in Indigenous Worlds*, Manchester University Press, Manchester, 2016, pp. 54–77.

Broome, Richard, 'Nicholls, Sir Douglas Ralph (Doug) (1906–1988)', *Australian Dictionary of Biography*, National Centre of Biography, Australian National University, https://adb.anu.edu.au/biography/nicholls-sir-douglas-ralph-doug-14920/text26109, published first in hardcopy 2012.

Carter, Sarah, '"The faithful children of the Great Mother are starving": Queen Victoria in Contact Zone Dialogues in Western Canada', in Sarah Carter and Maria Nugent (eds), *Mistress of Everything: Queen Victoria in Indigenous Worlds*, Manchester University Press, Manchester, 2016, pp. 78–99.

Curthoys, Ann, 'Good Christians and Useful Workers: Aborigines, Church and State in NSW 1870–1883', in Sydney Labour History Group (eds), *What Rough Beast? The State and Social Order in Australian History*, George Allen & Unwin, Sydney, 1982, pp. 31–56.

Curthoys, Ann and Jessie Mitchell, '"Bring this Paper to the Good Governor": Aboriginal Petitioning in Britain's Australian Colonies', in Saliha Belmessous (ed.), *Native Claims: Indigenous Law against Empire, 1500–1920*, Oxford University Press, New York, 2012, pp. 182–203.

Hart, PR and CJ Lloyd, 'Lyons, Joseph Aloysius (Joe) (1879–1939)', *Australian Dictionary of Biography*, National Centre of Biography, Australian National University, https://adb.anu.edu.au/biography/lyons-joseph-aloysius-joe-7278/text12617, published first in hardcopy 1986.

Horner, Jack and Marcia Langton, 'The Day of Mourning', in Bill Gammage and Peter Spearritt (eds), *Australians 1938*, Fairfax Syme & Weldon, Sydney, 1987, pp. 29–35.

Ingham, SM, 'O'Shanassy, Sir John (1818–1883)', *Australian Dictionary of Biography*, National Centre of Biography, Australian National University, https://adb.anu.edu.au/biography/oshanassy-sir-john-4347/text7059, published first in hardcopy 1974.

Jones, Philip, 'Unaipon, David (1872–1967)', *Australian Dictionary of Biography*, National Centre of Biography, Australian National University, https://adb.anu.edu.au/biography/unaipon-david-8898/text15631, published first in hardcopy 1990.

Lowe, David, 'Makin, Norman John (1889–1982)', *Australian Dictionary of Biography*, National Centre of Biography, Australian National University, http://adb.anu.edu.au/biography/makin-norman-john-14673/text25810, published first in hardcopy 2012.

Markus, Andrew, 'After the Outward Appearance: Scientists, Administrators and Politicians', in Bill Gammage and Andrew Markus (eds), *All That Dirt: Aborigines 1938*, History Project Inc., Canberra, 1982, pp. 83–106.

McLisky, Claire, "'All of one blood"? Race and Redemption on Maloga Mission, 1874–88', in Leigh Boucher et al. (eds), *Historicising Whiteness: Transnational Perspectives on the Construction of an Identity*, RMIT Publishing in association with the School of Historical Studies, University of Melbourne, Melbourne, 2007, pp. 408–15, <https://search.informit.com.au/documentSummary;dn=8636376 24565074;res=IELHSS>.

Miller, Jim, 'Petitioning the Great White Mother: First Nations Organizations and Lobbying in London', in his *Reflections on Native-Newcomer Relations: Selected Essays*, University of Toronto Press, Toronto, 2004, pp. 217–41.

Nelson, George E, 'James, Thomas Shadrach (1859–1946)', *Australian Dictionary of Biography*, National Centre of Biography, Australian National University, http://adb.anu.edu.au/biography/james-thomas-shadrach-10610/text18855, published first in hardcopy 1996.

Nugent, Maria, 'The Politics of Memory and the Memory of Politics: Australian Aboriginal Interpretations of Queen Victoria, 1881–2011', in Sarah Carter and Maria Nugent (eds), *Mistress of Everything: Queen Victoria in Indigenous Worlds*, Manchester University Press, Manchester, 2016, pp. 100–21.

Nugent, Maria and Sarah Carter, 'Introduction: Indigenous Histories, Settler Colonies and Queen Victoria', in Sarah Carter and Maria Nugent (eds), *Mistress of Everything: Queen Victoria in Indigenous Worlds*, Manchester University Press, Manchester, 2016, pp. 1–21.

Rowse, Tim, 'Genealogies of Self-Determination', in Joy Damousi and Judith Smart (eds), *Contesting Australian History: Essays in Honour of Marilyn Lake*, Monash University Publishing, Melbourne, 2019, pp. 136–51.

Ryan, Peter, 'Turnbull, Stanley Clive (1906–1975)', *Australian Dictionary of Biography*, http://adb.anu.edu.au/biography/turnbull-stanley-clive-11893/text21301, published first in hardcopy 2002.

Sayers, Andrew, 'McRae, Tommy (1835–1901)', *Australian Dictionary of Biography*, National Centre of Biography, Australian National University, http://adb.anu.edu.au/biography/mcrae-tommy-13074/text23649, published first in hardcopy 2005.

Souter, Gavin, 'Skeleton at the Feast', in Bill Gammage and Peter Spearritt (eds), *Australians 1938*, Fairfax, Syme & Weldon, Sydney, 1987, pp. 13–27.

Stokes, Geoff, 'Citizenship and Aboriginality: Two Conceptions of Identity in Aboriginal Political Thought', in Geoff Stokes (ed.), *The Politics of Identity in Australia*, Cambridge University Press, Melbourne, 1997, pp. 158–71.

Strahan, Frank, 'Selby, Isaac (1859–1956)', *Australian Dictionary of Biography*, National Centre of Biography, Australian National University, http://adb.anu.edu.au/biography/selby-isaac-11653/text20817, published first in hardcopy 2002.

Wright, Nancy E, 'The Problem of Aboriginal Evidence in Early Colonial New South Wales', in Diane Kirkby and Catharine Colebourne (eds), *Law, History, Colonialism: The Reach of Empire*, Manchester University Press, Manchester, 2001, pp. 140–55.

Manuscript

Scarlett, Philippa, *Warangesda: Daily Life and Events, 1880–1924*, 1994, https://indigenoushistories.com/warangesda/.

Theses

Atkinson, Wayne, Not One Iota: The Yorta Yorta Struggle for Land Justice, PhD, La Trobe University, 2000.

Barwick, Diane, 'A Little More than Kin': Regional Affiliation and Group Identity Among Aboriginal Migrants in Melbourne, PhD, Australian National University, 1963.

Davis, Fiona, Colouring within the Lines: Settler Colonialism and the Cummeragunja Aboriginal Station, 1888–1960s, PhD, University of Melbourne, 2010.

Gamboz, Chiara, Australian Indigenous Petitions: Emergence and Negotiations of Indigenous Authorship and Writings, PhD, University of New South Wales, 2012.

Goodall, Heather, A History of Aboriginal Communities in New South Wales, 1909–1939, PhD, University of Sydney, 1982.

McLisky, Claire, Settlers on a Mission: Power and Subjectivity in the Lives of Daniel and Janet Matthews, PhD, University of Melbourne, 2008.

Matthews, Patricia, 'Uplifting our Aboriginal People': The Victorian Aboriginal Group, 1930–1971, BA Hons, Department of History, Monash University, 1985.

Penney, Jan, Encounters on the River: Aborigines and Europeans in the Murray Valley 1820–1920, PhD, La Trobe University, 1989.

Ward, Michael Victor, The Cummeragunja Walk-Off: A Study of Black/White Politics and Public Discourse about Race, Ideology and Place on the Eve of the Second World War, Masters of Research, Macquarie University, 2016.

INDEX

THE MIEGUNYAH PRESS

This book was designed and
typeset by Cannon Typesetting
The text was set in 12 pt Bembo
with 15 points of leading
The text was printed on 80 gsm woodfree
This book was edited by Katie Purvis

THE
MIEGUNYAH
PRESS